WORD STUDY
THAT STICKS

K-6

What Your Colleagues Are Saying . . .

"Who said word study has to be boring? Not Pamela Koutrakos! In her book *Word Study That Sticks*, Koutrakos provides teachers with a host of highly engaging and easily implemented approaches for making phonemic awareness, phonics, spelling, and vocabulary instruction come alive in their classrooms."

—Timothy Rasinski, PhD, Professor of Literacy Education at Kent State University

"Pam offers so many practical and innovative ideas for word study, but even more than that, by highlighting the importance of student choice, engagement, and collaboration, Pam's book is a primer for planning instruction across the day. In addition to very practical and engaging ideas for word study, Pam helps teachers prioritize their time, organize their instruction, and offer children both individual choice and social opportunities across the day. Pam helps teachers envision and implement an engaging and effective approach to word study, one that supports students' growth and curiosity; one that invites student inquiry and agency."

—Kathy Collins, Literacy Consultant, Author of *Growing Readers*, and Co-Author of *I Am Reading* with Matt Glover

"*Word Study That Sticks* provides Grades K–6 differentiated support for making word study meaningful in any classroom. Chock-full of resources—including sample schedules, lessons, routines, tips for classroom set-up, even workarounds if your classroom is different—Pamela Koutrakos has pulled together the most popular and effective word study techniques being used in schools today. Her inviting writing style will make you feel like you have a master teacher by your side as you implement these ideas in your classroom.

What I like best about this book is that it employs the key characteristics of strong phonics instruction—active, engaging, and thought-provoking. Students don't just learn about words; they explore words like detectives uncovering aspects that will improve their reading and writing skills. Students are also taught to take ownership of their learning so that these skills can be more easily transferred to their independent reading. The result—students who more naturally develop into skilled, fluent readers.

A great resource that's a needed addition to every elementary teacher's professional library."

—Wiley Blevins, Author of *A Fresh Look at Phonics*

"As a presenter I'm asked if I know of a good book for word study. I found one in Pamela Koutrakos's *Word Study That Sticks*! She breaks it down for the novice and streamlines for the old pro. It's truly word study that sticks."

—Jeff Anderson, Author of *Patterns of Power*

"Whether you've been teaching word study for a few years or a few decades, *Word Study That Sticks* will change your mindset and open your eyes to innovative word study practices. Pam's enthusiasm for inquiry-based word study experiences, coupled with her classroom-rooted expertise, glimmers off the pages of this must-have resource. With features like practical prioritizing, teacher tips, and workarounds to common classroom challenges, Pam offers a no-excuse guide to providing students with the word knowledge needed for school and beyond. I guarantee that Pam's positivity will lift your teaching to new heights. If Pamela Koutrakos can't get you and your students fired up about joyful word study instruction—no one can!"

—Maria Walther, First Grade Teacher and Instructional Specialist,
Indian Prairie District 204, Aurora, IL and Author of
The Ramped-Up Read Aloud: What to Notice as You Turn the Page

"This book showcases the joy of word study not as an isolated skill, but as an essential ingredient in creating empowered, purposeful readers. The perfect combination of research and practice, Pam reminds us that word study is an engaging, inquiry-based, non-negotiable element in ELA instruction. With its practical lessons, easy-to-implement activities, and motivating games, *Word Study That Sticks* is a must-have for any reading teacher, literacy coach, or lover of language."

—Molly Ness, PhD, Associate Professor at Fordham University and
Author of *Think Big With Think Alouds*

"Professional texts about word study often are too technical and removed from the everyday realities of the classroom. Fortunately, Pamela Koutrakos serves her 'signature dish' of positivity and enthusiasm with a side of sincerity and practicality. Throughout *Word Study That Sticks*, Pam infuses her deep respect for students, teachers, and the learning process. Her explicit discussions of the what, why, when, and how of word study instruction feel like conversations with a trusted colleague. Alongside the voices of experts and researchers, Pam includes those of teachers and students—which are frequently excluded from professional texts. Recognizing a diversity of learning needs, Pam offers varying entry points for teachers who are beginning to practice word study or are interested in 'stepping up' their instruction. She takes the guesswork out of where to begin by prioritizing meaningful practices, lessons, and materials that can be implemented easily. She also thoughtfully anticipates challenges and offers doable workarounds. Pam reminds novice and veteran teachers alike that developmentally-appropriate word study instruction can be authentic, fun, and challenging. Her thoroughness and thoughtfulness ensure that readers feel prepared (and excited) to plan, teach, differentiate, and assess word study. With her words, Pam inspires and reconnects us with the power of studying words."

—Heather Frank, First Grade Teacher, Central School, Glen Rock, NJ,
and Doctoral Candidate, Montclair State University

"This book is so needed in the world! Wherever I go, teachers ask about word study—how to do it and when to fit it in with all of the other demands placed on their time. *Word Study That Sticks: Best Practices, K–6* is just the right resource at just the right time to answer these important questions. Pamela Koutrakos gives us a perfect blend of background knowledge (the what and why behind word study) and the practical day-to-day (the how) to get word study up and running. Her sample schedules, classroom blueprints, launch lessons, teaching tips, and options for assessment—just to name a few of the awesome tools—give us what we need to harness student engagement, gradual release of responsibility, student independence, and joy around word study. Thank you, Pam, for giving us your signature dish!"

—Julie Wright, Instructional Coach, Educational Consultant,
and Author of *What Are You Grouping For?*

"As an increasing number of schools and districts embrace a balanced literacy model, oftentimes, word study is an area that either gets overlooked or causes confusion. In *Word Study That Sticks*, Pamela Koutrakos cuts through the clutter and demystifies what word study is all about with a practical, research-based system that any educator could implement. This much-needed book is the first and only book I can recommend on the topic, and I could not recommend it enough for any school or district exploring word study."

—Ross Cooper, Elementary School Principal, Old Tappan School District
and Author of *Hacking Project Based Learning*

"In *Word Study That Sticks: Best Practices, K–6*, Pamela Koutrakos takes a fresh look at word study instruction and moves away from word study as discrete skills needed for reading and writing success to patterns and practices that help students leave their mark on the world. Grounded in best practices, authentic reading and writing, and joyful engagement, Pamela clearly shows educators how to teach students the power of words and word study. Focused on developing teacher expertise over knowledge of a program, Pamela invites teachers to honor their current practices, explore curious and creative word study instruction and foster engagement and independence in the classroom. She provides explicit, practical advice to weave word study instruction throughout the day, breathing the power of words into the classroom. Pamela's dedication to her work, her enthusiasm for teaching and learning, and her optimism for personalized, authentic word study instruction for all students are threaded throughout the pages of this book. Reading this book is like collaborating with a trusted literacy coach who understands the complexity and challenges of the classroom and supports teacher learning with real-life photographs of classrooms, word study routines and instruction, inspiring student samples and a clear set of lessons for use in classrooms. *Word Study That Sticks* provides educators with the tools they need to enact purposeful and authentic word study instruction into an elementary classroom framed around inquiry and joyful learning."

—Stephanie Affinito, PhD, Literacy Teacher Educator,
University at Albany, SUNY

"If you're seeking a comprehensive guide to differentiated word study aimed at building independent, inquisitive word explorers, you've got the right book in your hands! In *Word Study That Sticks*, Pamela Koutrakos offers practical and purposeful lessons to get started and set up and maintain inquiry-based, engaging word study routines across a variety of grouping options throughout a year of study. Her friendly, supportive voice makes readers feel as if they are sitting across the table from her being coached with expertise and care as they make critical decisions regarding learner-centered word exploration. Readers are guided through assessments, upping the rigor and relevance of word study for all learners at all levels K–6, incorporating word study across content areas, and transferring learning to everyday reading and writing all within an investigational, joyful classroom environment. Pam's masterful guidance coupled with the user-friendly features of this volume will be appreciated by both teachers who are new to dynamic word study and seasoned practitioners seeking to up their level of pedagogy. Thank you, Pam, for your thoughtful voice and all you offer teachers and learners through this book!"

—Janiel Wagstaff, National Literacy Consultant and
Author of *The Common Core Companion: Booster Lessons,
Grades K–2: Elevating Instruction Day by Day*

"Pam's passion for engaging children in purposeful, thoughtful, and joyful word study exudes in *Word Study That Sticks*. The framework she posits is elegant yet practical in daily teaching within a workshop structure. The lessons, grounded in research that supports the urgency of word study for our learners, convey a clear vision for developing a culture of word learning, exploration for words, active engagement, and positive, student-centered word study. These lessons will lead learners to powerful, joyful, and exciting word etymology that fosters student choice and celebration of words, covering phonemic awareness, phonics, meaning, spelling, and high-frequency work—all facets of word study. A thoughtful and visual format provides educators with lessons and clear examples to develop thoughtful word study in the classroom now. The framework presents real-time challenges faced by schools and districts with honest and considerate 'workarounds.' This is the exact approach to word study that our children need and deserve!"

—Deirdre Spollen-LaRaia, EdD, Principal,
West Brook Middle School, Paramus, NJ

"When reading *Word Study That Sticks*, you feel as though Pam has stepped inside your classroom and is with you each step of the way, cheering you on. She understands your word study concerns and provides you with an abundance of options that are responsive to your students' right-now needs which you can immediately use. As I was reading, I could envision my teachers flipping over the ready-made word study charts and lessons that Pam makes available. These charts are teacher friendly, but more importantly, they also help your students to become independent word experts in a flash! Creating students who lift the level of their vocabularies, reading, and writing."

—Yvonne Mortello, K–5 Literacy Coach and Primary Grade Educator

To my mom and dad.

If they could see me now . . .

Their constant example of what it means to be good-hearted,
relentlessly positive, and ceaselessly courageous individuals pointed me in the right direction,
and the memory of their boundless love and sacrifice keeps me going.

WORD STUDY THAT STICKS
BEST PRACTICES
K-6

PAMELA KOUTRAKOS

CORWIN Literacy

FOR INFORMATION:

Corwin

A SAGE Company

2455 Teller Road

Thousand Oaks, California 91320

(800) 233-9936

www.corwin.com

SAGE Publications Ltd.

1 Oliver's Yard

55 City Road

London EC1Y 1SP

United Kingdom

SAGE Publications India Pvt. Ltd.

B 1/I 1 Mohan Cooperative Industrial Area

Mathura Road, New Delhi 110 044

India

SAGE Publications Asia-Pacific Pte. Ltd.

18 Cross Street #10-10/11/12

China Square Central

Singapore 048423

Director and Publisher, Corwin Classroom: Lisa Luedeke

Acquisitions Editors: Wendy Murray and Tori Bachman

Editorial Development Manager: Julie Nemer

Senior Editorial Assistant: Sharon Wu

Production Editor: Jane Martinez

Copy Editor: Amy Hanquist Harris

Typesetter: C&M Digitals (P) Ltd.

Proofreader: Alison Syring

Indexer: Sheila Bodell

Cover Designer: Candice Harman

Graphic Designer: Anupama Krishnan

Marketing Manager: Brian Grimm

Printed in the United States of America

Library of Congress Cataloging-in-Publication Data

Names: Koutrakos, Pamela, author.

Title: Word study that sticks : best practices, K–6 / Pamela Koutrakos.

Description: First edition. | Thousand Oaks, California : Sage Corwin, [2019] | Includes bibliographical references and index.

Identifiers: LCCN 2018025224 | ISBN 9781544327242 (pbk. : alk. paper)

Subjects: LCSH: Reading—Phonetic method—Study and teaching (Elementary) | English language—Orthography and spelling—Study and teaching (Elementary) | Language arts (Elementary) | Student-centered learning.

Classification: LCC LB1573.3 .K68 2019 | DDC 372.46/5—dc23

LC record available at https://lccn.loc.gov/2018025224

This book is printed on acid-free paper.

SFI label applies to text stock

18 19 20 21 22 10 9 8 7 6 5 4 3 2 1

Contents

PART I: CURIOUS, CREATIVE WORD STUDY

CHAPTER FOUR   89

Assessment: A Less-Is-More Approach to Seeing Next Steps   89

PART II: FOSTERING ENGAGEMENT AND INDEPENDENCE

PART III: TEACHING FOR TRANSFER

Visit the companion website at
resources.corwin.com/wordstudythatsticks
for downloadable resources.

Online Resources: Printable and Reproducible Resources
  After-Hours Activities Letters (K–1, 2–3, Grades 4 and Up)
  Blend, Digraph, Prefix, Suffix, Root Cards
  Primary Minicharts
  Upper-Elementary and Middle-Grades Minicharts

Acknowledgments

The adage about it taking a village could not be any truer.

Thank you to my husband, Ike, and my children, Colby and Peyton. You are why I look forward to every new day. Your willingness to pitch in (beyond the usual) and your commitment to keeping the house quasi-quiet while I was writing are likely what made this book actually get published! Thank you to Michele, Tim, Liam, Linda, and Ron. Our family may be unique in structure, but there is none better! Your guidance empowers me, and your celebration of all the little steps reminded me that this could happen. Thank you, family and friends, for the laughs and needed distraction, which were equally important in this journey.

Thank you to my present teammates. I get to work alongside the most fabulous "dream team." Gravity Goldberg, Patty McGee, Laura Sarsten, Karen Finnerty, Julie McAuley, and Wendy Murray, your steadfast "of-course-you-can" belief is what set these wheels in motion. The discussions we have and experiences we share clarify all that is important in education.

Thank you, friends and family in Teaneck! The team at Thomas Jefferson Middle School helped me learn what *real* day-to-day teaching was all about. It was here that I began to understand the ingredients for learning (included in this book) of student self-efficacy, empowerment, and playfulness. The community at Hawthorne Elementary School gave me greater insights into the trajectory from kindergarten to eighth grade. You all made the idea of "collective teacher efficacy" crystal clear. There is no doubt we were better together, and my learning skyrocketed as a direct result of visiting and being a part of each of your classrooms. Amy VanLew and Carrie Williams, co-teaching with you both was not only ridiculously fun but also central to my understanding of what it means to make learning accessible to everyone. The district team of literacy coaches, and especially my everyday partner Janet Bus, taught me how to lend support to teachers and nurture schoolwide growth. Patricia Schwartz and Deirdre Spollen-LaRaia, you both saw more in me that I ever saw in myself. Your leadership, wisdom, and mentorship built me up and set on my way.

Colleagues at Brookside and Hillside Schools in Allendale showed me the impact a learning community can have. I am forever grateful to have been a part of this team of teachers! Brad Siegel, Mike Barcadepone, Bruce Winkelstein, Anastasia Maroulis, and Cathy Danahy: Thank you for helping me feel confident in taking the chances I wasn't sure I was ready for. The opportunities you provided led me to question, rethink, and outgrow my approach to teaching about words and inspired a journey that led to this book. To my once QUAD partner-in-learning and now teammate Laura Sarsten, there is no greater person to nerd out and talk shop with. You are my teaching soulmate and a tried-and-true friend.

Thank you to the team at Corwin. Wendy Murray, there are truly no words . . . your experience and mentorship energize me and clear the path to accomplishing goals I never imagined possible. Tori Bachman, your clear perspectives, voice, direction, and encouragement have made an impact that will surely outlast the writing of this book. Lisa Luedeke, Julie Nemer, Melanie Birdsall, Brian Grimm, Frank Krasilshchik, Jane Martinez, Amy Harris—the entire Corwin team constantly bowled me over with their expertise. The cover design by Candice Harman is every author's dream. Special thanks to Sharon Wu, who shepherded 400 image files without blinking and coached me in a thousand ways.

I have such gratitude for the teachers, administrators, and incredible coaches in the countless districts I get to work in as a consultant—or as I prefer to say, *traveling teacher*. Being welcomed into your schools has meant so much. I am appreciative of the reciprocal nature of the work we do together! Thank you to the educators who invited me into their schools and classrooms to try out this work: Irene Pierides, Krista La Croix, Deirdre Spollen-LaRaia, Yvonne Mortello, Viviana Tamas, Courtney Rejent, Dina Bolan, Heather Frank, Jennifer Winkel, Stefanie Goncalves, Rebecca Johnson, Jessica Boyle, Katie McGrath, Holly Bruni, Laurie Hemmerly, and all the teachers at Hamilton School, Coolidge School, Jefferson School, and West Brook Middle School. You are all rock stars!

Finally, there are no words to express the gratitude and love I have for all the students I have had the honor of working with. These learners and their incredible families are the direct cause of everything in this book. You are all the reason why I do what I do, have done what I have done, and look forward to what I will do next.

Publisher's Acknowledgments

Corwin gratefully acknowledges the contributions of the following reviewers:

Nancy Akhavan
Assistant Professor,
Department of Educational Leadership
Fresno State University
Fresno, CA

Melissa Black
Director of Instruction, K–12
Harlem Village Academy
New York, NY

Leslie Blauman
Teacher, Author, Consultant
Cherry Creek School District
Centennial, CO

Helen S. Comba
Consultant
Rutgers University
Westfield, NJ

Introduction: Word Study Now

My signature dish—made for me by a very special student!

I was once part of a summer literacy institute where poet and author Amy Ludwig VanDerwater gave an inspiring keynote address about finding our "signature dish." Our signature dish, Amy explained, helps us focus, even in turbulent times. Without a moment of hesitation, I knew my signature dish: my positivity and my desire to work together with others to make things happen—and whenever possible, happen with a cupful of joy. This "OK-where-do-we-start?" optimism is in my genes, and it was how I was raised. I come from a long line of strong women who, when hit with setbacks, never wallow in pity, but instead solve problems and forge ahead with both strength and a smile.

I have taught students from preschool through sixth grade in the roles of both classroom teacher and interventionist. I have had the tremendous opportunity to learn alongside students and collaborate with educators in numerous communities. Empathy and understanding—coupled with smiles, a positive demeanor, and a plan—help to not only offset challenging circumstances occurring both in and outside school walls but also to get learning jump-started and moving. I now bring this disposition to every school I visit and work in as a traveling teacher and coach. This is personally fulfilling because my signature dish is put to good use every day. This book is essentially an extension of my signature dish.

> Teamwork is all about cooperating with other people. A good team can get anything done if they work together. I think teamwork is important because it is something that is used to solve major issues. You can do so many more things working with others, than by yourself.

—Victoria, age 10

We all are aware of the ballooning demands on young learners. The academic pressures and learning standards students face can be daunting. As classroom, building, and district leaders, we tirelessly and creatively investigate ways to marry mandates with fun, active, developmentally appropriate practice. We are also aware of a constantly changing social and political climate. Words have remarkable power and an equally awesome impact in all of these domains. This book is a necessity because our students, as future citizens, need greater access to words. Words are a gateway to sharing our voices. Words allow us to be heard and allow us to listen to and, perhaps, better understand others. Through words, our stances and choices become clear. Through words, we have the chance to come together, even when we have distinct beliefs and philosophies. To this end, there is a clear and compelling need for systematic, thoughtful word study instruction.

Words give students a voice, help students express their beliefs, and enable students to compromise.

Word Study for a New Generation

I happily spend my days talking with dedicated educators from numerous districts. All hold different positions and work with students at a range of grade levels. In reflecting on these conversations, patterns emerge: We became teachers to make a difference. We feel alive when we collaborate with colleagues to create classroom experiences where *challenging concepts become fun, instruction is effective, and learning is personalized for each of our students.* Without fail, teachers say that those lightbulb moments for learners are the highlights of their days. Teachers talk about how lucky they are to witness the spark of curiosity when students come to new understandings. A friend called it a "perfect storm," when the feeling in the classroom is electric, unmistakable, and lasting. When she said that, I had chills and then a more subdued moment when I realized that *not one* of a multitude of aha moments was about word study. *Hmmm . . .*

These days, word study is sidelined due to the hyperfocus on tested areas and mandates. One teacher described to me the pressure to constantly push kids forward. She shared, "At times, it feels as though I don't have the space to afford children the time they need to grow and learn at their own pace." She went on to describe how hard it is to see children internalize the expectations of those around them and how it leads them to feel anxious about making mistakes and taking risks. When I asked other teachers why curriculum and lesson plans don't include robust language exploration, they shrugged their shoulders. When I asked if students found any joy in studying words and spelling, I actually got a couple of laughs. When I inquired about student perseverance in decoding tricky words while reading and willingness to take risks (and possibly make mistakes) in their writing by using interesting language (as opposed to more simple and bland language), the reaction was similar. *Hmmm . . .*

Curious

> ## TEACHER TIP
>
> Heineken's United Kingdom ad campaign titled "Worlds Apart" demonstrates how words, even in divisive times, have the power to bring together people with contrasting viewpoints.

My dogged optimism still in high gear, I kept asking teachers questions, knowing that my "yeah, buts . . ." were getting me closer to figuring out how I could help them reenvision word study. So I did what every right-minded action researcher does: I went to Trader Joe's; bought chips and guac, a wide selection of cheese and chocolate, sparkling water, and wine; then, I invited four teacher colleagues to my house after school. By sundown, they'd sung like canaries, telling me the real reasons they resisted the idea of professional learning around word study. The gist, they felt, was that if they were to open themselves up to all the possibilities, it would be like diving too quickly into the deep end of a pool. They wanted first to lean on a resource that gave them a framework for better word learning. One teacher said, "I wish something great was out there that checked *all* the boxes and fit every need—instead of just one or two." *Hmmm . . .*

And with that, I had *my* aha moment that galvanized me to write this book. As we polished off the last of those tasty snacks, the teachers described how they are tired of having to cobble things together. They are adding in, taking out, modifying, and tweaking what they have as a way to include what they feel is most important for their students. Many teachers feel there is not enough emphasis on phonemic awareness, phonics, or vocabulary. Many see current word study programs as one-size-fits-all and/or difficult to manage. Many see it as rote, surface, and heavily reliant on short-term memorization. Almost all share concerns about lack of transfer—and even lack of knowledge—once the Friday test is over.

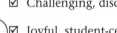
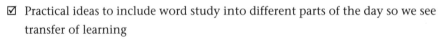

Word Study That Sticks sets out to be the resource we have been wanting but haven't yet found. It includes the following:

- ☑ Challenging, discovery-based practices

- ☑ Joyful, student-centered learning

- ☑ Personalized and differentiated instruction

- ☑ Developmentally appropriate routines

- ☑ Instruction in *all aspects* of word study, with enough phonemic awareness and phonics in the primary grades and balanced emphasis on spelling and vocabulary in all grades

- ☑ Practical ideas to include word study into different parts of the day so we see transfer of learning

- ☑ Something that intertwines a myriad of established best practices to support all learners

- ☑ An easy-to-implement approach that can be used to start up word study

☑ Built-in professional development so you feel prepared in moving forward with a stepped-up approach to word study instruction

☑ Access to words that precisely express ideas and viewpoints

Let's get started. We are in this together! We can do this, we will do it, and we will have fun doing it! (There's my signature dish.) I am in this with you, and together, we will bring curiosity, enthusiasm, and a sense of liveliness to word study.

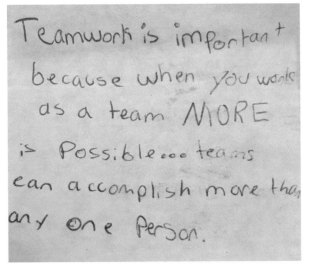

—Patty, age 10

How to Use This Book With Other Programs or as Your Sole Resource

This text can easily be used in conjunction with other programs your district may already have in place. It also can be used to help your district create its own approach to word study, seamlessly incorporating the best aspects of many different existing programs along with additional insights and ideas.

WE HAVE A PROGRAM IN PLACE

I am a big believer in holding onto what's working. If there are parts of your current approach to word study that you like and feel are relevant, effective, and joyful . . . by all means, *keep those practices in place!* Is there something you are not too fond of or feel is missing? Are you one of the many educators who believe your current approach is not checking off all your boxes? Are you hoping to step up your current word study instruction? Use this resource to easily and effectively enhance and lift the level of the word learning currently happening in your classroom and school.

WE HAVE NOTHING

Let's face it—there are positives and negatives to not having a set of consistent word study practices in place. The benefit (yes, always starting with the positive!) is that you have the power and capability to create it as you like and see fit. This freedom is empowering and is filled with opportunity, but it can also be overwhelming. This book will support you along the way! I am here to hold your hand and provide encouragement as you plan, tinker, try out, modify, and formalize word learning in your classroom and school.

Preview of the Three Parts

You may feel inclined to read this book cover to cover—go for it! You may prefer to read snippets and sections as you feel ready—another great plan. You may also choose to access certain features included in this book more than others; if so, you can bookmark, highlight, and return to these specific parts at your leisure. What follows is a sneak peek of each part of this book and the special features included throughout. By taking a few minutes to learn the structure and format of this book, you will be ready to use it in the way that *you* feel is just right!

PART I: CURIOUS, CREATIVE WORD STUDY

This section outlines the first steps to take in preparing for a rich year of word study. Think of Part I as your own personal launch unit for both you and your students. In this part, I will outline what is needed to roll out word study. We will review the foundations of word study, classroom setup, prioritized materials, and management of those materials. Advice is also given for inviting students into a world of word study. The included lesson ideas, charts, and student work explicitly show how to introduce word study routines to your class.

PART II: FOSTERING ENGAGEMENT AND INDEPENDENCE

This section covers all you need to know to solidify word study practices in your classroom. In this section, you will find research, advice, and ideas regarding what explicit word study will look like in the classroom each day. It is here we begin to empower students with greater choice, thereby increasing motivation and ownership of this important work. Multiple lessons and additional word study routines are laid out clearly. These additional routines highlight the different aspects of word study instruction: phonemic awareness, phonics, spelling, and vocabulary. These choices and routines support differentiated classroom practice. Additionally, support is provided for how to bring curiosity, inquiry, and discovery to all aspects of word study.

Part II also includes ideas on how to support our students' success. I address how to build meaningful classroom talk around words, provide purposeful small-group instruction, and coach into collaborative partnerships. Finally, goal setting, reflection, and celebration are all addressed in detail.

PART III: TEACHING FOR TRANSFER

In this section, we take word study to the next level. Explicit, clear, and practical advice is provided for how to embed word learning into *all* parts of the day so transfer happens! This part of the book is intended to be accessed after basic word study practices are fluently and confidently occurring in classrooms. It is here we will delve into how to sneak word study into reading, writing, math, social studies, science, and *more*!

Preview of Features

WHAT, WHY, WHEN

This regularly occurring feature gives the "just-right" amount of research-backed background info on each *best practice* described. It gives helpful information to explain what the practice is, when we might use it, and perhaps most importantly, why we would take the time to include this as part of our classroom practice. This feature is a user-friendly way to introduce each new idea and aspect of classroom work. Each time this feature occurs, it is followed by the more practical, accessible, ready-to-go advice, lessons, and ideas we all want and need to make sense of and implement these research-supported best practices.

INVITING INQUIRY

We all want students to make sense of and grow ideas with greater independence. Children are naturally curious. We want to do all we can to foster inquisitiveness about words in general and also about the way words work. This helpful feature lists questions and prompts (in language you can use) to promote student curiosity and discovery around words.

WORKAROUNDS

New work can be challenging! Even with explicit advice and examples, we may stumble here and there as we set out on this journey. As someone who has been there and lived the "mistakes," stumbles, and hurdles, I wanted to provide a little preventative medicine for others embarking on a similar path. This feature highlights and pinpoints areas of possible challenge and provides advice for avoiding or overcoming each encounter.

STARTING UP AND STEPPING UP

As educators, we can sometimes feel isolated. I believe we can feel more connected and supported by sharing experiences, advice, and encouragement more often. This feature includes the voice of actual teachers who have tried out the ideas in this book. You will hear from colleagues across the country on ways they used these practices to *start up* or *step up* word study in their own classrooms.

TEACHER TIP

Sometimes, it helps to have a tip (or two) to help things go a little more smoothly and efficiently. This feature intends to do just that—provide a little extra clarity, a suggestion, or advice on where to go to learn more.

PRACTICAL PRIORITIZING

New work can also be a bit overwhelming. I am huge believer in starting small and prioritizing so that we can play, reflect, celebrate, and then implement with both confidence and intention. At the end of specific chapters, I have included a *brief* checklist of first steps to take in carrying out most essential aspects of the classroom practices included.

BACKED BY THE EXPERTS

Whenever I especially want to arm you with specific, strong support for a lesson or routine, you'll find these references to research-based best practices. Remember, use these and any other sound bites in classroom letters home, faculty meetings, and conversations. A rising tide of expertise lifts all boats!

In *Big Magic: Creative Living Beyond Fear* (2015), Elizabeth Gilbert reminds us that we know more than we think! She encourages us to open our perspectives and shake ourselves free of the status quo. To that end, when we pursue what we love and derive joy from new adventures in our work, it helps us to grow, grow, grow. As Gilbert suggests, it's OK to "imitate before we innovate" (p. 142). I invite you to draw inspiration from the content included in the coming pages. Enjoy this journey with your colleagues, students, and yourself. Have fun taking chances, being playful, and seeing things differently. Let's get this party started!

PART I

Curious, Creative Word Study

CHAPTER ONE

What Is Word Study?

Learning about words is important because if there were no words then you couldn't read books and books Are how we learn. When You know about words You can Read. Write a book. know Sonds. Which words make Sense in a Sertain Sentence. and talk to Pepele about Stuuf like sports or anything!

—Liam, age 7

Seven-year-old Liam says it best—learning about words is important. Words are our ticket to life. The thousands upon thousands of words I will use in this book don't say it much better than he does. If I had to pick one idea of Liam's that expresses the "why" behind my writing this book, it is this: Learning words helps you talk to people about stuff. My approach to word study is that it *is* a social endeavor; it's creative, curiosity-fueled, and classroom community building. Word study is also a gateway to reading, writing, and thinking—sure, yes, you know that. There are lots of other books you could pick up on word study that will crack that open, but how is this book different? I'm going to show you that the key to successful word study is to keep it about playfulness and peer interaction. Words express you. Yourself. Words clarify and deepen connections to others. Make no mistake about it, too: Words are power. Knowing words opens doors. Vocabulary is thinking. So simple, but profound. The more words we know, the more nuanced our thinking. This is the kind of power we want for the children we teach.

11

Language is the universal currency of connection. Musicians use their language to create and compose pieces that entertain, connect, and move us. Artists use images and sculpture to make meaning and instill feelings—the buzz created when we view, feel, and share art is unmistakable. Athletes communicate nonstop with their teammates, opponents, coaches, officials, and fans. Our ability to listen, understand, speak, question, share, read, and write is paramount. Words penetrate all we do. As such, if we want word learning to stick and we want our students to use and apply their knowledge of words in every facet of their lives, we need to embed, highlight, and create opportunities to study words in each part of our days.

Just how do we go about systematic, joyful word study? The lowest hanging fruit may appear to be a program or some kit with a colorful lidded box that has it all—but no, as is true of many things in teaching, there is no one-size-fits-all easy answer. However, engaging in conversation with colleagues, looking to our students, and taking the risk to try out new ideas will result in more meaningful, playful, and productive learning than we might have first imagined.

WHAT: THE DIFFERENT FACETS OF WORD STUDY

Quite simply, word study is the study of words . . . in all kinds of ways. When we study words, we think about sounds, letters, and spelling patterns, but we also think about the meaning, connections, connotation, usage, and impact of these words. In 2010, Rasinski and Zutell wrote,

> Word study is the direct study and exploration of words. . . . When we store words in our brain, the sound, spelling, and meaning are usually consolidated. When we view a word on the printed page, we access the sound, spelling, and meaning simultaneously and immediately. (p. 6)

I greatly appreciate how Rasinski and Zutell *start* by making the connections between sounds and letters, spelling, vocabulary, reading, and writing. We can't separate one from the others. A well-rounded approach to word study incorporates phonemic awareness, phonics, spelling, and vocabulary. In this book, I focus on how to start up and step up all these crucial elements of word study. The ultimate goal of word study is for students to develop knowledge of spelling patterns in general and also increase their specific knowledge of words, including the meaning of individual words. In their third edition of *Words Their Way: Word Study for Phonics, Vocabulary, and Spelling Instruction*, Bear, Invernizzi, Templeton, and

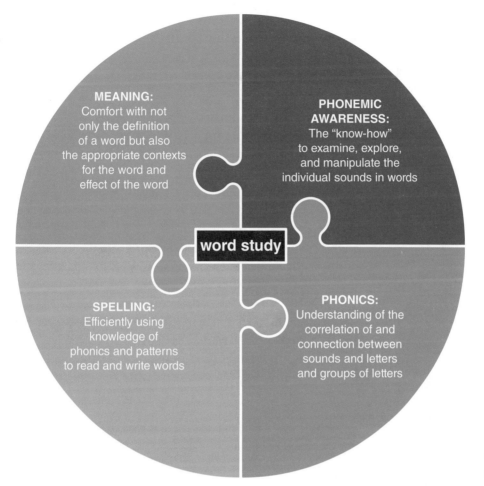

The different facets of word study.

Johnston explain, "Through word study, students learn how the spelling system, or orthography, works to represent sound, pattern, and meaning. Writing then exercises that word knowledge" (2004, p. 26).

This *learning how* aspect is critical; we want students to be strategic, *independent* word learners who do it on their own for a lifetime. Researchers Michael F. Graves, Steven Schneider, and Cathy Ringstaff emphasize this in a powerful article in *The Reading Teacher*, "Empowering Students With Word-Learning Strategies: Teach a Child to Fish" (2018). To bring about this learner independence, our word study approach needs to be multifaceted (Baumann & Kame'enui, 2004; Blachowicz, Fisher, Ogle, & Watt-Taffe, 2006; Graves, 2016; Kame'enui & Baumann, 2012; Stahl & Nagy, 2006) and "include providing students with rich and varied language experiences (in reading, writing, and discussion), teaching individual words, teaching word-learning

strategies, and fostering word consciousness (interesting and excitement about words)" (Graves et al., 2018, p. 553).

To me, the term *word consciousness* shows up in learners as curiosity. This is what we model and what we want learners to possess. In addition, we cultivate an analytical bent. For example, we might first get curious about students, investigate their current strengths and areas of readiness, and then design instruction that fits their stage of spelling development (Bear et al., 2004). We could then work to facilitate appropriate and relevant experiences where whole words are studied, phonemes are studied in real words, and we dig deep to study the *why* behind words—all the while consistently incorporating reading and writing into these practices. In this way, we would be working from student strengths and designing student-centered learning that is appropriate and within each learner's *zone of proximal development* (Vygotsky, 1962). The ideas in this book will help you do this. Over the course of the school year, students will learn how to use strategies for learning words when they are most ready. Most importantly, they will learn to employ the strategies flexibly, on their own.

STARTING UP

Pam recommends using a spelling inventory at the start of the year. She also taught me how to look for patterns in student work so I began to quickly see individual, small-group, and whole-class priorities. I used these patterns to help choose and match the words *to the students*. This method was much better than what I had done in the past, which was give everyone the same lists in the same order year to year. Check out Appendix B for a list of commonly used spelling inventories.

—Michele, Grade 6 Teacher

STEPPING UP

In our district, we use three different spelling inventories. They came with the program we use. Different grade-level bands (K–I, 2–3, 4–6) each have their own inventories. This creates a common language and an aligned approach to choosing words across the district. Pam then helped us learn how to use the results of this inventory to support student learning. See Chapters 4 through 7 for more information on using inventory results and more informally found day-to-day information to differentiate classroom practice.

—Jan, Literacy Coach

What Word Study IS	What Word Study ISN'T
Learning particular words and word features	Learning letter sounds in isolation
Recognizing and thinking about patterns across words	Reading controlled texts
Generalizing ideas about patterns we find	Passive
Phonics, phonemic awareness, spelling, and vocabulary	Only phonics
	Only spelling
	Only vocabulary
Developing strategies to study words	One-size-fits-all
Active	BORING!
Developmentally appropriate	
Collaborative	
FUN!	

Stages of Spelling, Reading, and Writing Development: Well-Regarded Research

Bear, Invernizzi, Templeton, & Johnston, 2004	Chall, 1983	Gentry, 1982
Emergent Letter–sound correspondence and alphabetic knowledge not yet solid; letter strings may be used.	**Stage 0: Prereading** Reader recognizes letters; expresses interest in words and reading.	**Precommunicative** Writer has message in mind to communicate; often uses letter strings and letter-like symbols to communicate this message.
Letter Name (Alphabetic) Letter–sound correspondence in place; phonetic spelling often includes first and last consonants heard.	**Stage 1: Initial Reading and Decoding** Reader has letter–sound correspondence; able to read some high-frequency words and many "phonetically regular" simple words.	**Semiphonetic Stage** Writer has some understanding of letter–sound correspondence, and words written have some "correct" letters (often beginning and ending consonants).
Within Words Able to spell most simple CVC words and able to conventionally write blends and digraphs in simple words; attempts to spell words with long vowel sounds; starting to attempt spelling words containing other vowel patterns (*ou, aw,* etc.).	**Stage 2: Confirmation and Fluency** Reader decodes simple words and has increased sight word vocabulary; as a result, can read an increasing number of texts with fluency.	**Phonetic Stage** Writer able to segment, hear, and write a letter for most sounds heard in a word; relies heavily on sounds heard to help with spelling.
Syllables and Affixes Conventional spelling of high-frequency words, words with short vowels, and many words with long vowel patterns; learning to spell multisyllabic words.	**Stage 3: Reading to Learn** Reader able to read more complex texts with unfamiliar vocabulary and take on a more syntactical and systematic study of words.	**Transitional Stage** Writer spells simple words conventionally; vowels present in most to all syllables; greater reliance on visual and morphological information.
Derivational Relations Conventional spelling of most words; greater understanding of the connection between vocabulary and spelling—accordingly, high understanding of word parts, prefixes, suffixes, and Greek and Latin roots.	**Stage 4: Multiple Viewpoints** Reader able to read complex, academic, and content-driven texts; has a highly systematic repertoire of how to study words and word parts. **Stage 5: Construction and Reconstruction** Reading comprehension now more efficient than listening comprehension.	**Correct Stage** Spelling is conventional; high level of sound–symbol understanding; writer relies on wider range of strategies, including knowledge of the orthographic system.

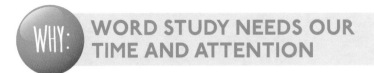

WHY: WORD STUDY NEEDS OUR TIME AND ATTENTION

It's time to recognize the power of words and the importance of word study in our classrooms. In 2000, the National Reading Panel reported that direct instruction in phonics and vocabulary are important factors in learning to read. Many of us likely knew this, but perhaps we still struggle to make the time for this direct instruction or figure out just how it "should" look. One thing we know for sure is that we can't continue to use one-size-fits-all spelling instruction. Bear and colleagues say it best when they write,

> Commercial phonics, spelling, and vocabulary programs are often characterized by explicit skill instruction . . . much of the repeated practice consists of rote drill, so students have little opportunity to manipulate word concepts or apply critical thinking skills. The best way to develop fast and accurate perception of word features is to engage in meaningful reading and writing, and to have multiple opportunities to examine those same words out of context . . . the most effective instruction in phonics, spelling, and vocabulary links word study to the texts being read, provides a systematic scope and sequence of word-level skills, and provides multiple opportunities for hands-on practice and application. (2004, p. 4)

In 2008, Rasinski deepened this professional conversation on the importance of making time for strong word study instruction. He and his colleagues remind us that there are more words in the English language than any other language in the world. Our students will need systematic, meaningful, in-and-out-of-context word work to make sense of the language with the most words!

As early as 1958, James taught us all, "Teaching is not telling." As part of word study, students actively examine, manipulate, and categorize words. They also pose theories and talk with peers to create larger, transferable understandings. We hope to support our students in becoming confident conversationalists, remarkable readers, and wicked-awesome writers. We know that we want students to take risks in using strong, precise words—even if they may not know how to spell these words. Word study instruction provides the background knowledge necessary to help students become more comfortable attempting to read and use words they do not yet know. We know that if students labor too long on decoding, accessing, or trying to spell a particular word, their motivation will be lost, and they may lose the intrinsic reward that accompanies success. Students who are more confident are more willing to take risks. Well-rounded word study instruction builds this mindset.

"What about spelling?"

www.CartoonStock.com

Making the time for
word study is important!

 WHEN: ## ANYTIME! AND COULD BE IN AS LITTLE AS FIVE MINUTES

In 2010, Simon Sinek tweeted, "Rule books tell people what to do. Frameworks guide people how to act." When it comes to the "when" of word study, keep Sinek's insight in mind because effective word study is all about you finding and tweaking a framework that works for *you*, your setting, your goals. Anyone who knows me knows well that I am not a believer in "one right way." I have been in countless classrooms spanning all grades and have seen diverse structures yield positive results. The common thread is that there is some time devoted specifically to word study *and* some time where word study is woven into other parts of the day.

We *all* have room for word study. We just need to make the space. In 2010, Rasinski and Zutell wrote, "Finding 5 to 10 minutes at the right time for examining and playing with words can make all the difference between deep and limited understanding" (p. 10). In *Words Their Way*, Bear et al. share that in 15 minutes a day, we can make space for students to compare and contrast words by sound, by consistent spelling patterns associated with patterns of sound, and by meaning, use, and part of speech (pp. 7–8). I have worked with students from kindergarten through sixth grade using a 15 to 30 minutes-per-day model. I have also had the opportunity to implement a language workshop block that allotted as much time for word study and conventions as it did for reading and writing. In Chapter 2, we will explore each of these models in more detail and with more specifics. Until then, pull out a copy of your daily schedule and start spinning those wheels, contemplating how you can carve out a bit more space for word study.

Word Study Is a Verb, Not a Noun

Dale Carnegie once said, "People rarely succeed unless they have fun in what they are doing." Albert Einstein proclaimed, "It is the extreme art of a teacher to awaken joy in creative expression and knowledge." And Simon Sinek noted, "When you use a framework, you are acting." You are doing, choosing—not merely dispensing spelling lists. One central concept presented in this book is that word study is the perfect time to get students *learning by doing*. We can explore words like scientists do specimens and social scientists do artifacts. We can wonder about words and look more deeply into these curiosities with peers. Word study is active, student-centered learning! The Before and After chart at the end of this chapter shows a peek into the world of Word Study That Sticks. I invite you to try it out with your students.

Word Study Invites Inquiry

I once witnessed a first grader slurp her chicken noodle soup at lunch and then begin freestyling, "Campbell! Campbell! Mmm, mmm, good!" as she bopped around the room. Charmed and forever on duty looking for those teachable moments, I made sure that by the time those first graders went home from school they had learned about Clive Campbell, aka DJ Kool Herc, the founding father of hip hop. In a fifth-grade class, I overheard a student tease a friend, "You go on autopilot whenever you play video games." Later in science class, he came across the term *autoimmune disease*. Hmmm . . . "Jake, didn't you just use the word *autopilot*? I asked. "Oh, yeah—wait," he replied. I could see his mental engines turning. "Auto, autho . . . self. Autoimmune . . . maybe it means a disease that gets started with, umm . . . the self, like from inside you?" I smiled. "You got it. I wonder what else we can discover when we delve into the prefix *auto*?"

Inquiry-based word study experiences allow students to discover patterns, connections, and meaning themselves. In *The Curious Classroom* (2017), Harvey Daniels describes children involved in inquiry as being "seized by curiosity, hungry to build knowledge, and fully in charge of their own learning" (p. xiv). I can imagine nothing worthier of our time and attention! The bottom line is that word study can be an engaging, individualized, meaningful, and *fun* part of our classrooms. Here are a few questions we can use to launch some thinking about words:

INVITING INQUIRY

- ☐ Why do we study words?
- ☐ Why is it important to learn about words?
- ☐ How do words impact our interactions with others?
- ☐ What do you notice about words?
- ☐ What would happen if we didn't spend time learning to read, write, and use words?

When we invite inquiry into one area of our instruction, it has a miraculous way of seeping into the entire culture of our classroom. When we embrace curiosity, learning becomes more engaging and playful. When we spark the inherent wonder in our students, they create and follow their own learning paths that supersede our greatest expectations. All we have to do is set the stage, make the time, and step out of their way.

BEFORE	AFTER
Word study as a noun: Passive, teacher-driven instruction Assignments, mandates, memorization (lackluster)	Word study as a verb: Active, developmentally appropriate, collaborative (fun)
When word study is a noun . . .	When word study is a verb . . .

. . . students feel bored. This "learning" is quite passive and definitely not joyful.

. . . students collaborate and may even giggle!

(Continued)

(Continued)

BEFORE	AFTER
Word study as a noun: Passive, teacher-driven instruction Assignments, mandates, memorization (lackluster)	Word study as a verb: Active, developmentally appropriate, collaborative (fun)
When word study is a noun . . .	When word study is a verb . . .

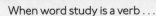

Photo by Holly Bruni

. . . students don't discover or collaborate. They instead complete surface tasks and one-size-fits-all assignments.

. . . there is a sense of discovery. Students experience "WOW!" moments all the time.

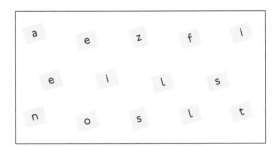

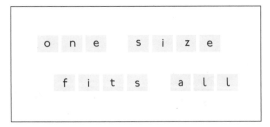

. . . it is tried to be made into a "thing." A workbook or a worksheet is not able to create student-centered, differentiated, active word study habits.

. . . students learn to make choices. Even young students make decisions about how they best learn.

BEFORE	AFTER
Word study as a noun: Passive, teacher-driven instruction Assignments, mandates, memorization (lackluster)	Word study as a verb: Active, developmentally appropriate, collaborative (fun)
When word study is a noun . . .	When word study is a verb . . .

SPELLING WORKBOOK

Match the letters to fill in the blanks on the words below. Hint: create!

. . . students move their bodies and learn in creative and nontraditional ways.

. . . students engage in high-level thinking, including sorting, categorizing, creating theories, defending viewpoints, and so much more.

. . . students nurture all facets of word learning!

CHAPTER TWO

Start It Up! Finding Time and Resources

> In a classroom, I look for an encouraging teacher, a warm learning environment, and a big supply of learning materials, as I am a visual learner. A classroom should be a comfortable and safe place for students to learn.
>
> —C. J., age 11

Chapter 1 clarified what word study is and isn't and explained that a well-rounded approach to word study includes phonemic awareness, phonics, spelling, and meaning/vocabulary. Now, we will delve into ways to do the following:

- Find the time

- Plan the physical space

- Gather the essential materials needed to start up and step up this multifaceted approach to word exploring

WHAT: MAKING THE ROOM FOR WORD STUDY

Making the space in our classrooms for word study is twofold: it's physical and it's psychological. It might be moving furniture to set the stage for small-group word work *and* moving our mindset to be open to trying new practices. In *A Fresh Look at Phonics* (2016), Wiley Blevins says something so delicate so beautifully:

> We need to constantly take a step back from practices and reevaluate them objectively—be open to evidence that original ideas might need some modifications . . . be open and flexible in our understanding as new information presents itself. (p. xvii)

It is comfortable to keep things status quo. I can understand not wanting to upset the delicate balance of all of the plates we are currently spinning. We may worry that if we switch the rotation or speed of one plate (how, when, or where word study happens), it could all come crashing down. But if we recognize any practice isn't the best it could be, how could we not consider switching it up? Some of our "what-if" worries are just that—worries, many of which will never come to fruition. How about we instead ask ourselves, *What if I could find a few extra minutes for word study? What if I looked long and hard at my day and identified areas that might need to be reevaluated? What if I carefully planned and created classroom spaces* with *the learners in the room? What if . . .*

WHY: OPEN-MINDEDNESS IS GOOD FOR OUR TEACHING SOULS

Research shows that those who are open to exploring change and seek out appropriate risks are more likely to succeed. In *The Happiness Advantage* (2010), Shawn Achor shares, "Constantly scanning the world for the negative comes with a great cost. It undercuts our creativity, raises our stress levels, and lowers our motivation and ability to accomplish goals" (p. 91). By worrying about the negative "what ifs," we are making those plates *harder* to spin! Essentially, by allowing ourselves the freedom to consider fresh perspectives, we become more motivated, creative, and ready to accomplish our word study goals.

THERE'S NO BETTER TIME THAN NOW

Now is the time! There are models of word study that can fit the hustle, bustle, pace, and priorities for every classroom out there. Word study *could* happen in as few as 5 to 15 minutes a day! In 2001, David Allen said that our brains can only hold so much without organization assistance. I wholeheartedly agree. Let's get a more "nitty-gritty" picture of where word study fits. *Any* increased time we devote to word study will make a difference. By looking through the schedules shared throughout this chapter, you will see the flexibility of word study and gain a better sense of how to organize classroom time and space. As teachers, we have to get away from that all-or-nothing perfectionist thinking—so grab even 5 minutes, and see what a great beginning that can be!

SAMPLE PRIMARY SCHEDULES

Use Responsive Classroom OR include poetry, oral language, math, and critical thinking challenges, art appreciation, etc.

Developmentally appropriate practice includes active learning, frequent opportunities to move, and time to relax.

Here, word study sneaks into a tiny pocket of time in between special time and lunch/recess.

SS, science, health, literacy, and math are woven into these playful and student-driven centers. This supports additional discovery, learning, and transfer.

MARVELOUS MONDAY and FUN FRIDAY:

Unstructured play time

	Monday	Tuesday	Wednesday	Thursday	Friday
8:15–8:30	A.M. Meeting	A.M. Meeting	A.M. Meeting	A.M. Meeting	A.M. Meeting
8:35–8:45	Calendar Math	Calendar Math	Calendar Math	Calendar Math	Calendar Math
8:55–9:35	Math Workshop/ Instruction	Math Workshop/ Instruction	Math Workshop/ Instruction	Math Workshop/ Instruction	Math Workshop/ Instruction
9:40–9:50	Shared Reading & Writing	Shared Reading & Writing	Shared Reading & Writing	Shared Reading & Writing	Shared Reading & Writing
9:50–10:05	Snack & Brain Break	Snack & Brain Break	Snack & Brain Break	Snack & Brain Break	Snack & Brain Break
10:10–10:45	Reading Workshop/ Instruction	Reading Workshop/ Instruction	Reading Workshop/ Instruction	Reading Workshop/ Instruction	Reading Workshop/ Instruction
10:50–11:30	PE	ART	PE	MUSIC	PE
11:35–11:50	Word Study	Word Study	Word Study	Word Study	Word Study
11:55–12:35	Lunch/Recess	Lunch/Recess	Lunch/Recess	Lunch/Recess	Lunch/Recess
12:40–1:15	Choice Time (Includes all subject areas!)	Choice Time (Includes all subject areas!)	Choice Time (Includes all subject areas!)	Choice Time (Includes all subject areas!)	Choice Time (Includes all subject areas!)
1:20–1:55	Writing Workshop/ Instruction	Writing Workshop/ Instruction	Writing Workshop/ Instruction	Writing Workshop/ Instruction	Writing Workshop/ Instruction
2:00–2:30	MARVELOUS MONDAY (Unstructured play, STEM challenges, makerspace, creative conflict resolution, etc.)	Discovery (Addl. SS/ Science)	Discovery (Addl. SS/ Science)	Discovery (Addl. SS/ Science)	FUN FRIDAY (Unstructured play, STEM challenges, makerspace, creative conflict resolution, etc.)
2:35–3:00		Interactive Read-Aloud or Interactive Writing	Interactive Read-Aloud or Interactive Writing	Interactive Read-Aloud or Interactive Writing	

Transition time has been added to the schedules. The full time of each period will be used for instruction.

	Monday	Tuesday	Wednesday	Thursday	Friday
8:15–8:30	A.M. Meeting	A.M. Meeting	A.M. Meeting	A.M. Meeting	A.M. Meeting
8:30–8:45	Shared Reading & Writing	Shared Reading & Writing	Shared Reading & Writing	Shared Reading & Writing	Shared Reading & Writing
8:50–9:20	Word Study/ Language Workshop	Word Study/ Language Workshop	Word Study/ Language Workshop	Word Study/ Language Workshop	Word Study/ Language Workshop
9:25–9:40	Calendar Math	Calendar Math	Calendar Math	Calendar Math	Calendar Math
9:40–10:00	Snack & Brain Break	Snack & Brain Break	Snack & Brain Break	Snack & Brain Break	Snack & Brain Break
10:00–10:40	Math	Math	Math	Math	Math
10:45–11:25	Reading Workshop/ Instruction	Reading Workshop/ Instruction	Reading Workshop/ Instruction	Reading Workshop/ Instruction	Reading Workshop/ Instruction
11:25–12:10	Recess/ Lunch	Recess/ Lunch	Recess/ Lunch	Recess/ Lunch	Recess/ Lunch
12:15–12:30	Interactive Read-Aloud	Interactive Read-Aloud	Interactive Read-Aloud	Interactive Read-Aloud	Interactive Read-Aloud
12:35–1:15	Choice Time (Includes all subject areas!)	Choice Time (Includes all subject areas!)	Choice Time (Includes all subject areas!)	Choice Time (Includes all subject areas!)	Choice Time (Includes all subject areas!)
1:20–2:00	Writing Workshop/ Instruction	Writing Workshop/ Instruction	Writing Workshop/ Instruction	Writing Workshop/ Instruction	Writing Workshop/ Instruction
2:00–2:30	SS/Science (Alternating or integrated units)	SS/Science (Alternating or integrated units)	SS/Science (Alternating or integrated units)	SS/Science (Alternating or integrated units)	SS/Science (Alternating or integrated units)
2:35–3:15	PE	ART	MUSIC	PE	WORLD LANGUAGE

Use Responsive Classroom OR include poetry, oral language, math, and critical thinking challenges, art appreciation, etc.

Here, word study is part of a language workshop that also includes grammar and vocabulary learning. If centers are used, they are active, meaningful, and do *not* include workbooks or worksheets.

Developmentally appropriate practice includes active learning, frequent opportunities to move, and time to relax.

SS, science, health, literacy, and math are woven into these playful and student-driven centers. This supports additional discovery, learning, and transfer.

Transition time has been added to the schedules. The full time of each period will be used for instruction.

SAMPLE UPPER-ELEMENTARY SCHEDULES

Use Responsive Classroom OR include poetry, current events, book talks, math, and critical thinking challenges, etc.

Here, word study provides the perfect way to transition back to classroom learning after lunch/recess.

Students move their bodies and/or work on relaxation/meditation techniques.

FUN FRIDAY:

Playfulness is important for all of us—big kids included!

?

	Monday	Tuesday	Wednesday	Thursday	Friday
8:15–8:30	A.M. Meeting	A.M. Meeting	A.M. Meeting	A.M. Meeting	A.M. Meeting
8:30–9:45	Math	Math	Math	Math	Math
9:50–10:40	Reading Workshop/ Instruction	Reading Workshop/ Instruction	Reading Workshop/ Instruction	Reading Workshop/ Instruction	Reading Workshop/ Instruction
10:45–11:30	PE	ART	MUSIC	PE	LIBRARY
11:30–12:30	Recess/Lunch	Recess/Lunch	Recess/Lunch	Recess/Lunch	Recess/Lunch
12:35–12:55	Word Study	Word Study	Word Study	Word Study	Word Study
1:00–2:00	SS/Science (Alternating or integrated units)	SS/Science (Alternating or integrated units)	SS/Science (Alternating or integrated units)	SS/Science (Alternating or integrated units)	Writing Workshop/ Instruction (1:00–1:45)
2:00–2:10	Brain Break	Brain Break	Brain Break	Brain Break	Brain Break
2:10–3:00	Writing Workshop/ Instruction	Writing Workshop/ Instruction	Writing Workshop/ Instruction	Writing Workshop/ Instruction	FUN FRIDAY (STEM challenges, Genius Hour, makerspace, etc.)

	Monday	Tuesday	Wednesday	Thursday	Friday
8:15–8:25	A.M. Meeting	A.M. Meeting	A.M. Meeting	A.M. Meeting	A.M. Meeting
8:30–9:15	Writing Workshop/ Instruction	Writing Workshop/ Instruction	Writing Workshop/ Instruction	Writing Workshop/ Instruction	Writing Workshop/ Instruction
9:20–9:50	Word Study/ Language Workshop/ Instruction	Word Study/ Language Workshop/ Instruction	Word Study/ Language Workshop/ Instruction	LIBRARY (9:15–10:00)	Word Study/ Language Workshop/ Instruction
9:55–10:40	Reading Workshop/ Instruction	Reading Workshop/ Instruction	Reading Workshop/ Instruction	Reading Workshop/ Instruction	Reading Workshop/ Instruction
10:40–10:50	Brain Break	Brain Break	Brain Break	Brain Break	Brain Break
10:55–11:40	SS/Science (Alternating or integrated units)	SS/Science (Alternating or integrated units)	SS/Science (Alternating or integrated units)	SS/Science (Alternating or integrated units)	SS/Science (Alternating or integrated units)
11:45–12:30	Lunch & Recess	Lunch & Recess	Lunch & Recess	Lunch & Recess	Lunch & Recess
12:40–2:20	Math	Math	Math	Math	Math
2:30–3:15	PE	ART	PE	Word Study/ Language Workshop/ Instruction	MUSIC

Use a community-building framework OR include poetry, oral language, math, critical thinking, art appreciation, etc.

Here, word study is part of language workshop. Word study and language conventions are explored, studied, practiced, and used each day.

Students move their bodies and/or work on relaxation/meditation techniques. *Tech-free 10 minutes!*

Transitions and time to pack up are included in the schedule.

Spending Time Exploring Words

There are countless possibilities for how word study time could look in your classroom. What follow are just a few of the many, many options.

TEACHER TIP

We will go much more in depth into what the whole-class, small-group, partner, individual, and center routines could include starting in the next chapter and continuing throughout the rest of this book.

I don't always use a Monday to Friday schedule when implementing a word study curriculum. A Monday to Friday schedule would be most appropriate when each week the class is studying the same pattern or types of words, and you are providing differentiation within that framework. If you are brand new to word study and your district does not use a balanced literacy framework, a Monday to Friday schedule is a perfectly appropriate and thoughtful way to begin this work. If your district uses a balanced literacy framework and you are comfortable and confident using workshop structures, you may prefer to work in cycles as opposed to weeks.

FOR GRADES K–2: WHEN I HAVE ONLY A FEW MINUTES EACH DAY . . .

Monday	Tuesday	Wednesday	Thursday	Friday
Whole-class minilesson or introduction (often phonemic awareness or phonics driven)	Small-group work OR one *meaningful* center rotation	Partner work OR one *meaningful* center rotation	Individual work OR one *meaningful* center rotation	Whole-class minilesson (often phonemic awareness or phonics driven)

FOR GRADES 3–6: WHEN I HAVE ONLY A FEW MINUTES EACH DAY . . .

Monday	Tuesday	Wednesday	Thursday	Friday
Whole-class minilesson or introduction with goal setting	Partner work with partner reflection	Individual work with self-assessment	Partner work with partner celebration	Check-in—how's it going? (many different models)

FOR GRADES K–2: WHEN I HAVE ABOUT 20 MINUTES EACH DAY . . .

	Monday	Tuesday	Wednesday	Thursday	Friday
Students	Whole-class minilesson, tip, or learning experience (often phonemic awareness or phonics driven)	Work with small group, on own, or in center doing "meaning" work Class share/ Reflection	Work with small group, on own, or in center doing "meaning" work Class share/ Reflection	Work with small group, on own, or in center doing "spelling" work Class share/ Reflection	Work with small group or on own doing "spelling" work Class share/ Reflection
Teacher	Facilitate whole-group learning experience	Work with one small group	Work with one small group	Work with one small group	Work with selected students

FOR GRADES 3–6: WHEN I HAVE ABOUT 20 MINUTES EACH DAY . . .

	Monday	Tuesday	Wednesday	Thursday	Friday
Students	Whole-class minilesson, tip, or learning experience related to words, recent observations, or a class wonder	Work with small group, partner, or on own to do "meaning" work Class share, reflection, or celebration	Work with small group, partner, or on own to do "meaning" work Class share, reflection, or celebration	Work with small group, partner, or on own to do "spelling" work Class share, reflection, or celebration	Work with small group, partner, or on own to do "spelling" work Class share, reflection, or celebration
Teacher	Facilitate whole-group learning experience	Work with one small group	Work with selected students	Work with one small group	Work with selected students

FOR GRADES K–2: WHEN I HAVE TIME FOR A FULL "LANGUAGE WORKSHOP" EACH DAY AND/OR ALREADY USE A BALANCED LITERACY FRAMEWORK . . .

	Sample Word Study Cycles (5–7 Days Are Most Typical)
Word Study Cycle or Unit	EACH DAY: • 5–8 minutes: Minilesson on a pattern, strategy, or habit most the class is ready for • 10–15 minutes: Independent, small-group, and/or meaningful center work ○ During this time, teachers provide differentiated support (more to come on this) • 1–5 minutes: Partner or whole-class teaching share/Closure
Grammar/ Language Cycle or Unit	EACH DAY: • 5–8 minutes: Minilesson on a convention or strategy most the class is ready for • 10–15 minutes: Independent, small-group, and/or meaningful center work ○ During this time, teachers provide differentiated support (more to come on this) • 1–5 minutes: Partner or whole-class teaching share/Closure

Many teachers choose to alternate word study and language by

• Cycle (5–7 days)

• Unit (4–6 weeks)

Some choose to alternate a full word study unit with a cycle of language work.

TEACHER TIP

Some classrooms follow a Monday to Friday schedule. Other classrooms work in **cycles**. A **cycle** of word study is often 5 to 7 days and does not follow a traditional Monday to Friday format. For example, Day 1 of a cycle could start on a Tuesday, and if school was closed on Wednesday, Day 2 of the cycle would be Thursday. Day 3 would be Friday, Day 4 would be Monday, and so on.

FOR GRADES 3–6: WHEN I HAVE TIME FOR A FULL "LANGUAGE WORKSHOP" EACH DAY AND/ OR ALREADY USE A BALANCED LITERACY FRAMEWORK . . .

	Sample Word Study Cycles (5–7 Days Are Most Typical)
Word Study Week, Cycle, or Unit	EACH DAY: • 5–10 minutes: Minilesson on a pattern, strategy, or habit most the class is ready for • 10–20 minutes: Individual, partner, or small-group work ○ During this time, teachers provide differentiated support (more to come on this) • 1–5 minutes: Partner or whole-class teaching share/Closure
Grammar/ Language Week, Cycle, or Unit	EACH DAY: • 5–10 minutes: Minilesson on a convention or strategy most the class is ready for • 10–20 minutes: Individual, partner, or small-group work ○ During this time, teachers provide differentiated support (more to come on this) • 1–5 minutes: Partner or whole-class teaching share/Closure

Many teachers choose to alternate word study and language by

• Cycle (5–7 days)

• Unit (4–6 weeks)

Some choose to alternate a full word study unit with a cycle of language work.

WHEN I AM PART OF A DEPARTMENTALIZED PROGRAM AND HAVE ONLY A CERTAIN NUMBER OF MINUTES A DAY TO TEACH "EVERYTHING" LITERACY

Example of a Six-Day Rotating Schedule

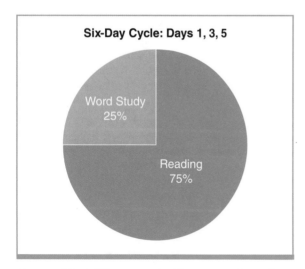

Literacy block (60 minutes)—15 minutes of word study followed by 45 minutes of reading

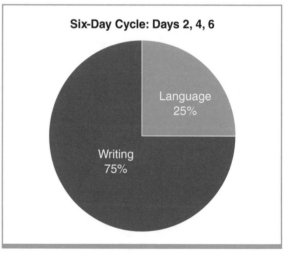

Literacy Block (60 minutes)—15 minutes of language followed by 45 minutes of writing

Example of a "Rotating Unit" Schedule

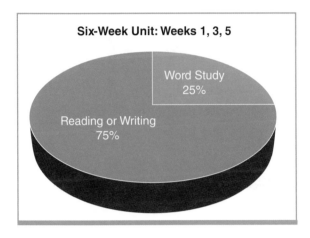

Six-Week Unit: Weeks 1, 3, 5

Word Study 25%

Reading or Writing 75%

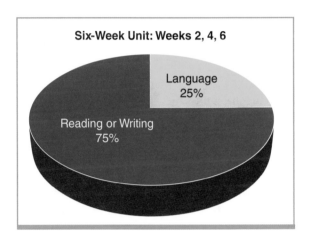

Six-Week Unit: Weeks 2, 4, 6

Language 25%

Reading or Writing 75%

60-Minute Literacy Block When It Is a Reading Unit:

Week 1, 3, 5: 15 minutes word study, 45 minutes reading

Week 2, 4, 6: 15 minutes language, 45 minutes reading

60-Minute Literacy Block When It Is a Writing Unit:

Week 1, 3, 5: 15 minutes word study, 45 minutes writing

Week 2, 4, 6: 15 minutes language, 45 minutes writing

TEACHER TIP

In both structures, I recommend doing the few minutes of word study or language *first.* If saved for the end of the period, these components are likely to get "bumped" fairly consistently.

Setting Up Structures

WHAT: CO-CREATING LEARNING SPACES, FINDING AND PREPARING MATERIALS

Walt Disney is said to have advised, "The way to get started is to quit talking and begin doing." Finding, choosing, and preparing materials seems like a purposeful (and F-U-N) way to "begin doing." I often share that when in doubt, I go see an early childhood educator. This position requires a tool belt filled with supplemental, super-creative, outside-the-box strategies in virtually every imaginable domain. Perhaps this is why I find myself referring to Renee Dinnerstein's book, *Choice Time* (2016), for ideas I can use, tweak, and apply across *all* grades in *all* contexts. I love what Renee has to say about classroom environments. She recommends setting up a space that fosters both collaboration and creative thinking. Ideally, this learning space is organized, lacks clutter, and possesses aesthetic beauty. Renee invites us to bring nature into our classrooms and plan spaces where children can access materials without adult assistance (p. 22). By doing this, she promises, we bring in a sense of co-ownership.

This is me getting the letters all by myself. My group shares them. I like making words. I don't think cleaning up is fun, but I do it. We all clean up because it's our classroom.

—Donovan, age 5

Most importantly, Renee shares ways to create a "room with a voice" suggesting we, too, find a sense of playfulness in creating our learning spaces. Specifically, she recommends removing nonessential furniture, looking for pieces of furniture that serve multiple purposes, creating quiet nooks, and considering the flow from one part of the room to another. While creating spaces, we can also consider the noise level of different areas of the room. Perhaps my favorite way to create a collaborative room with a heart is Renee's recommendation to highlight *collaboratively* created classroom charts "hung up like literacy laundry" (p. 30). What a beautiful image!

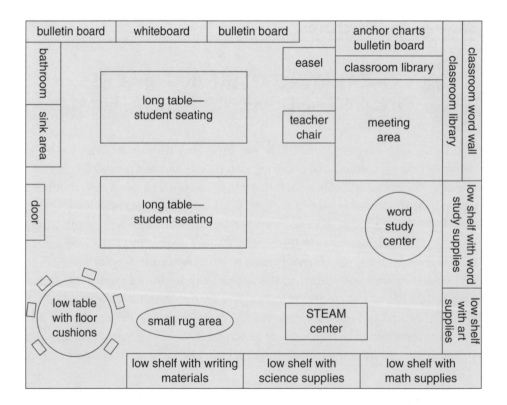

An early elementary classroom setup.

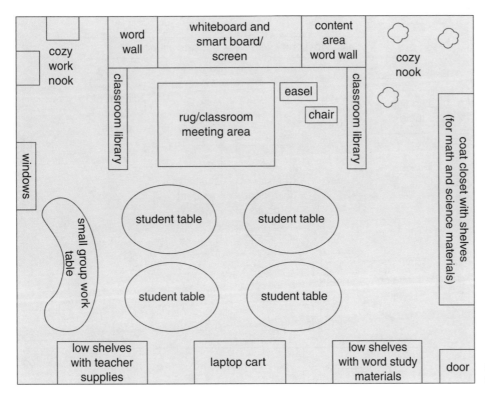

An elementary classroom setup.

An elementary classroom setup.

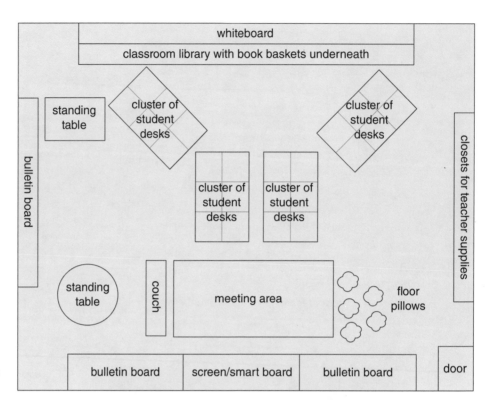

An upper-elementary/middle-grades classroom setup.

Alphabet chart made by kindergarteners. When students co-create classroom charts, they are more likely to refer to and use them.

WHY: CUSTOMIZED CLASSROOMS FIT AND NURTURE LEARNERS

It's fruitful to consider new ideas and revamp the physical layout of our classrooms because children grow into the spaces we create—and more importantly, it's wise to invite children's ideas, for they have plenty to offer regarding how we can improve our learning spaces. In *What Do I Teach Readers Tomorrow? Nonfiction* (2017), two of my mentors, Gravity Goldberg and Renee Houser, empower teachers in their role as intentional decision-makers. Although they were specifically speaking of making decisions for reading workshop, their advice can be transferred into almost any learning domain. I greatly appreciate their wise words, telling us to look at our students (not a manual) to decide what is most needed (p. 9). When we study our students and recognize both their strengths and appropriate next steps, we may have a better understanding of what *this* class needs right now. The physical and emotional environments we create in our classrooms and schools need to support and nurture the independence of learners in the room. Learning will flourish when we take the time to create a welcoming, creative, and collaborative space. Ask yourself this: When I look at my classroom, does it encourage learners to be self-sufficient—or dependent upon me? Trust me, you want the former!

The materials we select to enhance word learning are also an important consideration. In *Simple Starts* (2015), Kari Yates provides "Courage Rules" for teachers. I am positively googly-eyed over these guidelines, but the first courage rule can be applied to virtually every possible scenario. Kari recommends, "Start small, but start" (p. 170). When selecting materials, I wholeheartedly suggest you remember these words. It is easy to feel we need *so* much, and we need to have it all before beginning. The truth is, we need very little to begin word study. Most of what is *essential* is first, debatable, and second, found in your classroom. We don't want to postpone this learning in hopes of having it all look and feel perfect first. In fact, by starting simply, the management of these materials and routines for which we use these materials will become internalized by students so much more quickly. When considering which items you want to prioritize attaining, I would like to suggest you ask yourself three questions:

1. Will it help my students do more meaningful and thoughtful work?

2. Will it help my students create learning possibilities for themselves?

3. Will it help create joyful and exciting learning?

Whether outfitted with "the latest and greatest" in flexible seating options or more traditional classroom furniture, there's possibility in *every* classroom to co-create space, invite student choice, and build shared ownership.

Choice Time centers are immersed with words so students can create their own meaningful learning experiences through play.

Left: Tables (set at different heights) and chairs on wheels.
Right: Bean bags and comfy cushions. Flexible seating options make for endless, inviting collaborative work options.

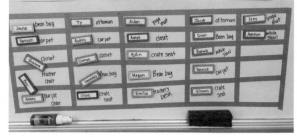

Left: Students decide where supplies are kept.
Right: Students decide where they will work. Both photos show student ownership of classroom materials.

WHEN: HOW OFTEN TO REFRESH LEARNING SPACES AND TIPS FOR SUCCESS

I have long considered trying to be "that teacher" who truly and fully co-created the classroom with students. Although I have moved away from having a fully functional classroom on the first day of school, I still find myself preparing the outline of our space before school even begins. I like a little "wow" when students walk into the room the first time, but I also leave a lot of our space *in progress* so that we can better define and refine it together. By co-creating some of the spaces in our classroom, I do find that students are more collaborative and respectful in those spaces.

I also try to be flexible in my initial decisions. If something isn't working or doesn't seem right, even if it was perfect for last year's class, I will change it for this year's class. If certain materials were favorites last year and are ignored this year, I simply tuck them away. If my current class is obsessed with something new, I try to find, add, and create more of it. "When" may start before the students walk into your classroom, but it is on an ongoing and continuous loop. We can alter our classroom spaces and materials at any point. We can try on different material management systems, and as Gravity and Renee suggest, *look to our students* to make those follow-up and ongoing decisions.

All that said, even starting small can be exhausting! Here are a few tidbits to help you "begin doing."

ESSENTIALS SHOPPING LIST

You likely have most of the needed materials for word study already in your classroom! Time to go "shopping" around your classroom. No purchase necessary.

ESSENTIALS CLASSROOM SHOPPING LIST

- Notebooks and folders
- Pens, pencils, paper, scissors, crayons, markers, colored pencils, markers, glue sticks
- Pocket chart
- Index cards or sentence strips
- Word-building manipulatives— basics include magnetic letters and/or letter tiles
- Mini dry-erase boards and markers (or a plain piece of paper inside a clear sheet protector)
- Magnetic boards or baking/ cookie trays
- Engaging, developmentally appropriate books
- Word games (Zingo, Scrabble, Bananagrams, Boggle, etc.)

As you can see, most of these items are already stored in either your classroom supply closet or building supply closet. Many of us with an indoor recess bin have some type of word games available. If necessary, upper-elementary teachers can also check in with their primary counterparts. There are often plenty of letter manipulatives available for sharing.

WORTH-THE-MONEY SHOPPING LIST

My suggested "Worth-the-Money Shopping List" includes the most commonly used materials that may need to be purchased. Many classrooms already have at least some of these materials. There are also easy, DIY (free or almost-free) options for each of these ideas.

WORTH-THE-MONEY SHOPPING LIST

- ☐ MORE engaging, accessible books
- ☐ Poetry books
- ☐ Blending boards and letter cards (K–2)
- ☐ Additional fun and meaningful word games
- ☐ Select other miscellaneous letter/word-building materials, including but not limited to these:
- ☐ Wikki Stix
- ☐ Pipe cleaners
- ☐ Legos or building bricks
- ☐ Magna Doodles
- ☐ Chalk
- ☐ Mini chalkboards
- ☐ Computer keyboards (even old keyboards with cords cut off)

Dry-erase boards and markers are easy-to-find word study materials.

Sixth graders (and students of all ages!) enjoy and benefit from word-building manipulatives!

WISH LIST SHOPPING LIST

Last, we have the "Wish List Shopping List." This list includes materials that could enhance practices—but are not completely necessary. You could factor these purchases into your grade-level or school's yearly budget.

WISH LIST SHOPPING LIST

- ☐ Even MORE engaging, accessible books
- ☐ Even MORE poetry books
- ☐ 3–5 iPads loaded with *well-reviewed* letter and word game apps (K–2)
- ☐ Chromebooks or other 1:1 devices
- ☐ Additional playful manipulatives, including these:
- ☐ Linking letters (Unifix Cubes, creature-themed, construction-themed, etc.)
- ☐ Translucent letters with lightboard
- ☐ Letter beads
- ☐ Clips and cards sets (various types available)
- ☐ Make-a-word tile sets and dice sets (for simple, starting CVC patterns through prefix, suffix, and root patterns)

These 1:1 devices are by no means a necessity, but they are worthwhile "wish list" items.

WHERE DO I PUT IT ALL?

We aim to create classroom spaces where energy and learning are optimal. We can *choose* to carefully plan our classroom environment and make materials available to students. As a result, students are more apt to explore, work, persevere, and problem solve with greater independence. When we consider storage of materials, we want to consider how to give student-friendly access to them. As teachers, we are incredibly busy and have better ways to spend our time than managing materials. Students will also feel more ownership when they manage supplies. Take some time to thoughtfully consider storage of word study materials—it is a win–win solution for us *and* students.

Teachers across grades find creative ways to store materials so students can access and manage supplies with greater independence.

WORKAROUNDS

Three things educators rarely have enough of? Time. Money. Space. And yet, teachers have a special way of circumventing hurdles (like these) with flair and know-how! Here's a bit of advice to set those wheels in motion.

CHALLENGE 1: *I don't have the money for the materials suggested! I checked around my building and don't see them and/or colleagues don't have any to spare.*

POSSIBLE WORKAROUNDS

☐ Beg, borrow, or steal (sort of kidding). Worst-case scenario, you can be like me and "steal" from the children in your own life to bring a starter set of letter manipulatives and/or games into your classroom . . . or ask the families of your students. Caregivers are often ready to part with (and are looking to get rid of) a lot of those "seemingly" early toys and tools.

☐ Be creative. Consider getting together with colleagues for a "tool-making," grade-level meeting/ party. If you are an administrator, you will be celebrated and receive never-ending accolades if you provide faculty meeting time to gather materials and create DIY versions of what are not budget-feasible items.

☐ Check the companion website for this book, resources.corwin.com/ wordstudythatsticks. I have included printable letter cards, blend and digraph cards, and common prefix, suffix, and root cards to help you get started. Ideally, you would print these on cardstock, possibly laminate, and be ready to go.

online resources

☐ Get help! PTO and other local grants are options to help you obtain a couple of your prioritized "wish list" items. DonorsChoose.org is another worthwhile avenue to explore.

CHALLENGE 2: *I gathered a lot of the "stuff" recommended, but I have no place to put it all.*

POSSIBLE WORKAROUNDS

☐ Purge. You *know* there is plenty of "stuff" in your classroom you don't need. A few years ago, a beloved parent (of a beloved student) lent me her copy of *The Life-Changing Magic of Tidying Up* by Marie Kondo (2015). This book is jam-packed with straight talk and advice, such as, "No matter how wonderful things used to be, we cannot live in the past. The joy and excitement we feel here and now are more important" (p. 114). Using this advice, I tackled my classroom, and the results were spectacular. The space became more organized and calm. What was removed was only the overwhelming clutter that distracted from what was most important.

☐ Ask for help. Who? Perhaps a young teacher in your building who just finished college and found ways to organize a small dorm room. How? Take a tour of your school. Find *that* teacher with *that* classroom. In this room, everything is organized and in its place, and even though your rooms are identical in size, his or her room seems so much larger. THAT person is your go-to resource! He or she likely has a passion for organizing—and may even do it for you—for the FUN of it!

PRACTICAL PRIORITIZING

☐ Look closely at your current classroom schedule. Investigate where you can carve out space for word learning.

☐ Consider your classroom setup. Think about how to create a space that invites thinking, creativity, and collaboration. Map out a few ideas.

☐ **Go "shopping" around your classroom.** Gather, purchase, and create starting materials. Organize materials in a way that encourages students to manage classroom supplies with independence.

☐ Get caught up in the excitement of kicking off a new year of word learning!

CHAPTER THREE

Launching a Year of Lively Learning

A good teacher finds time for learning and fun—usually together. For example, a teacher might lead a lesson but we would ALL have fun at the same time. A good teacher should have a good sense of laughter. When we have fun, we want to participate and we want to do even more. We don't want the learning to stop

—Theresa, age 11

Once we carve out the time, co-create the learning space, and gather some supplies, we are ready to start things up. Cultivating a culture of word learning starts with students. Getting students on board and recognizing the *why* is essential. This chapter includes two parts to help students understand the purpose of and practices inherent in a stepped-up approach to word study:

- The first part outlines lessons that kick off a year of meaningful word learning.

- The second part includes more than two weeks of high-impact lessons that can be used to help students learn how to actively explore all aspects of words.

WHAT: INTRODUCING THE IDEA OF WORD EXPLORING

Have you had "the talk" with students? There is no more appropriate way to begin our study of words than by using our words! I often used to rush into introducing content without making the purpose clear to students. Now, I always start with a conversation to help students understand what word study is, why they are learning it, and how that learning will look over the course of the year. Whether spritely kindergartners who can barely sit still on a rug for a minute or cynical sixth graders, children immediately appreciate and grasp the concept that word learning leads to them becoming confident, competent speakers, readers, writers, and communicators.

The research on teacher clarity goes back decades, and there has been a resurgence of interest in it in recent years. John Hattie describes the concept in terms of "visible learning" in his 2016 book, *Visible Learning for Literacy*, coauthored with Douglas Fisher and Nancy Frey, which popularized the research even more. They advise, "We need to make sure our students know WHAT they are learning, WHY they are learning it, and HOW they will know when they learned it" (p. 41, emphasis added). Further, Alfie Kohn (2011) reminds us that we shouldn't focus on what we teach, but instead on what students learn, and there's a greater likelihood of learning when the students have voice and choice in both the content and the process. Pulling from the words and ideas of these revered leaders, it is clear we need to talk to our students about word study, our hopes for word study, and expectations for this time—and invite students to do the same. Laura Robb, author of *Read, Talk, Write* (2017), says it beautifully when she writes, "Talk brings social interactions to learning and initiates deep thinking" (p. 3).

WHY: COMMUNICATING THE PURPOSE OF WORD LEARNING

In Simon Sinek's 2009 TED Talk "How Great Leaders Inspire Action," he tells us, "When we start with *why*, we have vision . . . all the decisions we make connect back to the why." When we start with *why*, we provide vision and make the invisible visible. For me, the *why* behind inviting our students into our world of word study is all about mutual respect. I am the kind of person who tends to rebel when words such as *must*, *should*, and *have to* are used. As a teacher, coach, or administrator, we do have certain leadership responsibilities. However, we certainly can't do *anything* without students. Classroom work is shared work. At its best, classroom "work" is creative, collaborative, learning play. When I start by setting goals *with* students and highlighting the *why* of the work we are taking on together, there is instant buy-in. When I listen to the ambitions, concerns, and ideas of students, I learn more than I could have ever imagined. This reciprocal respect breeds high-quality, high-quantity, joyful learning. Our first classroom word study conversations and lessons aim to do just this.

WHEN: WORD STUDY RIGHT FROM THE START

Day 1 . . . or OK, realistically, by the end of Week 1—that's the quick answer to *When do we share our invitation with students and start word study?* By the time the school year has started, we have set the stage. We have organized a skeleton classroom space that we plan to continue to co-create together with the class. We have found, purchased, and/or created prioritized materials. We have thoughtfully stored these materials in a way we imagined could be easily accessible for our students. We have set aside time in our daily schedule that is devoted to word learning. All that's left is to begin. We don't need to wait for all the stars to align for the feeling to be just right, or to have every *wish list* supply. This is one of those cases where we want to jump right in! In *Daring Greatly* (2016), Brené Brown reminds us that vulnerability is the "birthplace" and great source of joy, creativity, courage, and eventual clarity (p. 34). This is our time to embrace a bit of uncertainty—that is, have a plan, but also be ready to be flexible and reshape that plan, as students show us the path that is just right for them. The lesson ideas included in the rest of this chapter will help you to introduce word study and foundational (yet meaningful, student-centered, balanced) word study routines to your class.

Lessons That Introduce the World of Word Study

Speaking, listening, questioning, and—in the words of my close friend and colleague, Laura Sarsten—"engaging in spirited conversation" will be a huge part of word study learning. Because students often need practice and support in all parts of conversation, most launch units (across subject areas) dedicate a great deal of time on building class, partner, and "inside-the-head" talk. Word study will be no different—it will not bear the weight of this entire lofty task, but the different talk lessons and practice you do across subject areas will all synergistically result in a much stronger talking community. The kickoff lessons that follow intend to build excitement and an eagerness to talk and learn about words. You can use, modify, or adapt any of these lessons to make them appropriate for other grade levels or students with a distinct set of instructional needs.

> ### TEACHER TIP
>
> In this book, **lesson** refers to instruction that can be "one and done." **Routine** refers to a practice that students will be using regularly throughout the year.

> ### TEACHER TIP
>
> I recommend spending the first 8 to 12 weeks of kindergarten focusing solely on bolstering phonemic awareness, solidifying letter recognition, and *introducing* letter–sound correspondence. Most kindergarten teachers I know *first* focus on these essential building blocks. Once kindergartners are into the swing of school and have been immersed in the exciting world of sounds and letters, the routines in this chapter and the rest of the book can and will be used to continue building letter–sound correspondence, as well as all other essential aspects of a well-rounded approach to word study.

Favorite Words

Grades K–I, Kickoff Lesson I

WHAT?

Students will start their word study learning lives by partaking in a mini-inquiry of favorite words.

HOW?

1. Gather students for a "class meeting"–styled conversation about words and favorite words.

2. Model by sharing a few favorite words and the *why* behind what makes these words favorites. Choose one word. Sketch and write that word.

3. Invite students to think of, sketch, write, and share their favorite word and why they like it.

4. Create a class display of favorite words.

5. Increase enthusiasm by telling students that at the end of this year, they will know how to read and write so many more words and that they will likely all have *many* new favorite words.

WHY?

- To celebrate words
- To build excitement about words
- To practice speaking and listening
- To encourage sharing and trusting each other with our precious ideas

YOU NEED

- Sticky notes, index cards, sentence strips, or paper for "favorite word" sketches and writing
- Miscellaneous art supplies
- Chart paper or bulletin board space

TIPS

- If students are not *yet* writing conventionally, create a class chart: Students can sketch their word and orally share their word with the class. Teachers can create a class chart titled "Our Favorite Words" and list students' names and their favorite words. Student can then come hang their sketch next to their name/word written on the chart.

- FUN: Kids love trading cards (baseball, basketball, Pokémon, etc.). Have students trade their completed word card with another student in the class. Then, the partners will introduce each other's favorite word to the rest of the class. This promotes careful listening and confident speaking.

- Extension: Create a bulletin board display of the class's favorite words. This can become a "fun" word wall for students to use in their writing.

Why Do We Study Words?

Grades 2–3, Kickoff Lesson 1

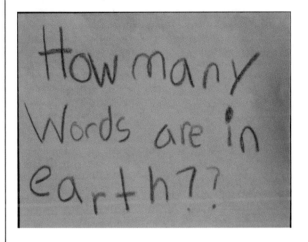

WHAT?

Students will begin to think about *why* we study words and why it is important to learn about words.

HOW?

1. Read aloud a short text on "words," with a word theme or with beautiful, especially entertaining, or interestingly formatted words (see Appendix C for plenty of suggestions).

2. Ask students, "Why do we study words?" Remind students there are no right or wrong answers and that you hope everyone will have different answers!

3. Give students time to think, talk, and/or write a bit about this question.

4. Share out responses. Talk about and chart student responses.

5. Increase enthusiasm by sharing that this year, the class will be able to do all of this and more by studying words together.

WHY?

- To celebrate words
- To build excitement about words and word study

- To model asking open-ended questions, employing inquiry-based thinking, and thinking beyond our first thoughts

YOU NEED

- A favorite book that is word-themed or begs you to notice the words (for my favorites, see Appendix C)
- Chart paper
- Markers
- *Optional*: Sticky notes, index cards, or sentence strips if students want to write their own responses

TIPS

- Create a class "wonder wall" and have the first round of wonders be about words! Students can pose interesting, open-ended questions about words on the wonder wall.

- If any wonders are researchable or debatable, make time for further exploration of student ideas.

- A few of the many possible word-themed read-aloud book titles are listed in Appendix C.

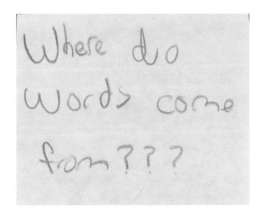

What Do You Think?

Grades 4–6, Kickoff Lesson I

WHAT?

Students think about the power, wonder, and importance of words.

HOW?

1. Share a famous quote about words. See Appendix D for suggestions.

2. Have students participate in a "written conversation" with a partner to share their thoughts, ideas, and questions about the quote.

3. Come together as a class and discuss thoughts, feelings, reactions, and ideas about the quote; then extend to words in general and finish with the importance of word learning.

WHY?

- To celebrate and build excitement about words

- To encourage sharing and trusting each other with our precious ideas

- To model asking open-ended questions, employing inquiry-based thinking, and thinking beyond our first thoughts

YOU NEED

- Paper and "fun" writing utensils for the written conversation

- Quote posted large enough for all to see (chart paper, smart board, screen, etc.)

TIPS

- Written conversation: Student partners write simultaneously for an allotted amount of time, switch papers, read what their partner wrote, and add to that. Partners keep writing and switching papers back and forth as many times as you ask. No out-loud conversation happens until after this "thought-gathering" time.

- Class conversation ideas: Instead of a written conversation, have students share

their thoughts with others using your favorite partner, small-group, or whole-class conversation model. A few ideas include "snowball discussions" (partnerships turn into ever-growing groups) or "speed dating" (two lines face one another and students have a short time to share their thoughts and ideas with a constantly changing rotation of classmates).

- Multiple quotes: Post different "word quotes" on chart paper around the room. Have students participate in a gallery walk, rotating from poster to poster and sharing their thoughts for each. Find something interesting or debatable to discuss further as a class.

- Use Padlet to allow students to respond to quote(s) digitally.

- Use a favorite digital platform—Google Classroom, Today's Meet, or Voxer—to have students post their responses and respond to one another's ideas digitally.

- Celebrate the words of students, too! Create a chart or dedicate wall space to pay tribute to the interesting, funny, and poignant words students share. Grow this space and collection over time.

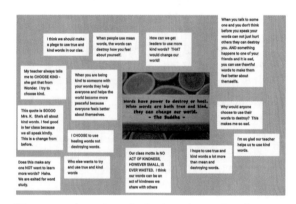

We post and use these Padlet boards as a "text" to spark more in-depth, whole-class conversation; then, we follow up with blogging to synthesize thinking from these quick initial posts.

Who Does What?

Grades K–6, Kickoff Lesson 2

	Day 1	Day 2	Day 3	Day 4	Day 5
Students	Meet together as a class	Work with group	Meet together as a class	Work with group	Work with group
Teacher		Meet with one group		Meet with one group	Meet with one group

WHAT?

If this approach to word study is new or different for students, it will likely be important to talk about what word study will look like this year. It will also be important to define the roles of different classroom members.

HOW?

1. Have a class meeting to discuss this model of word study instruction. Think of this as both an informational seminar *and* a pep rally.
2. Talk through what word study will "look like" each day and the across the week.
3. Together, co-create a chart to clearly define the teacher and student roles in the different parts of word study instruction.

WHY?

- To give a daily, weekly, and an overall vision for word study
- To define roles of classroom members and set the tone for engaged learning
- To highlight the interdependence of classroom members

YOU NEED

- Chart paper and markers
- *Optional*: Device and screen

TIPS

- While creating the chart, be sure to discuss the *why* behind the importance of each role. We want our students to see the importance of our work so it is not interrupted (or at least is interrupted much less). We also want students to understand the importance of their role so that routines are not assignments, but important, meaningful, and purposeful for students of all ages!
- Are you techy, or do you use 1:1? Instead of a traditional anchor chart, co-create a Google Slide or Doc to be posted on Google Classroom or shared in a class folder.

Teacher Roles	Student Roles
• Lead quick, whole-class lessons. • Work with small groups, partners, and individual students. • Coach, don't tell. • Ask questions. • Help make sure materials are cared for and organized. • Provide classroom time for word exploring. • Don't rush discovery—let students figure some of this out! • Share expertise . . . sometimes.	• Listen during instructional time. • Listen to partners and groups. • Ask questions of others and ourselves. • Keep going and going—we never finish. • Look at things differently. • Try different ways of thinking. • Take care of materials. • Observe, think, try, and do! • Have fun! Learn! Use new words in our speaking and writing. • Share learning with others.

A chart made by a sixth-grade class

WORKAROUNDS

CHALLENGE I: *I have a word study program I need to use, and this is not an outlined lesson.*

POSSIBLE WORKAROUNDS

- ☐ That's OK—add these lessons in! Word study is an attitude and set of active behaviors we use as we approach learning more about words. Studying words is an essential part of word learning and any spelling or vocabulary program. All the lessons suggested in this book can be added to any existing word study program. Feel free to incorporate and enhance away. Your students will thank you for it—and you will likely feel the joy, too.

CHALLENGE 2: *My kindergartners don't know how to write their favorite words.*

POSSIBLE WORKAROUNDS

- ☐ Yes, they can. Perhaps many kindergarteners may not yet write conventionally, but they sure can write. In 1971, Noam Chomsky expressed that emergent writers will write well before they learn to read—provided they are encouraged to do so. The youngest of learners feel empowered as they make their mark and scribble anywhere they can— including on our walls! Early writers can "write" their words using sketches, scribbles, random strings of letters, or quasi-conventional spelling. These are all exciting ways to share words! This will also give us a glimpse into the many, varied strengths and creativity our students are bringing to the table.

- ☐ During this lesson, as students share their favorite words with the class, students can help co-create the chart by adding the Post-it note or card with their sketch and/or writing representing this word. I suggest "mining" the strengths you see (Goldberg, 2015) in this student work and authentically celebrating these brave risks.

- ☐ I offer similar advice for students new to speaking English. How exciting it will be for the entire class to learn a favorite word in a different language! This also offers an opportunity to build language for every classroom member. Explore the similarities and differences in how this word looks and sounds across languages. This could maybe morph into another branch of class inquiry. This scenario also offers a student who may feel shy or nervous to be not only celebrated but also recognized as the expert on much the "rest of us" don't know! Maybe we can all learn our favorite words in *more* than one language!?!

CHALLENGE 3: *My students are reticent to share with one another.*

POSSIBLE WORKAROUNDS

- ☐ Do it first! Put yourself out there and model being vulnerable. Be the first to try something in a trust-building activity. Make mistakes—and laugh at them—regularly (not a challenge for me). Seek risks, model taking risks, and celebrate taking risks. Kids will follow your lead, and when they do, take the time to give a shout-out!

- ☐ Build classroom community. Early in the year, students are just getting to know each other—and their teachers! Sharing is understandably scary. Ice breakers and "get-to-know-you" games are a great way to build a sense of security and belonging. Participation could be encouraged and not mandated. Set up scenarios in which students can discover what they have in common with their classmates. Celebrate what makes us unique and stronger as a collective community.

☐ Take on class challenges—create something cool together, whether it be a classroom makerspace, a movie trailer for your classroom presentation at Back-to-School Night, or something else FUN—preferably not directly related to subject area learning. Let students discover that working toward goals is often easier when you are part of a team.

Introducing Routines Memorably

 WHAT: **TEN ROUTINES TO LAUNCH A YEAR OF LEARNING**

STARTING UP

I saw Pam do the Favorite Words lesson with a class last year and loved it. I actually plan on using it as an ice-breaker activity next year on the first day of school. This will also motivate me to jump right into word study.

—Jim, Grade 3 Teacher

The *way* you launch anything new is usually a key ingredient in the success of that undertaking. In this next section, I hope to help you set the groundwork for an entire school year of word learning. For many of us, this student-centered, active approach to word study may be different from our past experiences. Minilessons and whole-class, supported practice in the structures, routines, and management of materials will be essential in the kickoff to a successful year. Beyond these basics, during these early weeks we can also teach students the language of word study, the choices that are available, how to talk with and work with peers, and how to reflect on their learning. In "Making Learning Fun: A Taxonomy of Intrinsic Motivations for Learning" (1987), Malone and Lepper remind us that we can't just think about the cognitive processes that are inherent in learning, but we also could take the time to consider the intrinsic motivation that is just as essential to learning. Part of the importance of this launch is helping kids catch the spirit of word learning and wanting to partake—not because of possible external rewards or punishments, but because they feel it is purposeful and valuable. With that in mind, these first lessons intend to lead with laughter and elicit interest and adventure.

STEPPING UP

I work in a middle school and tried all these lessons with my classes. These lessons work for all grades. Students of any age will enjoy this type of kickoff.

—Aretha, Grade 6 Replacement Teacher

 WHY: **STARTING WITH WHOLE-CLASS WORD STUDY YIELDS A YEAR OF SUCCESS**

Everyone benefits from developing a full understanding of the *why, what, when,* and *how* of word study—students and teachers alike. Dedicating time to unpack the structures and processes of word study sets the wheels in motion for an efficient and productive year of learning. Solidifying this understanding breeds confidence. Confidence increases expertise. With expertise comes a sense of ease. Once students know and own these initial routines, they can focus on inviting more challenge and critical thinking into their word study practice. Students will also be more prepared to make purposeful choices, even in the earliest of grades. As we know, choice builds ownership and investment.

In 2016's *Choice Time*, Renee Dinnerstein proclaims that "during choice time, children have the freedom and opportunity to try out new ideas, seek answers, test predictions, navigate new social interactions, and experiment with a variety of materials in both structured and unstructured ways" (p. 2). In this way, building ownership of routines in word study offers much of the same to students. Also, once students have an understanding, solid competency, and fluidity in and with these routines, they will be prepared for decision-making in when and how they carry out these methods of word learning. We can also then begin to add in additional authentic routines to expand their repertoire, support their word learning, and provide additional choices. By providing a supported and strong foundation of word study practices, all subsequent and differentiated learning has room to grow and flourish. One of the world's leading business thinkers and multiple-time author Dan Pink shares that "control leads to compliance, but autonomy yields engagement" (2010). By taking the time to properly launch word study and carefully scaffold support at the start of the year, we build autonomy in practices for the remainder of the school year. Students become engaged in the study of words. Their investment is authentic and supersedes compliance.

WHEN: STARTING SOONER PROVIDES MORE TIME FOR LEARNING

When I was a starting teacher, most of my mentors did not offer advice on curriculum, but instead on how to get my classroom up and running. This tricky work is critically important, but it is often not taught or outlined for us. Most of our curriculum and provided materials offer information about what to do "once things are in place." But first, we need to get things in place! This leads educators, both new and highly experienced, to ponder, *Where do I start?* I imagine these launch lessons would generally be carried out over the first few weeks of school. Our exact pacing and final decisions on which lessons to include can be made with our students in mind. If you are not yet confident in your thoughts about the rollout, you are welcome to carry out these lessons just as outlined. However, please know—as with all educational practices—your classroom means your decision. Tweak, modify, and change what's here in any way you see fit.

Finally, we do not need to wait for a new school year to make changes and modifications to our practice. There is always an opportunity to adjust, no matter what the time of year. If you stumbled upon this book and half of the year is already behind you, remember that you have half of the year to go! Simon Sinek reminds us that progress is more important than perfect (2009). Progress does not have a start date. Even if the timing doesn't appear traditional, ideal, or perfect, we can still give things a go and try this all out. Fresh starts can happen at any time!

Launch Lessons: Introducing Routines

What follow are 10 routines for grades K–2 and 10 for grades 3–6 plus a bonus lesson—two school weeks of whole-class instructional ideas to introduce your students to the world of word study. In these introductory lessons, students will begin to discover the mindset of one who studies words, how to care for materials, and even some starting word study routines. There are brilliant minds that have developed and shared ideas for word study practices that teachers around the world already use. As such, some of the included routines, such as the popular meaning-based sorts that are research-backed and recommended by many experts in the field, may seem like practices you already know. In these cases, focus on the talk, choice, and more collaborative experiences highlighted in these "tweaks" of well-known and time-tested practices.

GRADES 1–6 LESSON 1: SET UP WORD STUDY NOTEBOOKS

Many teachers I know (myself included) keep their own reading and writing notebooks. We want to show students that we live this work alongside them. We love how our notebooks allow us to become a part of our classroom learning communities and not seen as someone "in charge." (Secretly, we also love being able to use our own notebooks in minilessons, small-group work, and conferring.) This got me thinking, *Why don't I keep my own word study notebook?* If I want my students to value words, feel invested in the study of words, and know that I also find purpose in this work, I need to live it just as I do in reading and writing . . . and yes, it could also be a great teaching tool for me to use from year to year! At the start of the year, I recommend setting up notebooks together as a class— yours included. We use our notebooks to learn with students and as an aid to our instruction. Students can take ownership of their word study notebooks and begin to see them as a useful tool they always have on hand.

STARTING UP

I was not sure which words to use in the launch. Pam reminded me that the launch is less about the words and more about learning the practices. Don't worry too much about the words. Choose a pattern that is "easy" for your class so they— and you—can focus on learning the new routines.

—Jen, Grade 2 Teacher.

STEPPING UP

Since I often start my launch before I have time to look closely at the beginning-of-the-year spelling inventory results, I usually choose simpler patterns that I know could always be reviewed by students. When I taught first grade, I often used beginning blends or short vowel sounds during my launch. Now that I have moved to fourth grade, I plan to start with r-controlled vowels or the /shen/ sound

—Tara, Grade 4 Teacher

Notebooks Are Tools!

Grades 1–6, Lesson 1

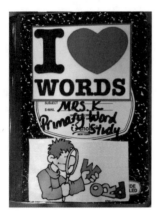

WHAT?

Students set up their word study notebooks to prepare for a meaningful year of word learning.

HOW?

1. Personalize the covers. I like fun photos and quotes about words. Some students will add "favorite words" to their notebook cover.

2. Divide the notebook into sections. I recommend a few specific sections: *Resources*, *Routines*, *Word Wonders and Collections*, and *Goals and Reflections*. An optional section is for *High-Frequency words* (some teachers mesh this work into the other sections; some separate it).

WHY?

- To give a vision for how word study will look and be recorded

- To promote independence (students will build a resource section with you and refer to it as needed to stay independent, accountable, and focused once the launch is complete)

- To highlight the role students play in word study and give them their own special space to document their learning

YOU NEED

- Notebooks (composition, spiral, and small binders could all work)
- Word study clip art, art supplies, and/or access to technology and a printer
- Clear packing tape or contact paper (to put over the glued photos on the cover)
- Flags, dividers, or Post-its to tab each section
- Scissors and glue sticks

TIPS

- Teachers can use the *Resources* section to roll out word study, teach word study practices, and foster independence. During the launch, students glue a minichart into the resource section each day a new practice is introduced. This minichart says the name of the word study practice, tells *why* the practice is useful, and has an example of what that practice looks like. This can be built upon throughout the year as new routines are introduced.

- Once small groups are up and running, students can refer to these minicharts (and first examples of this work done together) as needed. Notebooks become tools, and in turn, students are less likely to look to the teacher for redirection.

- Many word study routines are not written. However, any written work could be organized in the *Routines* section. Students refer to their written work often and use this section to reflect on their word study work habits and learning.

- If you choose to separate, the *High-Frequency* section not only lists the three to five words added each week, but it also provides space where students can play with these words.

- The *Word Wonders and Collection* section is where students can collect questions, ideas, and learning about any words of their choosing.

- The *Goals and Reflection* section has checklists to help students to self-assess and purposefully reflect on their work. Checklists are not only useful for reflection and self-assessment, but they also help students determine possible "next-step" goals (more on this in later chapters).

- There are many ways to organize a notebook. The setup discussed here is one possibility.

My own word study notebook!

GRADES K–2 LAUNCH LESSONS

Over the first few weeks of school, I recommend teachers introduce word study habits, routines, and expectations to the whole class. During the launch, the routines are the focus of instruction. Therefore, during this time, we study words that are accessible to *every* learner in the room. At this point, the prioritized learning is less about the actual words and more about the procedures that will help students eventually embrace choice, make purposeful decisions, and promote independence.

You will find that some routines coordinate well with particular programs and approaches to word study. However, all the following lessons can be used with all types of word study instruction and in conjunction with every existing program.

In kindergarten, the launch lessons that follow will often take place in the late fall. In the first two to three months of school, most word study time is spent building phonemic awareness, solidifying letter recognition, and introducing letter–sound correspondence. Phonemic awareness and phonics then become incorporated into more multifaceted word study routines to give all students—at all grades—more complete and well-rounded word learning experiences. Future chapters include lesson ideas exclusively devoted to the importance of and ways to build phonemic awareness and initial phonics skills.

TEACHER TIP

During the launch, the learning focus is the routine, not the patterns/words being used. I recommend choosing simple words and patterns. If you are STARTING UP word study, look in Appendix A for recommendations on where to find word lists you can use for the launch and for your whole year of word learning. If you are STEPPING UP word study, you will likely continue to use the words and patterns you already have access to in your district. *No matter what words you decide to use, I recommend you keep using the same set of words for all the launch lessons described.*

online resources

Don't forget! All of the notebook minicharts suggested in the launch lessons can be found at resources.corwin.com/wordstudythatsticks. Here's a sneak peek of a couple of these teacher- and student-friendly charts:

Meaning Day: Word Intro
Yep! Maybe...Huh?

Day _____

Why?
LEARN new words!

You Need:
Your word study folder, scissors, and a crayon.

How?

1. LISTEN and THINK, "Do I know this word?"
2. COLOR and CUT words.

Looks Like:

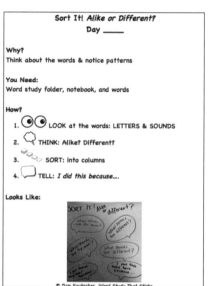

Sort It! *Alike or Different?*
Day _____

Why?
Think about the words & notice patterns

You Need:
Word study folder, notebook, and words

How?

1. LOOK at the words: LETTERS & SOUNDS
2. THINK: Alike? Different?
3. SORT: into columns
4. TELL: *I did this because....*

Looks Like:

TEACHER TIP

Word cards are provided by most publishers. If you are STEPPING UP word study, look through your printed and online materials and simply copy or print. When I was a classroom teacher STARTING UP word study with little guidance and minimal resources, I created my own larger sets of word cards by simply writing the words from each list/for each pattern being studied. Index cards are cheap, easy to get, and work perfectly. I also created my own reproducible student-sized sorting cards by creating a document and writing the words in a 3 x 5 or 4 x 5 table.

Photo by Laurie Hemmerly

Yep! Maybe . . . Huh?

Grades K–2, Lesson 2

WHAT?

It is important to make sure students know what the words being studied mean before they begin to look at what the word looks like, what it sounds like, or how it is spelled.

HOW?

1. Gather students.

2. Hold up each word being studied in the cycle, one at a time.

3. Each time you hold up a word, ask students to think about their understanding of the word.

4. If they know it and can use it, it's a YEP. If they heard it and recognize it, but perhaps can't use it, it's a MAYBE. If they don't know what a word means, it's a HUH.

5. Make three piles as you hold up words—one for YEP, one for MAYBE, and one for HUH.

6. Review all the MAYBE and HUH words together as a class.

Note: In the kindergarten launch, cards are usually pictures, often with the same starting sound. Phonemic awareness continues to be supported.

WHY?

- To learn the meaning of words (there is no sense in learning to spell words we can't use!)

- To model self-assessment of prior knowledge and reflection of understanding

- To provide essential background knowledge and kick off multidimensional word learning in a cycle of instruction

YOU NEED

- Teacher- or publisher-created word cards (one for each word being studied in the cycle). I often write words on index cards and keep them filed to use year to year. Other teachers make a Google Slides or PowerPoint presentation in which each slide is a new word to "flash" on the screen so all can see.

TIPS

- If even one student feels it is a MAYBE or HUH, put it in that pile. There's no harm in making sure everyone has a complete understanding.

- Students will need modeling to know how to distinguish between a YEP, MAYBE, and HUH. In the early weeks, you will want to model this process using tons of think-aloud.

- Some students may feel embarrassed to take the risk and share that they do not know what a word means, so I also suggest taking the lead and model being comfortable by adding a word to the MAYBE and HUH piles so that this becomes seen as a sought-out learning opportunity.

- Some teachers like to teach actions to symbolize each rating. For example, a thumbs-up or a nod for a YEP, a thumb to the side or the sign for maybe (like a palms-up seesaw) for a MAYBE, and a thumbs-down or shaking of the head for HUH. Others like to have mini dry-erase boards handy so students can jot and hold up the words *YEP*, *MAYBE*, or *HUH*.

MAYBE and YEP done with a small group.

Cut, Not Styled

Grades K–2, Lesson 3

  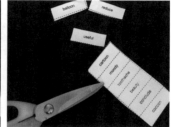

WHAT?

If you are using sort cards in your word study instruction, students need to learn to cut out their words in an efficient way. Keep in mind that sorting is a high-level thinking routine and many literacy gurus with diverse word study philosophies agree sorting is considered a "best practice."

HOW?

1. Explain that students will be using word cards with the teacher and also with small groups, partners, and independently. To use these cards, students will need to be prepared.

    Step 1: Five-second scribble on the back.

    Step 2: Picture frame—Cut along the border (the rectangle around all the words).

    Step 3: Columns—Snip top to bottom in each column.

    Step 4: Singles—Gather all columns together. Place on top of one another. Cut rows.

2. Model this start to finish. Model again, having select students "dip in" to help you. Have all students try, using one copy of the selected words. Go one step at a time, modeling and narrating the process as students work.

3. Provide a second set of words and try again—this time more quickly and independently.

WHY?

- To practice fine motor skills, listening routines, following multiple-step directions,

cutting words quickly, not perfectly (so that time is spent on studying and working with words, not cutting them).

- To make sure we, as teachers, spend our precious time on more important work than cutting sorts each week.

YOU NEED

- Many sets of words cards (same words introduced in the previous lesson) copied and ready to go

- Scissors and crayons

- Ziploc baggies or manila envelopes, labeled with student names (put word cards inside)

- Partially prepped chart that can be added to "in the moment" with students and hung to serve as a teaching tool for students in the coming weeks.

TIPS

- Assign each student in a group (or let them choose) a different color. Students in the same group do a "five-second scribble" with different colors. This is *their color* from now on. When a word card falls to the floor, the owner can check the color and grab it.

- Remind the students that this is word study, not art class. We are aiming for OK and separate, not perfect. Model this. Yes, K–1 students can do this with proper modeling.

What Do You Think?

Grades K–2, Lesson 4

WHAT?

The more connections we provide between a word and diverse contexts, the more likely students will add these words to their speaking, listening, reading, and writing vocabularies.

HOW?

1. Gather students to an area where a large set of word cards (being studied this cycle) are posted. These will serve as a visual reminder of the words being discussed.

2. Pose a scenario using a word and ask students which makes more sense. For example, if the word *wag* was being studied, a teacher may ask, "Would a dog **wag** its tail when you walk in the door after being gone all day or when it was sleeping? What do *you* think?"

3. Students turn and talk with a partner and tell their response using a *because* statement. Listen in on a couple of different partner conversations each time, informally checking for student understanding and coaching (not fixing) as needed. An example of a response is, "I think a dog would wag its tail when I walked in the door *because* dogs usually wag their tail when they are excited. Dogs are usually excited when their owners come home."

4. Encourage students to use the word, speak in full sentences, and when ready, ask a question back to their partner or add on to build a conversation instead of doing an "I go–you go" share.

WHY?

- To build speaking and listening skills
- To get students thinking about the meaning of words being studied

- To support the addition of new words to student vocabularies

YOU NEED

- Large word cards (or projected words)
- Prepared scenarios for using the words in different contexts

TIPS

- Hold up the targeted word or point to the word with a pointer as you use it. Make an implicit connection to the way the word looks and sounds, and what it means.

- Post sentence frames for early readers—for instance, I *think . . . because . . .* to help them speak in full sentences.

- Once students are comfortable with taking turns and speaking in full sentences, teach them to end by asking their partner a question, such as *Do you agree or disagree?*

- In time, teach students to repeat what their partner said before sharing their own ideas—for example, *I heard you say you think . . . I agree/disagree because . . .*

- Next, teach students to "add on"—for example, *To add on, I also think this because . . .*

- Create new sentence stems to model, practice, and post for visual reminders. Build up s-l-o-w-l-y, but continue to work on this language.

- This language is being taught and practiced in a high-scaffold, whole-group setting with the intention of transferring it to small-group and partnership talks with greater confidence and competence. Talk is a *huge* part of word study learning. We need to teach talk as much as we need to teach the different areas of word study.

Same or Different?
Grades K–2, Lesson 5

WHAT?

Students compare and contrast various objects to prepare for sorting words. By using items other than words, this high-level thinking becomes more accessible, developmentally appropriate. We are also teaching that there is not one way to sort and categorize. In addition, students are getting practice in making judgments and defending these ideas. All these skills will be used in word study instruction (and life)!

HOW?

1. Show two objects. Use think-aloud to model how the two items are alike and how they are different. Use full sentences such as these.

   - I think they are alike *because* . . .
   - I think they are different *because* . . .
   - After all of this observing, I now think they are more (alike or different) *because* . . .

2. Repeat with two new objects. This time, have students participate through turn and talks and sharing out. Chart thinking in a *T* chart (a two-column chart). Vote on whether items are more alike or different. Have students "defend" their thinking.

3. Send students back to seats to work with a partner or small group to compare two additional items, talk about similarities and differences, and decide/defend if they feel they are more alike or different. In some classes, teachers like to have the students go on a scavenger hunt around the room and choose two different classroom items. In others, teachers like to have student groups/partners choose from a gathered set of possible comparison items. Sometimes, teachers like to present two new items and have all students compare and contrast those same two items.

4. Close by having students not only share their observations and judgments but also by engaging in whole-class reflection on what was challenging and what was fun about this type of thinking and talking.

WHY?

- To prepare students for the conversations they will be having in word study all year
- To get ready to look at, hear, and think about similarities and differences between words
- To lay the groundwork for making and defending theories about words

YOU NEED

- Objects to compare and contrast—anything will work! I've seen teachers use two different-colored math counters, two items that are the same color but very different (e.g., a red coat and a red marker), or two seemingly *very* different items (e.g., a stapler and a bottle of water). The more different the items first appear, the more challenging (and sometimes interesting) the discussion.
- Chart paper and markers for charting

TIPS

- During whole-group discussion, model moving beyond the typical responses—model true "outside-the-box" thinking.

- Model how there could be different viewpoints on the same thing, such as "I imagine some people might think/say . . . because . . ." But others could respond by saying that both *could* be "right" and both "make sense"!

- While students work in partnerships and small groups, there is no need to record conversations or complete a written organizer. This is best as an oral discussion-based activity.

- The closing reflective (and celebration) piece can be used as an opportunity to create a class chart or checklist of reminders for comparing, talking, listening, and so on—the practices we want to foster development of now so that students can take on more responsibility later.

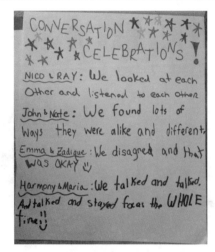

Students love adding their ideas to charts and writing on the charts! "In the moment" co-creation is incredibly important. Try not to worry about imperfections. They are beautiful!

BACKED BY THE EXPERTS

For those who are still hesitant to sort and feel that sorting cannot be part of a particular program, please take heart and remember that sorting is research-backed best practice. Gillet and Kita (1978) shared that categorizing is the way that we make sense of the world. They went on to note the active nature of sorting and the engagement inherent in the process of searching, comparing, contrasting, and analyzing. What I most appreciated was their idea that word sorting offers the best of both constructivist-based learning and teacher-directed instruction, moving students past rote memorization to the realm of high-level critical thinking and application of this thinking to make categorical judgments. They shared these ideas way back before any "sort"-based spelling program even existed!

Sort It! Alike or Different?

Grades K–2, Lesson 6

Kindergarten and first-grade students sorting coins.

WHAT?

Students begin to sort words based on similarities and differences. In kindergarten, students may start by sorting pictures with the same starting sound or sorting two different letters, written in different fonts and styles.

HOW?

1. Gather students. Explain how sometimes we will compare two items and say how they are alike and different and that sometimes we will compare lots of items and put them into groups. Provide some real-life examples, such as putting away laundry into different drawers, emptying the dishwasher, and sorting silverware into different sections. Share that there is often more than one way to sort items. Do not give too much information; this is meant to be a *discovery-based activity*.

2. Send students off in small groups—each with a collection of items. Have students sort the collection of items any way they like. However, they should make and agree upon the piles and be able to tell how the items in each pile are alike and how the various piles are different from one another.

3. Gather students. Spend time having students explain how they sorted and what the experience was like. Share that in word study we will be playing the Alike or Different game a *lot*, and we will practice grouping pictures, letters, and words in lots of different ways. We will then use words/conversation to share with others how these pictures, letters, and words are alike and different.

4. Send students off with the pictures, letters, or words being studied. Have students sort their cards into piles and be ready to explain how they sorted.

5. Return to discuss how students sorted— and the challenges and celebrations of the experience.

WHY?

- To support students in early sorting skills
- To begin to look at, hear, and think about similarities and differences between words
- To prepare students for making theories about words and defending their theories

YOU NEED

- Sets of nonword items to sort
- Larger class set of sorting cards
- Student sets of sorting cards

TIPS

- Commonly (and easily) found nonword sorting materials: math manipulatives such as teddy bear counters, pattern blocks, coins, and the like work well. Writing utensils, buttons, stickers, and even seasonal items such as leaves, apples, and acorns are all wonderful options.

- Do not provide many insights, suggestions, ideas, or guidance for sorting. Let students discover not only ways to sort but also ways to problem solve. Travel from group to group to coach students, but only as necessary. Try not to overscaffold or guide—this is *tough*, but worth it.

STARTING UP

My students LOVED going outside on a nature walk to find items we could sort for this lesson. We later used these items for an art project. Getting outside and then using what we found on our scavenger hunt was the highlight of our week.

—Amy, Kindergarten Teacher

STEPPING UP

My students have a writing unit in which they write about their own personal collections. This year, I will integrate this lesson into that writing work. I won't have to gather, prep, or find items to sort. It's a win–win situation!

—John, Grade 2 Teacher

Question Craze

Grades K–2, Lesson 7

Second graders asking one another meaningful questions in order to explore words more deeply.

WHAT?

Through talk and discussion, students get each other thinking about the similarities, differences, and patterns between words. By having students ask each other these questions, routines become more social and engaging.

HOW?

1. Gather students. Summarize the last sorting experience. Share that today we are going to find ways to help our classmates think even more carefully about words. Today is the day we will become word detectives and help each other find clues and secret information inside words.

2. Start to sort the large set of word cards into columns; it does *not* have to be related to the spelling pattern—sort any way you like. Use think-aloud as you sort to begin to show the thinking behind sorting.

3. Model by asking yourself a question: *Hmmm . . . I wonder where this word would go?* Then share an exciting idea: *I have an idea! My partner can be my coach. Together, we can be detectives. We'll look at these words and say them aloud for clues about where to put them. We will ask each other questions to try to find hints and clues!* Think of a first question (see Inviting Inquiry on p. 67) and jot it on a chart. Model asking this question to a partner.

4. Model asking questions and having students look to the words for hints and clues to find an answer. Continue to remind students that there is more than one "correct" answer—we just need to know *why* we are making these decisions.

5. Send students off to sort once again—this time asking each other questions.

6. Close by having students share how the questioning helped us think *more* and look more at the words.

WHY?

- To build excitement and curiosity about words

- To help students develop reasons to support their thinking

- To prepare students to sort more carefully and thoughtfully

YOU NEED

- Large sort cards (*Note:* Pocket charts make flexible sorting wonderfully easy!)

- Student word cards

- Chart paper and markers to co-create "questions to ask" chart in the moment with students

TIPS

- Start with two to three questions partners can ask one another. Build up *slowly* over the first couple of months of word study.

- Co-create a class chart so students are more likely to feel ownership and use it.

- Provide a "close-by" tool for students to have handy (minichart of questions, ring of index cards with prompts and questions, etc.).

INVITING INQUIRY

☐ How are these words alike?

☐ What is the same?

☐ How are these words different?

☐ Do you see a pattern? What is it?

☐ Where does this word go? Why?

☐ Why doesn't this word fit here?

Sound Search

Grades K–2, Lesson 8

First-grade student working in a word study center doing "sound search" with letters.

WHAT?

Students can use oral blending and segmentation to study sounds in words. Sound boxes are commonly used to help make oral blending and segmentation more visual and concrete for starting spellers.

HOW?

1. Gather students to the rug. Share that today we will be listening carefully to the sounds inside our words and taking words apart and putting them together, sound by sound.

2. Say a word being studied. Say the word a second time, this time segmenting the sounds in the word (e.g., CAT → C-A-T). As you segment the word, model putting a counter (any tangible manipulative) down to "represent" each sound heard. Count the number of sounds heard (CAT has three separate sounds). Blend the sounds together and say the word again (e.g., C-A-T→ CAT). Repeat this process, inviting students to join in.

3. Model this process a few more times with a few additional words.

4. For first and second graders (and those kindergartners that are ready), do a few additional examples where you replace each counter with the appropriate letter or letters. Work slowly and deliberately in your demonstration, and be sure to use plenty of think-aloud as you model.

WHY?

*   To support phonemic awareness, phonics, and spelling skills essential for primary word learners

*   To support reading and writing (oral segmentation and blending in word study are key in the transfer of word learning to more authentic and everyday experiences such as reading and writing)

*   To use manipulatives (like sound boxes) to make word learning more concrete and developmentally appropriate for primary students

YOU NEED

*   Words being studied available to you but not visible to students

*   Sound boxes (can be purchased or made)

*   Counters

*   Markers

TIPS

- You can do a "Day 2" of this lesson in which you gather students to review the process one time, then send students off to practice in partnerships.

- Once you have students try with partners, remember to rotate and coach students where needed— possibly on talk, material management, or oral segmenting/letter replacing.

- Some teachers like to use a visual like a rubber band or a slow toe touch to model stretching a word. Others like to teach students to tap out sounds. Involving actions, props, and movement is playful and effective!

STARTING UP

I made simple sound boxes and copied them onto cardstock. I laminated each set for extra durability. Students keep their own sound box page in their word study folder.

—**Sam, Kindergarten Teacher**

STEPPING UP

I have my students draw quick sound boxes on their desks or the table with dry-erase markers. At the end of the lesson, we use a wipe or a paper towel to clean off our sound boxes. They love this.

—**Karen, ELL Teacher**

Read It-Build It-Write It

Grades K–2, Lesson 9

WHAT?

Multisensory learning is often highly effective. When we use manipulatives, learning becomes more concrete and also more fun. Students say the word aloud (read it), then build the word using manipulatives (build it), and finally scribe the word conventionally (write it).

HOW?

1. Gather students to the rug. Share that since they have worked to discover so much about what their words mean and how they look and sound, we are now going to work on spelling the words with greater ease and speed.

2. Show two or three different fun letter/ word-building manipulatives. Sell this!

Make it an unveiling of something super special and exciting.

3. Model how to read it–build it–write it. Choose a word being studied. Model how the process looks, using each of the materials/manipulatives you are introducing today. Repeat for a couple of words. Use think-aloud as you work to model both the word study routine and careful, appropriate use of this "learning tool" (aka, not a toy!).

4. Send students back to their seats. Provide each group with a different set of word-building manipulatives and have them practice this new routine. Coach in to provide feedback to support both understanding and appropriate material management.

5. Close by having a quick class reflection and celebration on the day's work.

WHY?

- To practice reading and writing words
- To become more fluent in spelling
- To introduce appropriate handling of learning tools

YOU NEED

- Teacher set of word cards
- Student sets of word cards
- Letter manipulatives and word-building tools
- Grades 1 and 2: Word study notebooks (for writing words in the final step)

TIPS

- Start by introducing two or three different sets of materials. Over the coming weeks, slowly introduce new items students can use to build their words. This will maintain a sense of excitement throughout the year. Look at the suggestions provided in the shopping lists in Chapter 2.

- Some teachers like to use laminated (which become dry erase) word-building mats for this routine. Others have students build the word and then write the word in their word study notebook.

- Celebrate appropriate use of materials throughout this lesson.

These students are working together to listen carefully to the sounds in words and remember which letters match those sounds. They share and check their thinking together throughout the entire process.

Magnificent Material Management

Grades K–2, Lesson 10

WHAT?

Students need to be taught how to take out, use, care for, clean up, and return materials. Taking the time to teach appropriate material use now will make us better able to meet with individual students and small groups in the coming weeks.

HOW?

1. Gather students. Talk about what "positives" you noticed yesterday with material use. Discuss why we need to care for classroom materials. Brainstorm how we can best care for materials. Chart student ideas.

2. Invite selected students to model a "not so good" way to take out materials—and then a "thank you" way to take out materials. Have students orally annotate what they see their classmates doing. Discuss, again, the *why* behind the need to be so careful and follow the *hows* just brainstormed.

3. Repeat this "not so good" and "thank you" routine for using materials, cleaning up materials, and putting away materials.

4. Close by co-creating a class checklist detailing "telltale signs" of magnificent material management.

WHY?

- To model how to properly and respectfully care for items we care about and need to share with others
- To foster independence so students can take on greater ownership of materials
- To support much needed executive function and organizational skills

YOU NEED

- Chart paper and markers
- Word study materials introduced in prior lesson

Students create their own "how-to" book on material management and sign it like a contract.

TIPS

- Guidelines are not teacher-imposed rules, but instead are part of the way communities respectfully interact with each other and their environments.

- Hang the class-created checklist. Take a photo of the class-created checklist and make copies that the students glue into their notebooks. Hang another photo of the chart near where materials are stored. Material management makes a great first class goal to work toward and meet!

GRADES 3–6 LAUNCH LESSONS

Over the first few weeks of school, I recommend teachers introduce word study habits, routines, and expectations to the whole class. During the launch, the routines are the focus of instruction. Therefore, during this time we study words that are accessible to *every* learner in the room. At this point, the prioritized learning is less about the actual words and more about the procedures that will help students eventually embrace choice, make purposeful decisions, and promote independence.

You will find that some routines coordinate well with particular programs and approaches to word study. However, all of the following lessons can be used with all types of word study instruction and in conjunction with every existing program.

Don't forget: All the notebook minicharts suggested in the launch lessons are available on the online companion website (resources.corwin.com/wordstudythatsticks). They are reproducible. Here's a sneak peek of what these charts look like:

> ### TEACHER TIP
>
> During the launch, the learning focus is the routine, not the patterns/words being used. I recommend choosing simple words and patterns. If you are STARTING UP word study, look in Appendix A for recommendations on where to find word lists you can use for the launch and for your whole year of word learning. If you are STEPPING UP word study, you will likely continue to use the words and patterns you already have access to in your district. No matter what words you decide to use, I recommend you keep using the same set of words for all of the launch lessons described here.

online resources

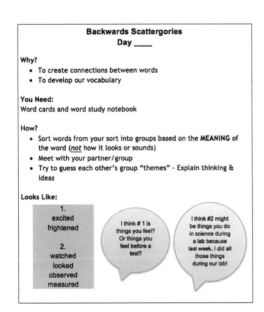

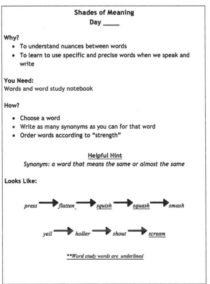

Word Introductions: None to Some

Grades 3–6, Lesson 2

Photo by Linda Day

WHAT?

It is important to make sure students know what the words on their list or in their sort mean before they begin to look at what the word looks like, what it sounds like, or how it is spelled.

HOW?

1. Gather students.

2. Hold up each word being studied in the cycle, one at a time.

3. Each time you hold up a word, ask students to think about their understanding of the word and hold up a number of fingers that shows their understanding of and ability to use the word. Zero fingers = *I've never even heard of this word.* Five fingers = *I know this word so well I could teach it.*

4. Review all the words that are not a 5 for even one student.

WHY?

- To learn the meaning of words (there is no sense in learning to spell words we can't use!)

- To model self-assessment of prior knowledge and reflection on understanding

- To provide essential background knowledge and kick off multidimensional word learning in a cycle of instruction

YOU NEED

- Word cards (one for each word being studied in the cycle). I often write words on index cards and keep them filed to use year to year. Other teachers make a Google Slides or PowerPoint presentation in which each slide is a new word to "flash" on the screen so all can see.

TIPS

- When in doubt, review it. Make sure everyone has a complete understanding of each word.

- Use student-friendly language in your definition of a word. Provide context for when and how a word might be used. Make sure contexts and references are relevant and accessible for all students.

- I first learned the 0/5-fingers routine by visiting classrooms: A third-grade teacher I knew used a "fist to three" approach, and a fifth-grade teacher I knew used a "fist to five" approach. Like everything recommended here, tweak practices to make them work for you/your class!

Backwards Scattergories

Grades 3–6, Lesson 3

WHAT?

Students learn words by using them. Making connections between words not only demonstrates high-level, creative thinking, but it also explores multiple contexts in which words might be associated.

HOW?

1. Gather students. Ask if anyone has ever played the game Scattergories. Tell students that in word study, we play Backwards Scattergories. We put words we are studying into categories based on their meaning, and our partner guesses what they have in common and what category all the words gathered fit into.

2. Use the words introduced in Lesson 2 to group a few words together (based on their meaning, *not* the way they look or sound). Have students try to guess what group/ category the selected words belong to. Repeat with a new group of words.

3. Send students off to create additional categories using the same set of words.

4. After an appropriate amount of time, have students work with a partner to see if a partner can guess the similar thread between words.

5. Close by sharing a few favorites as a class.

WHY?

- To have students see word study as playful and fun

- To create connections between words

- To think about and use the meaning of words

YOU NEED

- A teacher set of word cards and a pocket chart *OR* a smaller student set and a document camera

- Student sets of word cards

- Word study notebooks

TIPS

- Pre-prepare your categories before starting.

- Create an interactive bulletin board display for the whole class to try out some particularly challenging or impressive Backwards Scattergories in their free moments. "Can I Stump You?" and "Look How Many Words I Included!" might be nice headers. Students can decorate and post their most thoughtful groupings so others besides their partner can play.

Talk It Up!
Grades 3–6, Lesson 4

WHAT?

Talk is one of the most essential elements of word study. Students will spend a great deal of time working in partnerships and cooperative groups. Talk is a key part of word exploration, discovery, and thinking. By using the words while speaking, students are also more likely to transfer these words to both their reading and writing vocabularies as well.

HOW?

1. Gather students. Share this (or a similar) statement: *Talking helps me figure out new ideas. When I talk with others, I learn more.* Have students think about if they agree or disagree with this statement.

2. Students turn and talk to share viewpoints and provide explanations for this viewpoint. Partners listen to one another carefully.

3. Ask students to share out not what they think, but what they heard their partner say (to promote close listening).

4. Engage in discussion.

5. Explain that *talk* is a big part of word study this year and that students will frequently have an opportunity to talk with classmates about words and their thinking.

6. Together, generate and jot "talk moves" and conversation-building statements on a class anchor chart.

WHY?

- As per Gravity Goldberg and Renee Houser's advice in *What Do I Teach Readers Tomorrow? Nonfiction* (2017),

  Conversations serve as access points for making meaning in our everyday lives. . . . Conversation helps us build stronger language pathways to the brain. . . . Every time a neurological pathway is activated in the brain's language center, it contributes to the overall development of the pathways that are also reading pathways. The more pathways that are created (and used consistently), the stronger the brain becomes. . . . Conversations provide a platform where students can take risks in their thinking and develop their capacity to hear and negotiate multiple points of view. Over time, students learn to rely on their conversations to help clarify, question, confirm, and challenge ideas. (pp. 111–112)

- Teaching into talk is *always* worth it!

YOU NEED

- Low tech: Chart paper and markers
- High tech: A Google Doc or Slide to post on Google Classroom or place in a class shared folder

TIPS

- As much as possible, let conversation be front and center in this early word study work.
- Listen in on partnerships during turn and talks and model asking questions and adding on to build a more in-depth conversation between partners.

Questions we can ask our partner while looking at words:

- How are these words alike?
- What is the same?
- How are these words different?
- Do you see any patterns?
- What patterns do you see?
- Where does this word go? Why?
- Why doesn't this word fit here?

INVITING INQUIRY

- ☐ How do you think these words fit together?
- ☐ Do you notice anything all of these words have in common?
- ☐ Could it be . . .?
- ☐ Is there another word we could add to this group?
- ☐ What other words might "go" with this group?
- ☐ Why do you think I didn't put ___ in this group?
- ☐ Why doesn't that word fit?
- ☐ Is there another, different "group title" that would also make sense here? What is it?

Shades of Meaning
Grades 3–6, Lesson 5

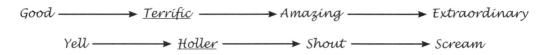

WHAT?

Shades of meaning describes the small, subtle nuances between similar words.

HOW?

1. Gather students. Review synonyms and antonyms. Play a quick round of "give one, get one" to generate synonyms and antonyms for select words being studied.

2. Model choosing a word being studied, writing as many synonyms as possible for that word, and ordering the words according to strength/intensity. Ask students if they agree or disagree with your ordering of the words. Have them share *why* they agree or disagree.

3. Select a second word. Together, generate synonyms. Have students each order synonyms on their slates (dry-erase boards). Students will share their order with a partner and compare thinking. Laugh and enjoy some debate!

4. Select a third word. Have students work with a partner to generate synonyms and order those synonyms. Share out as a class. Chart different shades of meaning. Combine words students thought of to create one giant class shades of meaning for this third word.

WHY?

- To create theories about and foster connections between words
- To help students see the nuances between words
- To support transfer of this knowledge and use the most specific and appropriate words when speaking and writing

YOU NEED

- Word cards
- Slates, dry-erase markers, and erasers
- *Optional:* 1:1 devices if also teaching students to use online tools to find synonyms

TIPS

- Preselect words that have multiple synonyms.
- Search online tools and apps that help students find synonyms. Wordhippo.com is one of my favorite sites for upper-elementary and middle-grade students.
- Don't skip the debates. Students *love* to debate the word orders—guaranteed laughs and fun!

STARTING UP

My students enjoyed seeing how long a chain of synonyms we could make. The collaboration and excitement around words blew me away!

—**Danielle, Grade 3 Teacher**

STEPPING UP

It was exciting to watch students debate the order of words listed in their Shades of Meaning word study routine. Students demonstrated a deep understanding of words, contexts in which the words might be used, and even connotations of words.

—**Vin, Elementary Principal**

Word Continuums

Grades 3–6, Lesson 6

WHAT?

The Word Continuums routine helps students explore not only synonyms but also antonyms of the words being studied.

HOW?

1. Gather students. Review the routine learned in the previous session (Shades of Meaning). Tell students that today they will learn a similar routine called Word Continuums.

2. Quickly review synonyms and antonyms. Play a fast round of "give one, get one" to generate synonyms and antonyms for select words being studied.

3. Model choosing a word, writing that word on one side of your line, thinking of an antonym, and writing the antonym on the other side of your line.

4. Ask students to think of words that might go in between. Share out ideas and jot a

word continuum. Make a quick symbol that coordinates with each word on the continuum.

5. Repeat a few times, each time having students do more and more of the work.

6. Ask students about what they foresee being challenging and fun about Shades of Meaning and Word Continuums.

WHY?

- To expose students to new words through the study of synonyms and antonyms

- To create and defend theories about words and the nuances between words

- To support transfer of this knowledge and use the most specific and appropriate words when speaking and writing

YOU NEED

- Word cards
- Slates, dry-erase markers, and erasers
- *Optional:* 1:1 devices if also teaching into online tools to help students find synonyms

TIPS

- Show and discuss the difference between quick sketches of symbols and detailed pictures. Remind students that this is not art class.

- High tech: Students can create word continuums on a Google Doc and use searched images to act as symbols of words.

Guess the Pattern
Grades 3–6, Lesson 7

WHAT?

In 1982, Darrell Morris shared that word sorts are an example of how students learn by doing. Word study sticks when it is active and students are *doing* the work. In Guess the Pattern, students participate in open sorts. In an open sort, students can categorize the words any way they like. We try to encourage creative thinking and promote the idea that there is not one way to do this work. Sort words by the way the words *look* and *sound*.

HOW?

1. Gather students. Explain how sometimes we compare lots of items and put them into groups. Provide some real-life examples, such as putting away laundry into different drawers, emptying the dishwasher and sorting silverware into different sections, and so on. Share that there is often more than one way to sort items. Do not give too much information—this is meant to be a discovery-based activity. Share that today they will be sorting the words based not on meaning, but instead by the way the words *look* and *sound*.

2. Send students off to work with a partner. Partners will sort their cards into columns and be ready to explain how they sorted.

3. Return to discuss how students sorted. Together, brainstorm a list of questions we can ask partners while sorting.

4. Send students off to *re-sort* in a new and different way, this time asking questions to push and extend each other's thinking.

5. End by choosing one sort and composing an interactive writing piece (teacher and students compose a paragraph together) to explain the way the words were sorted.

WHY?

- To encourage active exploration of words

- To encourage students to look closely at letters, sounds, and patterns within and between words

- To build partner talk

YOU NEED

- Student sort cards

- Low tech: Large sort cards (*Note*: Pocket charts make flexible sorting wonderfully easy!)

- High tech: Student cards to sort under a document camera

- Chart paper and markers to co-create "questions to ask" chart

TIPS

- Model sorting in untraditional ways.

- Coach students to ask each other questions to deepen thinking while sorting.

- Support strong thinking about patterns by using interactive writing of reflective paragraphs. This "we go" support will make a huge difference in student independence later on.

- After some time and practice with this routine, consider co-creating a progression to help students self-assess their reflective pieces.

INVITING INQUIRY

☐ How are these words alike?

☐ What do these words have in common?

☐ How are *these* words different from *those* words?

☐ Are you noticing any patterns? What are they?

☐ Where would this word fit best? Why?

☐ Why doesn't this word fit here?

☐ What could be the heading for this group of words? What makes you think this?

Multisensory Fun and Games
Grades 3–6, Lesson 8

WHAT?

Word study *is* word play. Students, even in the later grades, will enjoy word building and games with words.

HOW?

1. Gather students together. Share that since they have worked to discover so much about what their words mean and how they look and sound, we are now going to work on spelling the words with greater ease and speed.

2. Show two or three different, fun letter/word-building manipulatives. Sell this! Make it an "unveiling" of something super special and exciting. Model word building with manipulatives. Use think-aloud as you work to model both the word study routine and careful, appropriate use of this "learning tool" (aka, not a toy!).

3. Share two or three word games available (either online or in a word game center). Show students how to play.

4. Send students back to their seats. Provide each group with a different set of word-building manipulatives or a game to have them practice this new routine. Coach in to support both understanding and appropriate material management.

5. Close by having a quick class reflection and celebration on the day's work.

WHY?

- To practice reading and writing words
- To become more fluent in spelling
- To introduce appropriate handling of learning tools

YOU NEED

- Teacher set of word cards
- Student sets of word cards
- Letter manipulatives/word-building tools (look back to shopping lists in Chapter 2 for ideas)
- Word study notebooks
- Word games

TIPS

- Celebrate appropriate use of materials throughout this lesson.
- Consider extending this lesson by providing different materials/games to different groups to try out each day (rotate class materials).

Word Scavenger Hunts

Grades 3–6, Lesson 9

WHAT?

Word hunts are a way to get students to think beyond the words on the list or in the sort they are currently studying. Word hunts are an important step in transferring word learning beyond the context of word study. Students hunt for additional words that coordinate with those being studied.

HOW?

1. Gather students together. Remind students that word study is never just about memorizing how to spell the words on a list or providing basic definitions for words in a sort. Revisit the idea that word learners are interested in learning all about words so they can extend this knowledge to their reading, writing, speaking, listening, and life *outside* of word study.

2. Discuss noticings about what the words being studied look like and sound like. Identify a word part or pattern to extend beyond the confines of words we have been working with each day.

3. Model *rereading* a text or a short part of a text. While reading, go on a scavenger hunt for other words with this feature or that follow the pattern(s) being studied. A student volunteer can jot these words on the class chart.

4. Invite students to go reread and look for more words in their texts.

5. Come back and add to the class "master list" of found words.

WHY?

- To transfer word learning to new settings

- To make word study more meaningful

- To recognize that word learning extends beyond word study

YOU NEED

- Word cards/list

- A text that has been read (preferably as a class read-aloud or shared reading)— pre-plan to make sure the text has some examples to jot

- Low tech: Chart paper and markers

- High tech: Google Doc, Padlet board, Glogster multimedia compilation

TIPS

- Use think-aloud throughout to make the process more visible and clear for students.

- Incorporate different types of texts to grab students' attention

Students going on all kinds of hunts: (*top*) partners going on a hunt in their independent reading books and (*here*) a student using a shared-reading text for word hunts. In each of these experiences, students revisited a text they had already read.

Staying Accountable
Grades 3–6, Lesson 10

> I know that it's up to me.
> I am in charge of my decisions.

WHAT?

Students need to hold themselves accountable for putting in their best effort. Students can also help peers to do their best work. No one in the classroom needs to play police officer. This means we need to be intrinsically motivated to keep going, persevere, and problem solve obstacles and challenges that come our way.

HOW?

1. Gather students together. Tell students you are going to view a short video (I like, "What My Beagle Does When We Are Not Home: Beagle Gets Into Hot Oven" on YouTube) and want them to consider what they are learning about the dog in the video.

2. Play video. Discuss observations. Ask the students to think about how they could persevere and keep going, remembering to do their very best all the time, even when the teacher isn't watching.

3. Have students engage in triad conversations. Encourage students to ask each other questions and build off each other's ideas.

4. Come together and jot "Learning Lessons" (takeaways from video plus additional thoughts) on a class chart.

WHY?

- To set a standard of work expectations and co-create guidelines for word study learning

- To discuss the importance of self-accountability

- To continue to build speaking, listening, and conversational skills

YOU NEED

- Video clip
- Low tech: Chart paper and markers
- High tech: Google Doc, Padlet board, or class-friendly blog platform to share ideas on how students will keep themselves accountable for putting in best efforts (and why this is important)

TIPS

- Preview the video; if you don't like it, find another or read one of the many picture books featuring a character who perseveres, takes risks, and/or had a growth mindset. A few of my personal favorites include *Rosie Revere Engineer* by Andrea Beaty, *The Most Magnificent Thing* by Ashley Spires, *Jabari Jumps* by Gaia Cornwall, and *Courage* by Bernard Waber.

Photo by Linda Day

A "parking lot" share with a sixth-grade class. Students all had ideas about how to stay accountable.

Mirror, Mirror

Grades K–6, Bonus Lesson

WHAT?

In order to be a member of a classroom community, we all need to hold ourselves and each other accountable. No one can do their best work alone—there's interdependence in all we do. Teaching our students to celebrate and honestly reflect helps classrooms run so much more efficiently.

HOW?

1. Gather students to the rug. Review experiences from the first round of the launch. Discuss word study routines that have been introduced, what has been practiced in terms of partner talk, and what we learned about material management.

2. Discuss what it means to reflect . . . honestly. Name one of the previously mentioned areas of learning. Partners turn and talk about what's going well and what has been challenging in that area. Chart and repeat for each category of learning (content, talk, material management).

3. Celebrate what's in place, and both acknowledge and celebrate recognition of

challenges. Together, problem solve one or two class challenges.

WHY?

- To celebrate what's in place and going well
- To normalize challenges and struggle
- To bolster student independence and proficiency with learned routines

YOU NEED

- Chart paper and markers

TIPS

- Commit to a daily (or at least one or two times a week) "closing" share of word study to reflect on different focus areas.

TEACHER TIP

These routines will be done again and again throughout the year. They can be repeated each time students work with a new set of words or study a new pattern. To foster increased independence, I suggest that whenever you introduce a new routine, you hand out the corresponding minichart. Students will then glue these explanatory minicharts into the resource section of their notebook. The first example of this work (should it be a written routine) will go under/after this minichart. Students can then refer to this section whenever needed to refresh their memories and continue to work with confidence. As a reminder, all minicharts for the launch lessons can be accessed on the companion website, resources.corwin.com/wordstudythatsticks.

WORKAROUNDS

CHALLENGE 1: *I don't have some of the materials you mentioned in these lessons.*

POSSIBLE WORKAROUNDS

- ☐ Create or use something similar! Teachers are experts at modifying. Change it up in a way that works for you.

- ☐ Skip this part or this lesson if it seems like too much to create something similar.

- ☐ Friendly reminder—there is not "one right way" to do any of this work. Remember, these lessons are only suggestions I am sharing based off my experiences in the classroom and working with teachers in many different classrooms. When in doubt, trust yourself and give yourself permission to do what you feel is best—or for that matter, is possible.

CHALLENGE 2: *My students are not carefully cleaning up their materials, and everything is becoming a mess!*

POSSIBLE WORKAROUNDS

- ☐ Hold a class meeting. Review the checklist you co-created as a class. Celebrate the strengths (find at least one) and have the class generate a plan to overcome current challenges, check in to monitor progress, and implement "class-managed" accountability.

- ☐ Review teacher role–student role chart. Talk to the students honestly and ask for their help. Be sincere. Try to make it a community discussion and not a lecture.

- ☐ Temporary scaffold: Only when every other avenue has been exhausted should we scale back on available supply options and reintroduce each one slowly, one at a time, with a stronger emphasis on management.

- ☐ *Tip*: As much as possible, help students to figure their way out of this. Again, we do not want to become material police or managers. We have too much else to do that's far more important. This is not just a powerful "word study material" experience, but an important life lesson. Through this process, students focus on working together instead of accusing, finding solutions instead of problems, and accepting that it's OK when life is not smooth sailing but know that it is up to them to make the change and make a difference.

CHALLENGE 3: *Some of these lessons are too long. I only have a few minutes for word study.*

POSSIBLE WORKAROUNDS

- ☐ Modify the lesson so it fits into your time frame.

- ☐ Break the lessons in half: Day 1 is an "I go/we go" day, and Day 2 is a "we go/you go" day.

- ☐ Break the lessons into three sessions: an "I go" day, a "we go" day, and a "you go" day. Prioritize the lessons and routines you feel will have the greatest impact.

CHALLENGE 4: *I don't know how long to spend doing whole-class work or how much time to allot for these kickoff lessons.*

POSSIBLE WORKAROUNDS

- ☐ Different grade levels and classes may take different amounts of time for this immersion phase. Here are a few recommendations on how long the whole-class launch to word study often takes:

  - ☐ In kindergarten, whole-class immersion often takes about two to three months but often does not start until later in the year. I recommend that at the start of the year, most word study time is spent focused on building phonemic awareness and letter–sound relationships. Once more formal word study begins, learning these basic routines takes about two to three months.

  - ☐ In first and second grade, I often see classes being immersed in word study practices for about one to one-and-a-half months. Teachers often go through some of these kickoff lessons twice. The first round would be with one set of (simple) words and *plenty* of support. In the second round, the teacher often selects a new (second) set of simple words, and the students practice new routines with a bit less support.

  - ☐ For third grade and up, students often need two to three weeks for a whole-class kickoff.

- ☐ *Note:* During the kickoff, teachers can begin to informally gather information about students' word knowledge and look through the results of more formal spelling inventories. This formal and informal information will help teachers make instructional decisions.

PRACTICAL PRIORITIZING

☐ Chose one (or more) whole-class kickoff lessons to use with your class.

☐ Set up your own word study notebook and gather materials to help students personalize and organize their word study notebooks.

☐ Decide on patterns/words you will use for the launch. Prepare teacher and student word cards using the provided suggestions.

☐ Start teaching launch lessons. Laugh, smile, enjoy, and *have fun*!

CHAPTER FOUR

Assessment

A Less-Is-More Approach to Seeing Next Steps

I Am Many Things

I am many things.

I am a student, but also a teacher.

I like to play outside but also read inside.

I enjoy wondering, exploring, and creating.

I am more than meets the eye, I'm just not ready
to share it all.

I am full of connections, surprises, and
just-what-I-thoughts

So don't try to conform me to one thing.

because I am many things.

—John, age 12

John's poem is a gorgeous reminder that no one day, no one assessment, or even no one school year gives us the full picture of a child. Why, then, is education so addicted to the weekly spelling test? For most of my life, as a student and as a teacher, word study assessment meant a weekly spelling test. As a student, I numbered down the left margin, sometimes skipping lines. Despite my own challenges with spelling, I was confident I would spell the words correctly because I knew every word that would be assessed, and I practiced those exact words the night before. As a starting teacher, I felt so grown-up and professional, carrying my spelling book around the room as I called out spelling words and created funny sentences involving myself and my students. Most of my students would do well. It was calm and . . . expected. Later in my teaching career, I felt very creative as I moved toward replacing my traditional test with a blind written sort. Students needed to not only spell the words correctly but also sort the words according to their patterns. Several years later, I had a lightbulb moment while participating in professional development. We discussed alternative ways to assess students in word study . . . and it rocked my world!

In this session, a group of smart, talented, fabulous teachers (all with different teaching styles and philosophies) shared our approaches to assessment. Many of us used similar methods. We started talking about what information we could glean from these assessments—and what we *weren't* getting the chance to see through these assessments. At this point, we started brainstorming ideas of alternative assessments and began discussing the different types of information we could find (and use) from each of these methods. We did not judge any type of assessment; instead, we simply discovered the "lens" each type of assessment provided

Many teachers appreciated the affirmation that traditional spelling tests and blind written sorts do have value! It was exciting to discover that pattern generalization reflections, shared reading, interactive writing, and self-assessments also provide meaningful information. One powerful conclusion I drew was that some types of assessments give us more information than others, but there could be a time and place appropriate for each type of assessment. Driving home that day, I imagined discussing these ideas with my class and seeing what other ideas they had. I looked forward to all that might result from varying assessments. That next day, we had a moving discussion in our class morning meeting. The students not only offered additional assessment ideas but also brought up the idea of having a greater role and increased choice in assessment practices. The thrilling part of teaching is that there are always opportunities to fine-tune current practices while also incorporating new ideas. This may be hard to believe, but our classroom community became interested in and actually excited about assessment. In the months ahead, we tried many of the brainstormed ideas. Students appreciated the variation, and I enjoyed seeing their enthusiasm and the additional information each type of assessment provided.

WHAT: TURNING NOTICINGS INTO TEACHING

Formal and informal assessment are necessary and natural aspects of strong classroom practice. Earlier, I recommended using a spelling inventory or doing another type of preassessment to gather information about what students already know, understand, and use when it comes to word learning. This information, when used in conjunction with classroom observations and everyday student work, is helpful to teachers as we create flexible small groups and decide on prioritized patterns learners will study.

Teachers often strive for a balanced and diverse assessment diet, combining both formal and informal assessments. With the overemphasis on testing and evaluation these days, teachers are trying to reclaim assessment as a meaningful and helpful instructional tool. Keeping that in mind, a few examples of assessment we may use in our classroom include the following:

- Observing students' work in partnerships or word study groups

- Looking through written work in student word study notebooks

- Studying student writing samples in other subjects (especially unedited early drafts)

- Listening to students read aloud

- Formally assessing patterns studied

Photo by Katie McGrath

Looking at student writing is a useful form of informal assessment.

WHY: ASSESSMENT HELPS DRIVE INSTRUCTION

Teaching (even solid, strong teaching) doesn't always equal learning. Using both formal and informal assessment helps us see what students have learned. Equipped with this information, we are better prepared to plan next steps. Whenever we use available information to tweak, alter, or bolster our plans, we are providing *responsive instruction*. Assessment functions formatively when we use it to help us make future decisions. Although formative assessment seems to be a current buzzword in education, the idea is far from new: It was first coined by Michael Scriven in 1967. Later, in Black and Wiliam's (1998) famous and groundbreaking work, they wrote that formative assessment was *essential* in student learning. In 1999, Cowie and Bell shared their belief that formative assessment is "the process used by teachers and students to recognize and respond to student learning in order to enhance that learning, during that learning" (p. 101). Seeing a trend? More recent definitions of *formative assessment* are more likely to not only mention "instruction" but also mention "students." This makes perfect sense, as there has been a marked shift in education to remember students are at the center of all we do. This coincides with a shift from teaching the whole class the same 10 spelling words each week to implementing a more personalized and responsive approach to word study instruction. It only makes sense that this shift would also extend to the way we assess student learning. A repetitive weekly spelling test won't tell us all we need to know to support student progress.

WHEN: ASSESSMENT IS HAPPENING ALL THE TIME

When we use assessment (formal and informal) to guide our instruction, we are being responsive to students and student-centered in our approach to instruction. This does not need to occur only at the start of the year or at the end of a word study cycle or unit. Looney (2005) told us that formative assessment should be frequent and interactive, note student progress, identify learning needs, and be used to help us appropriately adjust our teaching. If assessment is all about figuring out what learners already have in place, deciding where they are going, and figuring out how we can help them get there, it needs to be a consistent classroom practice. Assessment, feedback, and instruction work together and are part of a continuous loop. Most everything we hear and see in our classroom can be used formatively if we alter or modify instruction because of these observations. Here are a few key points:

- Preassessment takes place at the start of the school year, often through use of a spelling inventory. As a reminder, Appendix A lists commonly used inventories.

- Follow up administration of a spelling inventory is *sometimes* given at specific intervals (beginning, middle, and end of the year).

- Informal assessment happens every day.

- More formal check-ins (this is *not* synonymous with *test*) may take place at the end of a word study cycle and/or at the end of a word study unit.

- All types of assessment can help us adjust, guide, and be more intentional in our instruction.

- All types of assessment can help us decide which of the many routines included in Part II (Chapters 5–8) we will teach to classroom learners.

Expanding Our Repertoire: Rethinking Assessment Options

Seven different assessment routines are given in the pages that follow, followed by an "at-a-glance" chart with even more ideas to help you check in on student progress and make follow-up decisions with greater confidence and ease.

Find & Fix Up: Using and Applying Our Smarts

WHAT?

- Students go back to "old" work on a hunt for words that include the pattern(s) recently studied. Students can go hunting in their word study notebook—but might also go hunting in their writing notebook, reading notebook, or even their math, social studies, or science notebooks!

- Each time students find a pattern word they have spelled correctly, they will celebrate (tally instances, highlight, underline, etc.).

- Each time students find a pattern word they spelled incorrectly, they will celebrate (tally instances, highlight, underline, etc.) their *new* acquired knowledge and FIX IT UP.

- *Optional:* Students can share different celebrations with partner, group, and/or teacher.

WHY?

- Students use an authentic context (their own work) to practice applying and transferring their gained word knowledge.

- Students concretely see their progress: "Wow! Before, I didn't know, but now I get it!"

- Students hold themselves accountable for applying word knowledge to all contexts— even outside of word study!

TIPS

- Remind students the goal is not to find out they have always been perfect but to celebrate prior knowledge and gained knowledge.

- Model looking for and finding pattern words in your own work.

- Celebrate "fixing up" just as much—if not more than—merely "finding."

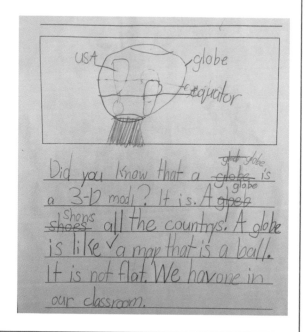

Self-Assessment and Reflection: Look At Me Now!

- Students share their reflections and self-assessments using the decided method (see the following tips).

WHY?

- Metacognitive thinking deepens understanding.

- Reflecting and self-assessing honestly will help students create "next-step" goals and/or guide "next-unit" goals.

TIPS

- Students might share their self-assessments via a "guided" partner conversation, a student–teacher conference, a simple and straightforward self-reflection form, or a written reflection.

- Students could create their own reflection and self-assessment tool!

WHAT?

- Students revisit and reflect on work toward set goals.

- Students check set goals (whether on class goal board or in the goal section of their notebook).

- Students skim their notebook for evidence of progress toward their "concepts" goal and mark these pages with a Post-it.

- Students skim their notebook for evidence of progress toward their "habits" goal. This may or may not be found in their notebook.

Photo by Holly Bruni

A fifth-grade student thoughtfully composes a written reflection.

Interactive Writing: Use It or Lose It

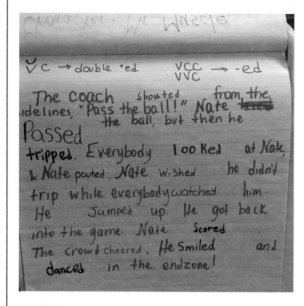

WHAT?

- Students gather with teacher and together decide on a writing topic (which may or may not be tied to any content area learning).

- Teacher and students compose a piece of writing that includes pattern words (those recently studied *and* other words that follow that pattern/those patterns). The students participate by sharing ideas. The teacher does *almost* all the physical act of writing.

- While composing, when getting to a pattern word, the teacher pauses, asks students to use their learning, and spell the word.

- Students either turn and talk with a partner to rehearse the spelling or stop and jot their attempt at spelling the word. The teacher watches, listens, and records observational notes.

- The teacher invites a class member to come up and spell that word on the class piece before continuing to draft the "other words."

WHY?

- Interactive writing is a helpful structure that supports "in-context" conventions work.

- In interactive writing, students use the words authentically and appropriately, thereby emphasizing both meaning and spelling.

- Students need to not only spell words correctly in isolation and during word study, but *whenever* they are writing.

TIPS

- To make this assessment routine more formal (although it's not necessary to do), students can stop and jot pattern words on paper, on index cards, on a dry-erase board/slate, or on an iPad/tablet app (e.g., AWW app at awwapp.com).

- Students can color-code words to lift the level of the routine.

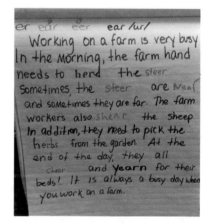

Here is an example of interactive writing that was done as a word study assessment. During interactive writing assessments, students often write pattern words on their individual slates.

Shared Reading With Scavenger Hunt: Use It or Lose It

WHY?

- Students want to use their knowledge of words while they write but also as they read. Knowledge of spelling patterns helps students with their accuracy, fluency, and comprehension. Students can even delve deeper to do additional meaning-based work with identified words.

- Transferring knowledge of words beyond word study is essential in word learning.

- Students need to be accountable for applying knowledge of word parts and words while reading and writing.

TIPS

- Students can record found words in their word study notebook. They can also share with partners, small groups, and/or the teacher.

- Students can do additional work beyond just locating the word; they can also generate other words in that word family, synonyms, antonyms, or related words. Shared reading partnered with word hunts bring endless learning and showing opportunities!

WHAT?

- In shared reading, students revisit the same short text or part of a larger text for several days in a row. Each day, there is a different focus, such as literal comprehension, word work, language standard work, inferential comprehension, fluency, response, and compare/contrast or synthesis work.

- On a "word work" day, students can help the teacher identify pattern words in the text. Students can share knowledge of the meaning of the words, how the words "work" in the sentence, and the spelling patterns in the words.

- Students can then follow up with rereading independent-reading books and finding additional pattern words in context. Students can share the words they found and again talk in depth about different pattern words they located.

Shared reading "assessment" followed by a scavenger hunt in students' own book-box books. Highlighter tape makes the activity extra fun for students!

Next-Level Sorting Challenge

Words studied	walked	skipped	studied
	jumped	flipped	carried
	watched	clapped	emptied
New words	bumped	trapped	married

WHAT?

- In a blind written sort, students are asked to not only spell words but also categorize those words in groups based on the way they look and sound. By having the students both spell and sort words, the level of rigor involved in the task increases.

- Often while doing a blind written sort, a teacher will call out words recently studied for students to sort and spell on their own paper.

- A teacher may also choose to include "other" words. These are words that follow the pattern that was studied but were not on the "list" students worked with across the cycle. This additional level of depth allows teachers to also see if the students can apply and extend knowledge of the pattern studied to other words.

WHY?

- This formal assessment helps teachers see if students can spell the words studied, if they understand the similarities and differences between the words being studied, and if they can transfer their knowledge of the pattern(s) studied to other words.

TIPS

- If formally assessed, teachers often give one point for each word spelled correctly and one point for each word that is sorted correctly. For example, if 10 words were all spelled *and* sorted correctly, students could score a maximum of 20 points.

- Teachers do not include "trick" words when including other words. Chosen "other" words are straightforward pattern words with expected spellings.

- Some teachers include the "other" words as bonus words. Other teachers include the "other" words as part of the actual assessment.

Explanation of Learning: Show Off (Part 1)

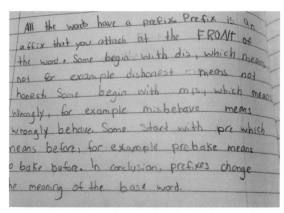

All the words have a prefix. Prefix is an affix that you attach at the FRONT of the word. Some begin with dis, which means not for example dishonest means not honest. Some begin with mis, which means wrongly, for example misbehave means wrongly behave. Some start with pre which means before, for example prebake means to bake before. In conclusion, prefixes change the meaning of the base word.

A fourth-grade student shows his understanding of studied patterns by demonstrating his learning in a synthesized paragraph.

WHAT?

- Students share their knowledge of recent learning.

- Explanations may include the meaning of words or word parts (particularly if students are working with roots or affixes), the features recently studied, and/or how they use this knowledge to help them develop learning across the day.

WHY?

- Word study is not about partaking in activities or completing tasks. Word study is about developing a deeper understanding of words, word parts, and the ways words work. By explaining learning, students are not asked to regurgitate ideas, but instead to articulate the ideas, theories, and information they now understand.

- When students can explain their ideas, it is clear they fully comprehend those ideas.

TIPS

- Students can share their explanations in a variety of ways.
  - Orally: Students can summarize recent learning in a conversation with the teacher, with a partner, or with a small group.
  - Written: Students can write a written explanation or create an infographic in their notebook.

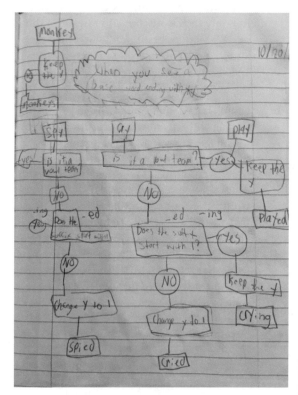

The same student also showed his understanding of studied patterns by creating an infographic to show when we usually "keep the *y*" and when it often "turns to an *i*."

Student Choice: Show Off (Part 2)

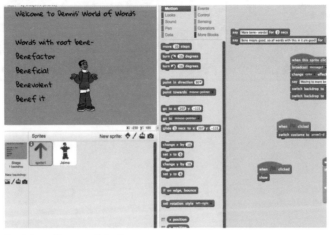

Scratch-coding word study game.

WHAT?

- Once familiar with different check-in routines, students can choose which assessment routine they want to use at the end of a word study cycle or unit.

- Students may also offer other meaningful ideas to show and apply recent learning.

WHY?

- By increasing student choice and voice (yes, even in assessment), students have more ownership of their learning.

- When students have more options available, they often step up the level of challenge and end up doing more varied and meaningful work.

- When we ask students for ideas about how else we can share our learning, we get countless new ideas from the most current experts on learning—students!

TIPS

- I suggest more time-intensive ideas be used for end-of-unit (not end-of-cycle) assessments/check-in routines.

- Techy: Students can use apps and software to share their learning and "teach" others. Examples include the Show Me app, Screencastify, Wevideo, Voice Thread, Animoto, FlipGrid, or a voice recording overlapping Google Slides. Be sure to check privacy guidelines and information before using any particular technology with your class.

- Gamey: Students can create a game that other future classes can use. I have had students create card games, word ladders, analogy-driven word puzzles, and even coding games (my former students used Scratch to create these games).

ASSESSMENT TYPES AT A GLANCE

Type of Assessment	Information Gleaned From Assessment					
	Can They Sort?	Spelling	Meaning	Explain Why	Transfer to Writing	Transfer to Reading
Glue word cards	x					
Traditional spelling test		x				
Blind written sort using studied words	x	x				
Reflection on learning				x		
Look back (own entry or published piece), recognize patterns, and fix up errors		x	x		x	
Notebook self-assessment with co-created tool (progression, simple rubric)	x	x	x	x		
Write paragraph/ poetry with studied words		x	x		x	
Dictation		x				
(Oral) Explanation of learning	x			x		
Act out or draw words			x			
(Written) Sort— new words!	x	x			x	
Look at published pieces and correct spelling of the patterns and parts studied		x			x	
Shared reading, guided reading, or conference				x		x

WORKAROUNDS

CHALLENGE: *I am worried parents will complain if I don't give a weekly test.*

POSSIBLE WORKAROUNDS

- ☐ You might be surprised. One district I work with (six schools, grades K–8) had the exact same concern. Lo and behold, a full year of no tests on Friday went by, and not one caregiver complained. This may sound hard to believe, but I promise it is true!

- ☐ Provide information to parents. It is understandable that some caregivers might worry about a practice that is so different from what happened when they were in school. However, by tackling this challenge head on with up-front discussion and well-substantiated ideas, most families will get on board.

- ☐ Get caregivers involved and excited about this more meaningful and playful approach to word study. Go to resources.corwin.com/wordstudythatsticks for printable PDFs of "After-Hours Activities" letters to caregivers with suggestions for simple activities that can be done to bolster home–school partnership in word learning. There are three letters available: one for grades K–1 families, one for grades 2–3 families, and one for families of students in fourth grade and up.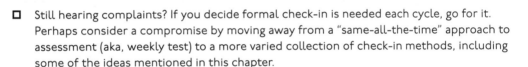

- ☐ Still hearing complaints? If you decide formal check-in is needed each cycle, go for it. Perhaps consider a compromise by moving away from a "same-all-the-time" approach to assessment (aka, weekly test) to a more varied collection of check-in methods, including some of the ideas mentioned in this chapter.

CHALLENGE: *I know certain districts use more frequent parent–teacher conferences in lieu of report cards or have standards-based report cards. But we give formal grades on our district report cards.*

POSSIBLE WORKAROUNDS

- ☐ Sometimes, district mandates don't perfectly align with our personal philosophies. That's quite common. I find educators are the most resourceful, creative problem-solvers I know. Talk to your colleagues and see what they are doing. Share and talk over different ideas.

- ☐ In *Feedback That Moves Writers Forward* (2017), Patty McGee offers thoughtful advice on how to separate feedback and assessment. Her advice for getting started: The clear majority of our time should be spent providing formative, strength-based feedback, and we need to be clear in separating when we are giving feedback and when we are formally assessing. Once we do this and communicate it to students, they know when we are in the coach/mentor/partner role and when we are in the more formal "I-also-need-to-submit-grades" role.

PRACTICAL PRIORITIZING

☐ If you will be using differentiated spelling lists, begin gathering information—administer a spelling inventory and look at student work.

☐ If you are using whole-class lists or differentiated-spelling lists, begin observing students, jotting strengths and areas of readiness.

☐ Choose a couple of different kinds of "check-in routines" that seem interesting and low stakes. Try them out!

☐ Enjoy watching students come alive during this special time of the day!

PART II

FOSTERING ENGAGEMENT AND INDEPENDENCE

Photo by Linda Day

Photo by Linda Day

Photo by Linda Day

CHAPTER FIVE

The Value of Choice and Protocols That Support It

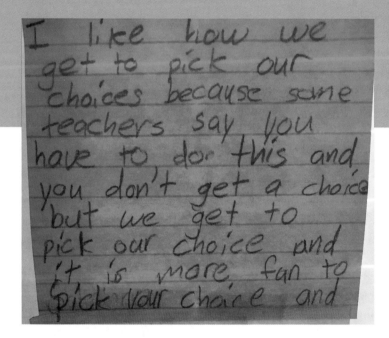

I like how we get to pick our choices because some teachers say you have to do this and you don't get a choice but we get to pick our choice and it is more fun to pick your choice and

That makes me feel appreciated and it make me feel joyful when I pick my choice

—Jayden, age 9

In Part I, the launch to word study was outlined. Students caught the fun of word study and became familiar with many of the initial routines. They learned that word study is proactive, not passive. They learned to value curiosity, risk taking, and exploration, and they learned that focusing solely on "correct" and "incorrect" spellings and answers is "oldthink." They began to see the rewards of the *process* of word learning. Once this whole-class kickoff is complete, it is time to build from the strong foundation that has been set. In this chapter, we deepen our understanding of what we mean by choices, why choices are important, and how to introduce choice-making and accountability to students.

WHAT: THE TYPES OF CHOICES OFFERED IN WORD STUDY

Giving students choices in their weekly word study routines begins with figuring out the kinds of options that best fit the learners in the room. Teachers know that formal assessment provides helpful guidance on who is ready for what, but only when paired with other information. Spending time kid-watching—noticing who often works with independence, who frequently finds it challenging to collaborate, who gets going right away but peters out almost as quickly, who doesn't yet trust themselves, and who has a tendency to take instruction to the next level—these are the kinds of tidbits that help teachers make responsive decisions and plan for "just-right" classroom choices.

Here's how it might go: As we teachers kick off word study early in the school year, we spend time observing students, looking at and discussing student work with colleagues, and closely examining the results of a spelling inventory. During this time, teachers find small-group patterns among classroom learners. These patterns are used to help teachers form flexible groups. Once word study is up and running, students then work collaboratively in these groups to study words (ideally, students delve into word learning most appropriate for their stage of spelling development). Each day, students spend time deepening their own word learning by engaging in thoughtful word study routines while teachers coach individual students and mentor small groups. Teachers can also offer additional choice routines (see Chapters 6–7) to support the learning of each small group. In this way, classroom learning is responsive to each learner's strengths and areas of readiness. As you might imagine, building collaborative, efficient, and meaningful practices for word study takes quite a bit of careful thought and focused effort.

TEACHER TIP

See Appendix A for where to find patterns/words appropriate for each stage of spelling development

Before this can all happen, you will want to think through questions such as these:

- How we can prepare *this* group of students for making choices?

- What number and kind of choices are appropriate?

The answers to these questions shape the parameters we may—or may not—include and provide needed direction for how we might go about teaching students to make the choices that feel (and are) most right for them.

WHY: GREATER CHOICE YIELDS HIGHER SUCCESS

If you feel yourself questioning why we would take the time to teach choice-making—or even doubting the idea that classroom learners *can* make appropriate choices—know that I do not stand alone in my belief that they can—and yes, we need to trust that they will. If we guide them, they will learn. So let's start to better understand the importance of student choice in word study with a powerful research finding about teacher choice.

Russell Quaglia and Lisa Lande surveyed over 4,000 teachers and found that when teachers have a voice, they are three times more likely to value setting goals and to work hard to reach those goals (2014). Can we imagine how the same is true for students? Catlin, Lewan, and Perignon's action research (1999) on increasing student engagement through goal-setting, cooperative learning, and student choice speaks right to this point. Their results indicate that there is an improvement in student engagement when students have choice in tasks. Students not only become more involved with the tasks, but they also set and achieve appropriate goals. When offered choice, students move beyond simply completing assignments and produce work that is more in-depth.

Still not convinced in the power of choice? A 2008 meta-analysis of 41 studies found a strong link between giving students choices and their intrinsic motivation for doing a task, their overall performance on the task, and their willingness to accept challenging tasks (Patall, Cooper, & Robinson, 2008).

> ## STARTING UP
> If you are piloting this approach to word study or this is the first year students are using this model of learning, you will likely need the full amount of time Pam recommended for immersion in Chapter 3's WORKAROUNDS. Use the provided time frames for each grade level as a guide, and then start adding in choices slowly once everyone is starting to feel more confident.
>
> —Debbie, Grade 2 Teacher

> ## STEPPING UP
> If similar word study practices are being used building- or districtwide, expect to need less time for the initial kickoff phase. You can begin adding in choices more quickly if students are already accustomed to *stepped-up* word study.
>
> —Charles, Instructional Coach

Daniel Pink states all these ideas much more simply: "Control leads to compliance; autonomy leads to engagement" (2009, p. 108). When we provide appropriate choices, we help students become not only more engaged, but also more responsible for their own learning. In Mike Anderson's 2016 book *Learning to Choose, Choosing to Learn*, he writes that when teachers offer choices that are "compelling and appropriately challenging," students make decisions about which options will help them best learn. He later notes the win–win–win–win–win results of choice: deeper and richer learning, more on-task behavior, increases in social and emotional learning, greater collaboration, and yep—more fun!

WHEN: STUDENTS GUIDE OUR DECISIONS AROUND CHOICE

Rest assured: Students let us know they are ready to make more choices. In Part I, I shared insights for immersing students in the world of "stepped-up" word study. I recommended taking the time necessary to build confidence and competence with initial routines. I will, however, caution you about taking *too long*. It is just as important to notice class readiness to move past immersion.

As students become more fluent and ready to follow their own group schedules, we begin to incorporate increased choice and greater freedom for students to make decisions. Looking for some telltale signs that students are ready to move past immersion? The room has a productive buzz, students aren't all coming to you after every single bump, and you feel as if you can actually breathe.

Expect and prepare for some stumbles (teacher and student), but keep going!

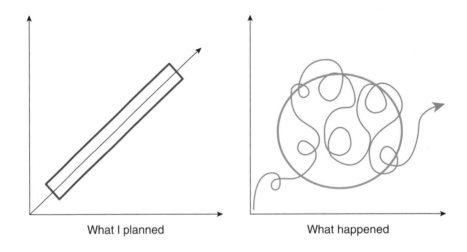

What I planned   What happened

EMPOWERING STUDENTS: LESSONS AND ROUTINES THAT OFFER STUDENT CHOICE

Once we understand why we offer choices and when we might start, the next obvious thought is *How will we do this?* The lesson ideas on the following pages intend to guide you through this exact process.

This or That?

Whole-Class Lesson to Introduce Choice-Making

sort and categorize routines based upon whether they emphasize meaning, spelling, or both (for primary and academic support classrooms, also add in phonemic awareness and phonics). Discuss the *why* behind student thoughts and decisions.

4. Share with students that on "meaning" days they might choose from certain meaning-based routines and on "spelling" days they might choose from taught spelling/pattern routines.

WHY?

- Choice bolsters engagement, ownership, motivation, and quality of work.

- Student voice can be honored in all parts of the school day.

- Students need to be aware of the choices they have and when these choices are available.

WHAT?

Meet with students to discuss choices available to them during word study.

HOW?

1. Invite students to the meeting area.

2. Play a quick game of "Would You Rather" in which students make a choice between two options and explain why they made the choice they did.

3. List on a chart the different word study routines learned this year. Together,

TIPS

- As students learn additional routines, additional choices may be added to the chart. This will keep engagement, interest, and motivation both consistent and high.

Routine Rundown

Whole-Class Lesson to Introduce "For-Now" Choices

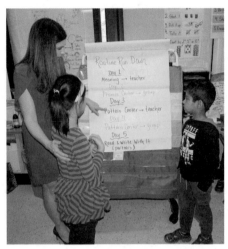

Photo by Linda Day

WHAT?

In this lesson, students will learn about the word study schedule and when they will make choices about which routines they will work on.

HOW?

1. Call students to the meeting area. Perhaps open by asking students what would happen if they had pancakes for every meal . . . or hot dogs . . . or even carrots. Subtly lead students to the idea that having a varied diet helps us to become nourished and helps us grow and develop.

2. Refer to chart of sorted word study routines. Summarize discussion from the previous word study session.

3. Share the classroom word study schedule— either a weekly or cycle schedule. (Reminder: Check out Appendix E for sample cycle schedules.) Share the importance of a well-balanced and varied word study diet and the need to nourish all aspects of word learning.

4. Together, add to the posted weekly or cycle schedule. Outline the focus of each day and the options students have on certain days.

5. If using small groups in your classroom, show students how you will track each group's movement through the cycle.

WHY?

- Following a schedule (especially if not whole class) takes practice and guidance.

- Taking the time to set up structures and routines helps students work with greater independence and accountability later in the year.

- Once students follow the schedule with fluency, the teacher is freed up to support more personalized next steps through conferring and small-group work.

TIPS

- Type up and copy the weekly/cycle schedule with options. Have students glue a copy of the schedule on the front, inside cover of their word study notebook.

- Enlarge a copy of the schedule (with choice options) and post in one or more places in the classroom.

- For the next several days, practice following the word study schedule, making choices, and making choices quickly and efficiently. End each day with a short reflection and/or celebration.

- Go through the cycle at least once (likely more) whole class before splitting the students into groups and having them follow separate group schedules.

- Refer to Chapter 2 and Appendix E for a few possible schedule options.

Sample Word Study Cycles

Here are a couple of sample word study cycles—one that highlights center work and one that highlights specific routines. See Appendix E for additional examples of word study cycles across all grades.

	Day 1	Day 2	Day 3	Day 4	Day 5	Day 6	Day 7
Routine	High-frequency word work center	Meaning intro Cut, Not Styled	Meaning practice center	Pattern intro Pattern practice	Pattern practice center	Phonemic awareness and phonics center	Informal assessment and/or center reflection

	Day 1	Day 2	Day 3	Day 4	Day 5
Routine	Meaning intro Cut, Not Styled	Meaning practice	Pattern intro Pattern practice	Pattern practice with emphasis on fluency	Assessment and/or reflection
Suggested practice routine options **(Choices)**	Intro: Yep! Maybe . . . Huh? Intro: None to Some	Backwards Scattergories Shades of Meaning Picture It	Guess the Pattern Nice to Meet You Word Scavenger Hunts	How Fast Can You Go? Read It–Build It–Write It Multisensory Fun and Games	Next-Level Sorting Challenge Interactive Writing: Use It or Lose It Find & Fix Up

WORKAROUNDS

CHALLENGE I: *My class is spread out across several developmental stages of spelling. I want to be responsive to everyone's needs, but I am not sure how I will manage six groups!*

POSSIBLE WORKAROUNDS

- ☐ I hear ya! I once tried to truly individualize instruction so every student had his or her own word list—and I had over I00 sixth-grade students. It was incredibly overwhelming! *Less is more.* Prioritize doing a fabulous job supporting *fewer* groups with meaningful word learning over an "ehhh" job trying to manage *too many groups.*

- ☐ If you are *starting up* word study, start by breaking your class into two groups. Yes, this may not be perfect and students may not all be in their exact developmental stage of spelling, but learners will still likely be much closer to this range than they ever were in the past.

- ☐ If you are *stepping up* word study and are comfortable with some of these structures, aim for no more than three or four groups.

- ☐ As with all small-group instruction, these groups are meant to be flexible and will likely need to be shifted and shuffled throughout the year.

- ☐ Remember: The strong instructional practices you are using trump everything else. By creating the time and space for meaningful word study, you are already lifting the level of instruction. By teaching meaningful ways to study *all* words, you will build the repertoire of every student.

CHALLENGE 2: *The idea of customized word lists, small-group work, and choice seems so exciting, but my district has a clear scope and sequence (with accompanying whole-class word lists) that needs to be used.*

POSSIBLE WORKAROUNDS

- ☐ When districts opt to use an approach centered around whole-class spelling lists, teachers feel understandably apprehensive about what differentiated practice looks like within these confines. But where there's a will, there's a way! Remind yourself that a little creative thinking will yield fruitful results.

- ☐ Observe student engagement, work habits, in-context success, and transfer of word learning. Create flexible groups based on this information. More personalized instruction will nurture the habits, practices, and unique expertise of classroom learners.

- ☐ Even if students are studying the same patterns and words, you can customize word study instruction by teaching different groups of learners different word study routines that are just right for them (see Chapters 6–7 for ideas).

CHALLENGE 3: *I'm interested . . . but also not sure these lessons seem quite right for my class.*

POSSIBLE WORKAROUNDS

- ☐ As many say, nothing in teaching is new. Many of my own instructional strategies were inspired by both *in-print* and *in-person* mentors. Over time, I made them my own to meet the needs of classroom learners. These lessons are ready and *meant* to be tweaked by you!

- ☐ Please try on and twist any or all the previous and upcoming word study routines to support greater student voice in phonemic awareness, phonics, meaning, and spelling-based practices.

PRACTICAL PRIORITIZING

☐ Make a list of the routines you have already introduced to your class. Sort these routines by type (phonemic awareness, phonics, spelling, meaning, or hybrid combination).

☐ Take some time to consider your priorities and what types of structures and routines you feel are most essential. Create a word study cycle that reflects these priorities. Remember: This can always be tweaked and modified as the year progresses!

☐ Weigh out the different number and types of choices that currently seem to fit classroom learners.

☐ Introduce your students to choice-making in word study and get ready for next-level word exploring!

CHAPTER SIX

Power Practices
Next-Level Word Exploring

> _A learner:_ A learner is always up for a challenge and is ready to gain knowledge. They want to participate and have a 100% positive addic itude.
>
> —Ava, age 11

It is December. I am teaching third grade, and the spirit of the holiday season has permeated the classroom. The building bustles with assemblies, concerts, and special activities. The social nature and talk of word study is a comfort in our day. The buzz of the classroom is a bit louder than typical, but still not quite at the point of becoming unproductive noise. I pull up a chair to a small group of students working collaboratively to complete a synonym and antonym chart. Once upon a time, this group felt excited and challenged to collect as many words as they could to grow their charts. They even engaged in a bit of informal, playful competition to "outdiscover" teammates. Today, they have decided to share with me that times have changed.

"Mrs. K, we wanted to talk to you," David began.

"This isn't really fun anymore," Kevin added.

"Also, we don't really even find it challenging. We feel like robots," Dahlia interrupted.

Eek, I thought to myself. _Robots?_ I took a breath and nodded empathetically.

"We had an idea for something else we could do, but we also thought maybe you might have some ideas," Dahlia continued.

David, Kevin, Dahlia, and the rest of their group could not have been more correct! They were a particularly curious and imaginative group of thinkers, but I also had no doubt that others might have felt the same way. It was undoubtedly time to enliven our classroom word study practice. That day, I learned the importance of regularly introducing new routines to keep the class interested in word study.

Choices in Word Study Routines: Lessons to Bolster Engaged Word Learning

In the previous chapter, I shared the structures and routines to establish during the immersion phase of word study—how we *start up* a *stepped-up* approach to word study over the course of the first few weeks. In this chapter, I offer what I like to call icing on the cake. These additional word study lessons can be taught once students show independence and confidence with the foundational practices. These experiences jump-start flagging student engagement—and you certainly know you need one when learners declare they are beginning to feel like robots!

In introducing these routines, find the pace that works for your students. For example, in kindergarten and first grade, I often add one to two new routines every two months. For second grade and up, plan to introduce one or two new whole-class choice routines each subsequent month throughout the school year. Try to balance *tried-and-true comfort* with a consistent blast of *new and fresh*! These recommended time frames seem to provide enough time for students to try out, practice, and get comfortable with new routines while also sparking curiosity, expectation, and interest at regular intervals throughout the entire year. (Please see Appendix E for the schedule ideas these routines drop into and management tips for groups.) The lesson ideas in *this* chapter are meant to be tailored and tweaked to honor the students you teach. The important thing is to stay true to the core concepts of this stepped-up word study work: active learning, collaboration, inquiry, talk, and most important, JOY!

Many teachers choose to introduce these routines during whole class instruction. Others target specific routines for specific small groups of learners. If you prefer to introduce additional practices to small groups, suggestions are included on which students might most benefit from each routine.

> ### STARTING UP
>
> I am easing into high-impact word study. In my first year, my whole class studied the same pattern at the same time. I pulled the word lists from *Fountas & Pinnell Phonics Lessons*. I differentiated classroom practices by teaching many of the suggested routines to small groups of students. This worked well!
>
> —Angie, Grade I Teacher

> ### STEPPING UP
>
> In my class, students study different patterns. I introduce new routines about once a month. I teach these new routines whole-class. When I teach new word study routines, I either use one group's words, high-frequency words, or content area vocabulary words. I do this purposefully so students see from the start that the routine being introduced can and will be used with any words we want to study.
>
> —Sam, Grade I Teacher

Note: The words being used to teach these routines reflect the pattern/words the class or group of students are currently studying. These routines are meant to be flexible and may be taught and used with *any* patterns/words!

Please read through the following routines, make notes, see what sparks interest for you, and get going!

ADDITIONAL CHOICE ROUTINES:
PHONEMIC AWARENESS AND PHONICS

Tap It

WHO?

Use this with any student or group, especially:

- Kindergarten and Grade 1
- Those working on developing phonemic awareness
- Students who need support in segmenting words

HOW?

1. Invite students to join you. Share that you are going to model a fun, new routine to practice pulling words apart (segmenting sounds).

2. Hold up a picture card. Say the word. Segment the sounds in that word.

3. Tap out the sounds—one tap for each sound. There are countless fun ways to Tap It! See the tips that follow.

4. Repeat with several word cards, having students participate a bit more each round. Try echo style, in which you say the word, they say the word, you segment the word, they segment the word, and so on.

5. Share when and why students will use this new routine (in partner work, in small-group work, with a teacher, or in a meaningful literacy center).

WHY?

- Segmenting (breaking apart) words is a superstar practice to develop phonemic awareness.
- Segmenting helps children to hear the different sounds in a word and eventually (or also) match the sound to the appropriate letter(s).

TIPS

- Free Tap It ideas: Students can tap the words up or down their arm, tap their hands on their desk/table each time they hear a sound, tap their feet on the floor for each new sound, tap their pencil on the desk/table each time they hear a sound, tap their hands on their head each time they hear a sound, and so on.

- Cheap Tap It ideas: Students can tap a drum using drumsticks each time they hear a sound, turn on cheap "tap lights" each time they hear a sound, tap a xylophone using a mallet each time they hear a sound, and so on.

Hold It, Say It, Sort It

WHO?

Use this with any student or group, but especially:

- Grades K–2

- Students developing phonemic awareness and phonics confidence

- Those working toward hearing specific sounds in words

- Those with strong phonemic awareness who are ready for more phonics work

HOW?

1. Invite students to the meeting area. Explain that you are going to model a new routine to practice listening for sounds and comparing the sounds (and letters) in words.

2. Identify two to four target letters or sounds (e.g., /b/ /m/ /sh/). Write each targeted sound at the top of a sort column or put each sound in a different sorting circle.

3. Hold up an object. Say the word. Stretch the word to emphasize the starting sound.

4. Place the word in the column with the corresponding starting sound; for example, a ball would go in a *B* column, a marker would go in the *M* column, and so on.

5. Repeat with several objects, having students participate a bit more each round.

6. Share when and why students will use this new routine (partner work, small-group work, with a teacher, or in a meaningful literacy center).

WHY?

- By holding, saying, hearing, and moving the object while sorting, students are engaging in multisensory word practice.

- Being able to hear specific sounds in words and match these sounds to specific letters is a critical word learning skill.

TIPS

- Sort boards and objects could be gathered ahead of time and ready for students to hold, say, and sort.

- Students can add to the sort using other readily available objects from the classroom.

- This same routine may be differentiated to focus on ending sounds, short- or long-vowel sounds, digraphs, blends, or word families.

- If this routine will be done in collaborative partnerships, teach students to take turns choosing, holding, saying, and sorting objects. When their partner is sorting, partners can ask, "Why did you put the ___ in that column?" or "Why do you think the ___ doesn't go there?" or even "If you changed the first letter of that word and made it a ___, what would the new word be?" By engaging in this metacognitive, reflective conversation, students are continuing to use the words and think more deeply about the *why* behind their practice.

- Close by having students reflect with this statement: "I/we put __, __, __, and __ in the *B* column because . . ."

Switch It, Change It

WHO?

Use this with any student or group, but especially:

- Grades K–2

- Students developing phonemic awareness and phonics confidence

- Those working toward hearing specific sounds in words

- Those with strong phonemic awareness who are ready for more phonics work

WHAT?

1. Invite students to the meeting area. Explain that you are going to share a new routine to practice listening for sounds and seeing how sometimes the sounds (and letters) in words can be switched and changed to make *new* words!

2. Hold up a picture card or object. Say the word. Segment the word to hear each sound. Replace each sound with a letter(s).

3. Hold up a second picture card or object (from the same word family). Say the word. Segment the word to hear each sound. Use think-aloud: *Hmmm . . . which sounds are the same? Which are different?* Keep the rime (middle and end of the word the same) and replace the onset (starting sound) with a new letter(s).

4. Repeat with several objects/picture cards, having students participate a bit more each round.

5. Share when and why students will use this new routine (in partner work, in small-group work, with a teacher, or in a meaningful literacy center).

WHY?

- Segmenting, replacing sounds, rhyming, and blending sounds are all powerful and meaningful phonemic awareness practices.

- By replacing the letters, students are transferring their word knowledge and building their phonemic confidence and competency.

TIPS

- If you do not have picture cards or objects, you can simply say real (not nonsense) rhyming words.

- This routine can be done with letter cards, letter tiles, and magnetic letters on a chart, on a dry-erase board, or on an enlarged screen.

- Extension: Create a running list of words used in this lesson/word family. Practice using these words in conversation and writing. Celebrate authentic, correct use of these words.

- Notice when you see a word from this family in a book or in environmental print. Tally the number of times you can find a word.

- Extension: Students showing readiness can complete a written word ladder. I like to call these "Chutes and Ladders," depending on if they are working their way up or down a page.

- Extension: Students can also create their own word ladders or "Chutes and Ladders" games using words they are studying.

(Continued)

(Continued)

Two sets of first-grade students doing this routine in very different ways.

Left: Students are using words being studied to spell new words (by adding endings).

Right: Students are using manipulatives to change the onset of a word and spell new words (in the same word family).

ADDITIONAL CHOICE ROUTINES: MEANING AND VOCABULARY

Homophones, Homographs, or None (Nun?) of the Above

WHO?

Use this with any student or group, especially:

- Grade 1 and up
- Those who have phonemic awareness and phonics confidence in place
- Students in the "within words" stage of spelling development (when the learner benefits from a focus on vowel patterns—homophones and homographs are particularly common in this stage of spelling development)
- Those who frequently interchange words while writing

WHAT?

1. Invite students to the meeting area. Have a sample of past student work (names removed) or "made-up student" work available to show where the student confused homophone/homograph words in their writing. Normalize the struggle—and remind students that although it can happen to anyone, it does not have to happen to them. They have the "word power" necessary to figure out which word to use in each scenario.

2. Review and chart student-friendly definitions of *homonym, homophone,* and *homograph* together so students understand each of these terms. *Hint:* Use a simple icon to help students differentiate between these terms. Provide an example of each.

3. Introduce and model the new routine. Students in first grade and up might identify a word currently being studied that is either a homophone or homograph and sketch a picture/icon for that word and its partner. Students in Grades 2 and up could make a "Homophone, Homograph, Neither" chart.

4. Complete the routine together. Provide students a new routine chart for the resources section of their notebook. Share when and why students will use this new routine (partner work, small-group work, with a teacher, or in a meaningful literacy center).

(Continued)

(Continued)

WHY?

- Homophones and homographs are common in the English language. Students need to build their vocabularies so they quickly know the differences between words and use the correct word at the correct time.

TIPS

- The whole class can be introduced to the same version of the routine (either simple icons or a more formal chart).

- Small groups of students could be introduced to a second version of the routine to provide differentiation.

- When appropriate, the whole class could be introduced to both versions of the routine to provide even greater choice.

"Picture It" version of the homophones/homographs routine.

Picture It

WHO?

Use this with any student or group, especially:

- Those who could use reinforcement in the meaning of words

- Students who enjoy drawing

- Those who are currently learning English as a second (or third or fourth) language

WHAT?

1. Invite students to a meeting area. Play a few rounds of charades, acting out a few words currently being studied. Then, play a few rounds of Popcorn—where the students say *one* word that "goes with" or is a clue for a word being studied. This is a three-for-one lesson!

2. Tell students that today you will introduce a new routine that is the *written form* of charades or Popcorn.

3. Choose one word just acted out or called out. Use think-aloud to model using what was done/said as a springboard for an idea of what you could draw to represent the meaning of that word. In an effort to promote flexible thinking, think of a second icon/picture that could be made for that same word. Be mindful: Show that the picture does not have to be *of* the word, but simply something that shows the student clearly understands the meaning of the word.

4. Together, create icons for a few more words. Provide students a new routine chart for the resources section of their notebook. Share when and why students will use this new routine (partner work, small-group work, with a teacher, or in a meaningful literacy center).

WHY?

- When students come up with an appropriate visual representation of the word, they have carefully considered the meaning of the word.

TIPS

- High-tech follow-up: Students can use Google Drawings, search permission-available clip art, or video themselves acting out a few words they are currently studying.

- Students can use the letters of the word *in* their sketch; the letters can be shaped/formed to show the image that correlates to the word.

- Students can trade "picture cards" with a partner to see if their partner can guess the word, based on the visual representation of the meaning.

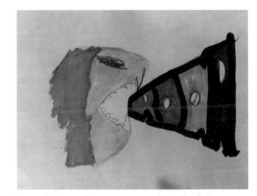

This is a picture of roar composed by the letters r-o-a-r.

I Might Be . . .

WHO?

Use this with any student or group, especially:

- Grades 2 and up
- Students especially interested in the meaning of words and word histories
- Those who could benefit from seeing/using a word in multiple settings
- Those currently learning English as a second (or third or fourth) language

WHAT?

1. Call students together. Talk about the "teacher scientists" who have done research on our brains and learned that when we know how to use a word in many different contexts, we remember that word, are more likely to recognize it as we read, and will begin to use that word when we speak and write.

2. Pose a scenario using a word currently being studied. Model using the word in different scenarios. For example, if the word being studied is *moody*, you can start by modeling different scenarios where you might feel moody—or evidence of feeling moody. For example, *I might be moody if my friends aren't listening to me; I haven't yet had my coffee; I was feeling excited but then something bad happened; or I was laughing one minute, crying the next, then went back to laughing again.*

3. Have students contribute and add additional scenarios.

4. Review the chart co-created with students and send off students to practice this new routine with another word being studied.

5. Provide students a new routine chart for the resources section of their notebook. Share when and why students will use this new routine (partner work, small-group work, with a teacher, or in a meaningful literacy center).

WHY?

- By exploring multiple scenarios in which students would use a new word, they are more likely to deepen their understanding of the word and transfer their word learning to other contexts.

TIP

- Have the students say the full sentence aloud as they share their idea—this way they get practice in saying, hearing, *and* writing the word.

POSSIBLE EXTENSIONS

- Practice using the word in a conversation with a partner after charting scenarios and contexts in which the word might be appropriately used.

- Add additional scenarios of *not* being the word you're studying (e.g., *moody*) to extend understanding even further.

- Add a quick sketch or icon for some of the scenarios/evidence listed on the chart.

Figurative Language Fun

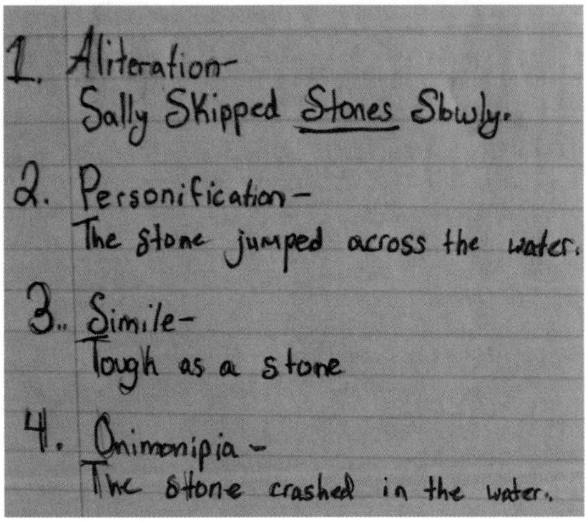

(handwritten note)
> 1. Aliteration—
>   Sally Skipped Stones Slowly.
>
> 2. Personification—
>   The stone jumped across the water.
>
> 3. Simile—
>   Tough as a stone
>
> 4. Onimonipia—
>   The stone crashed in the water.

WHO?

Use this with any student or group, especially:

- Grades 2 and up
- Those who have already learned about figurative language
- Students looking for a challenge
- Teachers trying to transfer learning from one part of the day to another

WHAT?

1. Gather students. Read aloud a couple of excerpts of text (published or student written) that include figurative language. Discuss the type used, why the author might have chosen to use this type of craft in their writing, and the impact on the reader. Share that students can practice getting more comfortable with using figurative language by taking some time to focus and playfully try out using figurative language in word study.

2. Do a bit of modeled writing, followed by some interactive writing where you share and jot examples of different types of figurative language using the words currently being studied.

3. Provide students a new routine chart for the resources section of their notebook. Share when and why students will use this new routine (partner work, small-group work, with a teacher, or in a meaningful literacy center).

WHY?

- This is a fun, challenging routine that dares students to apply and synthesize learning from different parts of the day.

TIPS

- Collaboration will allow students to experiment and play with nonliteral language, and it may increase the likelihood of success.

- Students can return to their writing notebooks/folders and find places to add figurative language (using word study words) to their current and past writing work.

(handwritten notes)
> The cot in Cape Cod was as bouncy as a trampoline.

> The rain was dotting our window as thunderclouds rolled in.

ADDITIONAL CHOICE ROUTINES: SPELLING

Stepped-Up Word Scavenger Hunts

These students are doing a stepped-up word scavenger hunt out in nature.

WHO?

Use this with any student or group, especially:

- Grades 1 and up

- Students ready to extend word knowledge outside of word study

- Those who could use an organized and prioritized method to transfer knowledge from word study to other contexts

- Those who would benefit from additional support in applying their knowledge of words and patterns studied in word study

WHAT?

1. Invite students to the meeting area. Explain (or have students use their own prior knowledge to explain) the *what, when*, and *why* of scavenger hunts.

2. *Optional:* Invite students to go on a scavenger hunt (for things you have already "planted") around the classroom, school, or playground. Come back and discuss strategies students used to find items.

3. Explain that in word study we can also be on high alert for patterns, parts, and words we have learned. Name a simple pattern. Have students look around the classroom and identify as many items as they can with this pattern. *Hint:* Make a list yourself ahead of time in case the class needs help getting started.

4. Share other places and ways we can go on word scavenger hunts. Model. See the following list of suggested starting sources for word scavenger hunts.

5. Provide students a new routine chart for the resources section of their notebook. Share when and why students will use this new routine (partner work, small-group work, with a teacher, or in a meaningful literacy center).

WHY?

- Word hunts are an established and celebrated method for word study. These "tweaks" of traditional practice lift the level and engagement involved in research-backed practices.

- Students should understand that they are not only studying these 5, 10, or 15 words, but instead, they should learn to focus on the transferrable parts of words.

- By staying on the lookout for places to recognize and extend word study learning, students are more likely to apply and truly internalize word study learning beyond one particular word study week, cycle, or unit.

TIPS

- K–2 students traditionally spend a lot of time on decoding strategies in reading and encoding strategies in writing. Capitalize on this knowledge—students can not only look for a word they know inside another word, but they can also look for similar word *parts* across words.

- All students can hunt "in their head" using their own prior knowledge, around the room (classroom charts, etc.), or in any type of digital or print text.

- K–1 students can use environmental print, word wall words, shared-reading texts, prewritten shared and interactive writing texts, and informational text features as accessible places to go on word scavenger hunts.

- Students in Grades 2 and up can use the abovementioned sources. They might also search for pattern words in their independent reading books or mentor texts for reading, writing, math, social studies, or science units. Additionally, they may look for pattern words in their own writing, a partner's writing, research, conversations, advertisements and commercials, YouTube videos, social media screenshots, infographics, and the like. Encourage students to find ways to apply their word study learning to "real-life" scenarios.

- Some teachers like to ask students to share "word sightings" in a morning meeting, on an interactive bulletin board in the classroom, or on a digital platform.

Photo by Linda Day

Here, a small group of first-grade students going on stepped-up word scavenger hunts in a graphic text.

How Fast Can We Go?

WHO?

Use this with any student or group, especially:

- All grades
- Students working to become more fluent in applying knowledge of word study
- Those who have the background knowledge, but tend to make "silly mistakes"
- Those who often rely more heavily on one source of information about a word (either how a word looks *or* how a word sounds) and are ready to become more balanced in their approach
- Those who find repetition is a helpful strategy
- Those who do *not* get flustered or stressed when "time" is added in as a variable

WHAT?

1. Gather students to the meeting area. Talk a bit about why and how it is helpful to be comfortable with math facts (whatever type of facts are appropriate for the grade level). Typically, once students have a high level of comfort and automaticity with basic facts, they can focus their brain power toward the more critical-thinking elements of a task.

2. Discuss how sometimes working collaboratively toward a goal can be both fun and motivating; however, working "against" someone else is only comfortable for some people.

3. Share that today's new routine has multiple goals: (1) to use how a word looks *and* how it sounds to categorize it and (2) to improve our "I-got-this" confidence for the pattern being studied. In kindergarten, this would sound something like this: "*We are going to study how our words look and sound so that we can put them into groups. We will do this again and again and again so that after a lot of practice, we can do this more quickly. Practice helps things get easier, like how we practice zipping our coats, tying our shoes, getting our lunch boxes, and getting in line.*"

4. Model independently sorting words two or three times. As you sort, be sure to say the word aloud and use think-aloud to recognize features and show the process of figuring out where to place a word. Afterward, check the sort for accuracy. Use think-aloud to confirm placement of words.

5. Model working collaboratively (with a partner, or a few students, or as a class)

to sort words two or three times. Make sure to say the word as you move it. As in previously mentioned strategies, we want to involve as many senses as possible and encourage students to rely both on how a word looks *and* sounds. Afterward, check the sort for accuracy.

6. Discuss how collaboration *helped* and *hindered* the process. Discuss what was helpful in deciding where to place a word. What made things go more quickly? What helped us be sure we were placing words in the correct spot? How and why was it easier and quicker this time around?

WHY?

-   Fluency is essential in both reading and writing. Students need to quickly see parts of words they know and use this information to decode. Students also need to listen for parts of words they know and use this knowledge to help them write. Fluency with recognizing and using word parts allows students to instead focus on the loftier challenges of a reading or writing experience.

-   Speed sorts and buddy sorts are commonly used word study practices. By having students collaborate to sort words (not necessarily compete against each other) and reflect on their experience and results after each round, the level and intensity of this practice is raised.

TIPS

-   Students can do these fluency races independently, with a partner, in a small group, or as a class. If working with others, I encourage stressing collaboration over competition.

-   Some teachers like to use counting, a clock, a timer, or another visual time model to keep track of their pace for each round and monitor improvements. Others choose not to do this. Even without a timing apparatus, students will be participating in repeated practice and reflection, which are the core elements of this routine.

-   This routine is often implemented later in a word study cycle, after students have participated in both meaning- and spelling-based practices for a set of words.

-   Create a couple of charts, such as "Tips for Fluent Sorting" and a list of questions students can ask themselves after each sort to reflect on the experience ("How Fast Can We Go Reflection Questions"). Glue a copy of these charts in their notebooks under or beside the routine information chart.

-   *Note*: I am not a fan of timed math fact tests or timed spelling assignments. However, I do recognize the importance of developing a high comfort and confidence level with both. There are plenty of ways to increase automaticity without competitive, punitive, or reward-driven systems of learning.

Word Webs and Word Riddles

WHO?

Use this with any student or group, especially:

- Grades 1 and up
- Those who display readiness
- Students working to develop a more rounded approach to studying words

WHAT?

1. Gather students to the meeting area. Play a quick round of I'm Thinking of a Number, 20 Questions, or any other deductive reasoning guessing game. Share strategies for eliminating possibilities and finding an answer.

2. Share that today students will learn two new routines that can be used together or separately.

3. Model choosing a word currently being studied and creating a word web. Often, the word and a quick sketch related to the word goes in the center bubble. The outside bubbles are often a mix of meaning, spelling, and when appropriate, phonics details about the word. Suggestions include synonyms, antonyms, related words (e.g., *infer/inference*), part of speech, number of syllables, type of vowel sound, distinguishing word parts (blends, digraphs, roots, prefixes, suffixes), and so on. Try creating a second one together. Have students create a third word web in their own notebook and then "turn and talk" to share their web with a partner.

4. Model using the information from a word web to create a three-clue riddle. I often create riddles in which the first clue is phonics- or spelling-based, the second clue is anything, and the third clue is meaning-based. The fourth line of the riddle can be "Who Am I?" Beneath that, the answer can be written. Model orally sharing a few additional precreated riddles and having students refer to their current word list to figure out which word is being described.

5. Reflect by asking students how each clue eliminated possible words and how they used the clues to find the answer; possible replies might include, "I knew it could maybe be *perplex* because the second clue said the word had an *r*-controlled vowel in the first syllable," or "I knew it couldn't be *sight* because the first clue said it has a short *i* vowel sound." This reflective practice and articulation of thinking deepens the level of the learning.

6. Discuss how to make sure the riddle gets more and more specific with each clue (how not to give away too much too quickly) and how to make sure the clues are specific enough that there is only one possible answer.

WHY?

- Both routines encourage students to integrate multiple aspects of word study (phonics, spelling, vocabulary).

- Riddles (creating and solving) are not only wonderful for building critical thinking, but they are also *fun*!

TIPS

- Some students benefit from breaking down a larger task into smaller parts. For these students, I recommend suggesting they first create word webs and then use the information from the web to create the word riddles.

- If appropriate for your class, teach word webs and riddles on two separate days. Younger students generally benefit from this separation; older students are often fine to learn both together.

- Instead of assigning what goes in each bubble or what the clue on each line must entail, I suggest providing possibilities students can choose from; this will help create more personalized, engaging learning. If you feel guidelines are needed, decide *together* how many "bubbles" students, at minimum, should create for each word.

- Students can create simple webs and riddles in their notebooks—there is no need for copied graphic organizers (unless in a student's personalized learning plan).

- Webs don't even need to be webs! Some students like creating "graffiti boxes" or their own mini–sketch notes for each word. Once students become comfortable with one method, feel free to introduce other possible formats for doing the same sort of work.

- In kindergarten and first grade, interactive writing can be used to create word webs. Teachers can also use webs to create riddles for students to guess which word is being described, or the teacher can put up two different words and play Could It Be?, an exercise in which the teacher says the riddle, one clue at a time, and students use deductive reasoning to decide the following: *Could it be this word? Or is it that word?*

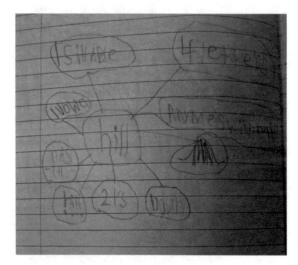

Examples of student word webs: At the top, *jog* is a first attempt. Here, *hill* is from the very next word study cycle. Look at the quick growth!

Workarounds

Challenge I: *My very young students would love more variety, but they are struggling with using new routines with independence.*

POSSIBLE WORKAROUNDS

- ☐ Take the month to slowly scaffold the rollout of a new routine. During Week I, introduce the routine to the whole class, use explicit modeling, and practice together as a class. The next week/cycle, review the same new routine, practice it together, and have students then repeat it in partnerships. The third week/cycle, model and practice the routine together once more, this time having the students go off and try to repeat the practice with greater independence. By the fourth week/cycle (now the end of the month), students will be able to complete the routine with independence. At this point, you can "maintain" the current menu of word study options for a month *or* start introducing the next "new" routine in the same supported, slow manner.

- ☐ Instead of immediately making the new routine an independent center, support use of the new routine during small-group instruction. For example, you could introduce the routine to the whole class, using explicit modeling and whole-class practice. Then, for the next month, keep the "old" routines as independent/partner/small-group center choices. Make the *new* routine the work you do with small groups when you meet with them. Having four weeks of small-group support will prepare students to then move to using this routine with competent and confident independence. At this point, the supported routine would move to an independently run center, and you could spend the next month supporting students in learning an additional new routine.

Challenge 2: *Despite the time I take introducing new routines, some of my students often choose to do the same practices over and over.*

POSSIBLE WORKAROUNDS

- ☐ If we are honest, we may admit to sometimes feeling this same way, as many of us are creatures of habit! Talk to these students and inquire about why they do the same routines week after week. Listen to their perspective. Based on their responses, decide whether to nudge or accept their decision (for now).

- ☐ Help students set a small, stretch goal. Talk to students about the routines they often choose and why they select these practices. Try to play matchmaker and select a new routine that aligns with their preferences. Instead of pushing students to revamp their current practices, nudge them to try out one new practice for a certain amount of time. Be careful to take the time to celebrate these attempts. Once a new routine becomes incorporated into their practice, perhaps they can even encourage other peers to try it, too!

- ☐ Make peer pressure work for you! Quickly survey the class to see who is using what routine(s). Match up classmates using different routines and have them support one another in trying out new word study practices.

PRACTICAL PRIORITIZING

☐ Read through the different choice routines.
Mark the ones that seem most appropriate and exciting for
your current group of students.

☐ Try out the routine(s) yourself. Create sample pieces of work.
By getting comfortable with the practice, you will be more
confident teaching and supporting students as they try.

☐ Prepare the needed material for new routine(s).

☐ Decide how and when you want to teach new routines. Think
through how you will support students as they start using
each new routine.

☐ Give it a go!

CHAPTER SEVEN

Supporting Students
Routines for Meaningful Differentiation

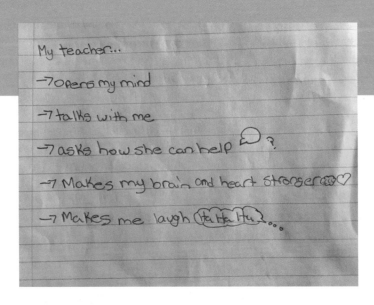

—Keira, age 10

In the previous chapter, we focused on strategies for keeping word study fresh for students and provided ideas for supporting each aspect of word study. The million-dollar question we explored was *What are the students actually doing during word study?* Now, we turn to answering the *billion*-dollar question: *What are some ways that you, the teacher, can support students during this time?* In this chapter, I walk you through these scenarios:

- Finding time to meet with different groups of students

- Believing you *can* differentiate instruction (and that taking small steps is totally OK!)

- Utilizing different routines to help each child grow, develop competencies, stretch curiosities and learning, and perhaps most importantly, feel successful

WHAT: FEEDBACK AND SMALL-GROUP INSTRUCTION MAKE LEARNING STICK

We want all classroom learners to thrive. We also know students come to school with a vast range of prior experiences and areas of readiness. Because of this, sometimes teaching doesn't stick the first time around. Fisher, Frey, and Hattie remind us that as teachers, we need to constantly reflect, not just on what we have taught, but on what students are learning (2016). Isn't that true! These researchers remind us that flexible, small-group instruction is a great way to ensure all students learn. The lessons described in this chapter show how more personalized instruction (sometimes in small groups and sometimes one-on-one) can make a real difference. By providing this kind of responsive, just-right instruction, we help students move beyond current strengths and continue to flourish.

It is also important to note that personalized instruction can do more than encourage students and revisit strategies. It can also extend and drive more rigorous, creative, playful learning. We can use small-group instruction and one-on-one conversations (aka, "conferring") to support and continuously challenge all students. I got chills when I first read Kate and Maggie Roberts's (2016) words:

> When we find ways to differentiate our teaching that conserve our energy, we are able to do more than just deliver lessons. We are able to imbue our teaching with the best part of ourselves—our love for the kids, our sense of humor, our deep compassion—for students and the world. (p. 72)

Yes, yes, yes! So what are *we* doing during word study? Just this! The variety of lessons shared in this chapter aim to support, extend, and bring an even-greater sense of playfulness to word study.

Fifth graders ready to learn: Small-group work happens in word study, too!

WHY: WE CAN DO MORE THAN HELP STUDENTS LEARN TO SPELL

Teacher feedback (conversations and instruction we provide in response to what we see students doing and not doing) in word study does more than help students become better spellers. In *Feedback That Moves Writers Forward* (2017), my close friend and respected colleague Patty McGee shares that feedback fosters a growth mindset (Dweck, 2012) and also nurtures risk taking, perseverance, engagement, and ownership. She believes that the feedback educators provide can help create passionate, invested, proficient writers. I agree and submit that feedback does the same for the readers, mathematicians, social scientists, explorers, and, of course, the linguists and logophiles we work with each day! We are reminded of the words and work of greats such as Carl Anderson (2000), Katherine Bomer (2010), Ralph Fletcher (2017), Carol Dweck (2006), and Angela Duckworth (2015) when it comes to providing students with growth-mindset, asset-based feedback. Inspired by all these brilliant minds, we can see why taking the time to provide meaningful, student-centered feedback/ instruction is a best practice. It helps students become more proficient word decoders and encoders, as well as more driven, focused, motivated learners (and people)!

Photo by Julie McAuley

Conferring with students is another great way to provide meaningful feedback and support student learning.

WHEN: ADVICE FOR FINDING THE TIME TO SUPPORT CLASSROOM LEARNERS

TEACHER TIP

Look through Appendix E for sample word study group schedules, including how we, as teachers, can prioritize time to meet with each learner in our classroom.

STARTING UP

As a kindergarten teacher, I found using centers helpful in creating the time and space I needed to meet with small groups in word study. I have used centers for years and am comfortable with this format. During our word study block, I start off with a 5-minute, whole-class minilesson. Then, students spend the next 20 minutes working in small groups in different word-focused centers. Students visit two centers each day. During the first center rotation, I meet with a small group. During the second center rotation, I observe students working and confer as needed. Using this model, I meet with each student at least twice per week in a small group or one-on-one situation.

—Lisa, Kindergarten Teacher

It can be challenging to be equitable with our time, especially as class size and the variety of "next steps" expands. As a classroom teacher, I often found that when I was trying to meet with all my students, looking across a single day was overwhelming and unsuccessful. By zooming out and looking across the week, I miraculously "found" time to meet with each student and provide more meaningful instruction. As I started to become comfortable moving away from all-the-time, whole-class instruction, I set small goals for myself. Initially, I worked toward meeting with each student in either a small group or through 1:1 conferring once per week. After this habit was in place, I eventually nudged myself to get more creative and efficient with my time. For example, I began working toward keeping my words concise, consistent, and clear. This helped to make each small group and 1:1 conversation go a little more quickly. I also took time to "pre-plan" my week and set goals for who I would meet with and when. This also resulted in me supporting *more* students in the little time I had. It takes a lot of creativity, experimentation, and risk taking to find ways to support all our students, but man, does it produce extraordinary results! Teaching is monumental—personalized teaching is magical.

The more time we allot to word study, the easier it is to meet with each student. However, it is very possible, and just as necessary, to find time to personalize instruction, even if we have only a few minutes per day for word study.

Providing Purposeful Small-Group Instruction

As teachers, we often, through best intentions, see what is amiss with our student and go into "fix-it" mode. We may focus on what seems problematic and jump in to help our students at the first sign of trouble. However, imagine the possibilities if we instead identified what's going well and planned instructional next steps from there. In *Mindset and Moves* (2015), Gravity Goldberg challenges educators to see their students differently. She asks us to view our students with promise, expectation, and admiration. Why? "Doing so requires us to build a different sort of relationship with our students. Rather than approaching students through a deficit lens, looking for what they are not doing or doing wrong, we approach them through an admiring lens" (Goldberg, 2015, p. 41).

Dr. Goldberg encourages us to see the potential in our students and imagine what "could be." When we work from a strength in place, the instruction we provide is in the learner's zone of proximal development (Vygotsky, 1978). Our instruction then keeps learners propelling forward. As teachers, we can always ask *ourselves* if the teaching we provide matches the developmental needs of the students in the room. We can also ask our *students* for their input. Imagine what might happen if we regularly took a few moments to ask the students themselves about what's going well for them and what strategies are working best. By doing so, we are not only encouraging metacognitive reflection, but we are also fostering ownership. Perhaps the most purposeful small-group instruction will result from mining the strengths we see and practices already in place. By observing students, listening carefully, examining student work, and asking for student input, we can instruct students in the "next steps" that are most needed and will have the largest impact. Keep it simple: Remind yourself to look for strengths, not deficits.

STEPPING UP

Using one of the models Pam outlines in Appendix E, I meet with two small groups most days in word study. On these busier days, I work hard to keep my words concise and be efficient with my time. On the days that I only meet with one group, I breathe a little more deeply and take the "extra" time to simply observe my students. Pam suggested that slowing down and taking the time to do some good old-fashioned kid-watching would provide me with more information than I might expect. She was right! By taking the time to observe how students work without me next to them, I see where they are excelling and where I can provide additional, targeted support.

—Roger, Grade 5 Teacher

During word study, we will spend our time providing more personalized instruction. Consequently, students develop their word knowledge and proficiency. The following are some additional routines you can implement to support different pockets of classroom learners. Remember, these lessons can be used in small groups or even one-on-one.

It is incredibly rewarding to help learners see what they are already doing well—and what they are ready for next!

ENGAGEMENT

"Kevin" was a member of my fourth-grade class. At the start of word study, he often sighed . . . audibly. Sometimes, he would make a comment like, "Again?" Inside, I would smile. I had to admit that there was a part of me that genuinely appreciated Kevin's frankness. I also told myself that he must feel very safe in our room if he felt comfortable enough to share his thoughts so openly! There were times and days when Kevin would start slowly but end up jumping in and losing himself in the collaborative word work of the day. There were also days he would ask to use the pass, repeatedly sharpen an already pointy pencil, or volunteer to do anything if it did not involve word study.

As I stepped up my approach to word study, I had fewer and fewer "Kevins" in my classes. However, there were still times where I felt the excitement fading. Instead of ignoring the issue or getting angry with any Kevin-like student, I chose to view these situations as personal missions. Our classrooms are filled with students with diverse interests, preferences, and learning styles. We can honor these unique traits while also working to help each student reach his or her potential—we all have one

or more Kevins in our classes. Small-group work can support students in building their interest and commitment to word learning.

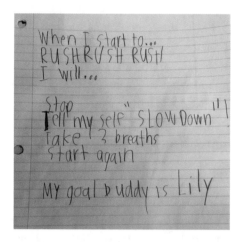

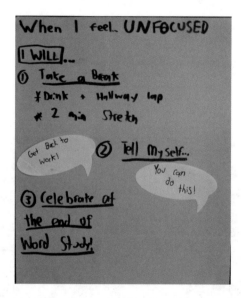

I love these reminder posters that second- and fifth-grade students made for themselves! It takes reflective thought to acknowledge areas of struggle . . . and even more courage to put a plan in place to work toward improving. WOW!

BACKED BY THE EXPERTS

"We are able to shift currents in our teaching when we step back, reflect upon the root issue for a student, group of students, or class, and offer a concrete, practical, visual tool to help address the bigger problem."

—Kate and Maggie Roberts (2016, p. 72)

Sample Lesson to Bolster Engagement: Why?

WHO?

Use this with any student or group, especially:

- Those who are ready to take on more ownership of their learning

- Students who may *appear* checked out, or disinterested, or seem to be working out of compliance, not true engagement

HOW?

1. Pull a small group of students you have identified as open to becoming more engaged. Review what's going well and what's already in place.

2. Normalize the struggle: Share genuine empathy for students' feelings (and perhaps a personal anecdote). Talk briefly about the role of engagement and explain that you hope to help students feel interested in word study.

3. Ask students to share what they feel is getting in the way of feeling engaged. Be prepared to wait to allow students to think through this big question. Prompt thinking only as needed. List their ideas and show acceptance and understanding of these struggles.

4. Invite students to be their own problem solvers. Choose one type of challenge. Together, brainstorm possible actions students can take to overcome this hurdle. Invite students to pick an action that they feel will work for them. Jot down a simple sentence frame, such as the following:

    - When I start to ____, I will ____.
    - When I feel ____, I will ____.

5. Repeat for the most commonly named challenges.

6. Choose "goal buddies." Goal buddies will support and check in with one another on how they are doing—and will remind partners of their "action" when things are not going well.

WHY?

- Engagement needs to come first. Learning won't happen if students are not engaged.

- Being explicit about helping learners name a personalized purpose is motivating. Students see the value in exerting effort and how it will have a positive impact.

- Learning needs to be fulfilling. Engagement is the precursor to the joy of deep learning.

TIPS

- Remember that each student may have a different hurdle or viewpoint. We work alongside unique and multifaceted people each day—this fact always supersedes the actual curriculum. Work with students to personalize the "why" behind word learning. Think through how word learning will impact and help each student: How will it nurture their existing strengths and interests? How can it help them overcome obstacles that might be leading to frustration?

- Follow up with this group regularly. Check in: Is the action working? Do they need another idea? Do they see or feel any progress that can be celebrated?

- At times, students who struggle with engagement may relapse. This is fairly typical. Students often experience a honeymoon period when a goal/action works wonders . . . and then things start to fizzle. Creating new habits is tough work! Instead of building shame about the (quite natural) ebbs and flows of engagement, simply call students together—find *something* to celebrate and brainstorm a new action that students can try out.

TEAMWORK

I had the pleasure of teaching a kindergarten enrichment class one year. There was an adorable and precocious student named Mina. Mina entered kindergarten reading. She was a leader and not only followed the classroom routines, but considered herself responsible for making sure others did as well. Mina cared for her classmates, and in an effort to help, she often told peers what to do and what to say. Yet when we sorted picture cards in a group, she was uncomfortable exploring different ways to categorize the cards. She also had a hard time accepting the "outside-the-box" ideas of her classmates. Mina loved working with a partner to play a word game but often insisted on choosing the game. When it was time to talk together at a Conversation Station, she preferred to start and guide the conversation. Mina was hard working, well intentioned, and interested in learning. We worked together on expanding her ideas about right and wrong. We also worked on teamwork. Sometimes, when we think of students who have a hard time with collaboration, we think of students who grab, speak unkindly, or simply prefer to work alone. These students, like all students, could spend time working on teamwork strategies. But there are other students who, like Mina, are social and focused but also uncomfortable with trusting others and

compromising. If you are like me and have ever had students like this in class, Team *We-Got-This!* is an idea for 1:1 teaching or small-group work.

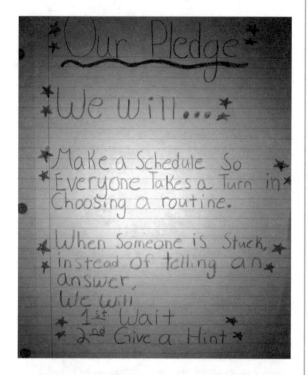

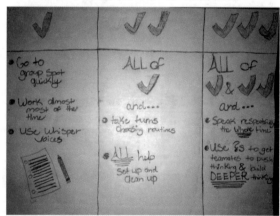

Shown are a "teamwork pledge" created by a small group of third graders and a "teamwork progression" made by a small group of fourth graders.

BACKED BY THE EXPERTS

"Individual commitment to a group effort—that is what makes a team work."

—Vince Lombardi, NFL Coach

Sample Lesson to Strengthen Teamwork: Team *We-Got-This!*

WHO?

Use this with any student or group, but especially:

- Those who are ready for more strategies for productive partnership and/or cooperative work time
- Students who are ready to face the challenges of working collaboratively
- Those looking to share the responsibilities of work with greater equity

HOW?

1. Pull a small group of students you have identified as ready for more proficient teamwork. Review what's going well and what's already in place.

2. Share your recent observations as objectively as possible (*I saw . . . and heard . . .*). Normalize the challenges by sharing genuine empathy for students' feelings: *We are not here to get in trouble, blame anyone, or fight. Instead, I wanted to talk together and share some ideas for how we could help things feel more comfortable when you are working together with your classmates.*

3. Share two to three *realistic* suggestions. Invite group members to add a few additional ideas to the list. Discuss appropriate language that would be used to support and remind others of these ideas. Decide on a pledge or promise together.

4. Create a microprogression (see photo on the previous page) of teamwork together with the group, keeping that promise in mind. Co-creation provides students with ownership of this process. Have students identify where they currently fall on the microprogression. Create a goal of getting to the *next* "step" using the idea suggested.

WHY?

- Collaborative problem solving is a life skill we need to teach and nurture.
- Practicing conflict resolution and teamwork strategies in an academic setting boosts learning and enhances productive social interactions (playground, hallway, PE class), too.
- Effective teamwork develops students' independence and EQ (emotional intelligence).

TIPS

- This small-group lesson has a peer mediation tone. However, a specific conflict between two students would best be worked out in a more traditional conflict resolution setting.
- Additional class team-building and trust games may be beneficial. Check out Project Adventure (www.pa.org) or talk to a school counselor for fun activities that seem feasible for your class and setting.
- Be on the lookout for positive changes—give a shout-out to students in the moment.
- Foster student leadership: Once you see progress, ask students to be the experts and lead a quick class share/debrief using these starters:
  - *One thing we struggled with was . . .*
  - *We decided to try . . .*
  - *At first it was . . .*
  - *Then it became . . .*
  - *Now . . .*
  - *If you have a situation like this with your partner or group, we recommend you try . . .*
- Watch impactful videos clips that highlight the importance of teamwork—YouTube always has dozens of suitable ones for K–6 (e.g., "Make a Difference" short film).

MATERIAL MANAGEMENT

"Where do I get the Wikki Stix?"

"Am I allowed to use a computer today?"

"Mrs. K, Michael just left all his stuff out. I always end up cleaning it up. Not fair."

"Ugh, these letter tiles are all mixed up. I'm going to spend my whole time just trying to organize this *mess*."

Sound familiar? Despite our best intentions and most explicit instruction in managing materials, organization remains a common classroom challenge. I can't count the times I have opened my supply closet and been aghast (and annoyed and exhausted) upon seeing how the materials were put away. Use the lesson that follows to inspire periodic reflection, celebration, and community problem solving. We are *all* likely to occasionally mess up, but when material management issues regularly pop up, we can recognize the opportunity to work on executive function or time management strategies.

BACKED BY THE EXPERTS

"I believe that if you have good organizational skills, then creativity can come out of that, but it's hard to be really creative when everything is a mess."

—Anne Burrell, Acclaimed Chef and Restaurateur (Hirsh, 2013, para.16)

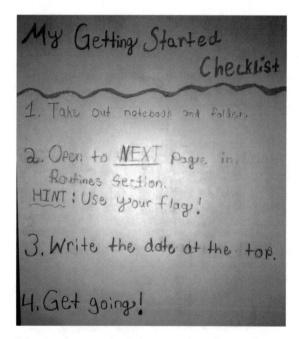

When students create their own tools and reminders, they are more likely to follow through.

Sample Lesson to Reinforce Material Management: All Hands on Deck

WHO?

Use this with any student or group, especially:

- Those who are developing new strategies for getting, cleaning up, or putting away class materials
- Students who are ready to use class materials more productively
- Students who desire to work toward organizing and using their own materials (notebook, etc.) with greater ease

HOW?

1. Pose a challenge: Take out three sets of "messy" materials that need to be organized. Have one group member work independently to organize the materials. Have a partnership work together to organize the second set of materials. Have a group of three organize the third set of materials. Afterward, discuss observations and feelings about the experience.

2. Explain to students that they are exceeding expectations in certain areas (name specifically) and are now ready to focus on managing materials.

3. Name the next step students are ready to take in this endeavor. Use opening clean-up experience to demonstrate the importance of working together and extend to talk *briefly* about collective responsibility (trying not to make it sound like a lecture).

4. Share ways students can gain ownership of material management responsibilities. Elicit other ideas from students. Decide which type of tool would be the most helpful. See suggestions below.

5. Spend a few minutes being artsy and creating the decided-upon tool. Discuss how it will be used and review expectations together.

6. At the end of word study, have the group participants briefly share with the class how others could use the tool.

WHY?

- Being a respectful classroom citizen involves respectfully using shared materials and spaces.
- Some students do not see the impact of their actions on others. We can help students develop an awareness beyond themselves and empower them with simple actions they may take to be a respectful, contributing member of a community.
- We, as teachers, spend plenty of our own time, resources, and money purchasing and creating materials—and we would like them to last as long as possible before having to replace them.

TIPS

- Separate groups by type of material management challenges. Some different areas to address might be organizing written work on a page and in a notebook, taking out and putting away materials neatly, and being respectful of materials and others' space while using materials.
- Students (including primary) may create labels to show where different materials belong on the shelves.
- Students (including primary) may craft written reminders for how to care for classroom materials.
- Students (including primary) can create their own simple, personalized checklists to serve as reminders for step-by-step plans for taking out and/or putting away materials, preparing to work with materials, and/or writing in their notebook.

PHONEMIC AWARENESS

It is late fall in a first-grade classroom. The students are comfortable with one another and are beginning to carry out routines with greater independence. Most students come in, unpack, and check the options for the day's morning meeting. A few minutes later, the class decides to start the meeting by working together to build a long, extremely silly tongue twister using alliteration. While we laugh and giggle together, I notice Heather sitting quietly. When we get to Heather and ask her to add on our next word, she struggles to share a word with the same beginning sound. A neighbor provides support by whispering two ideas and suggesting Heather chooses the one that she thinks will be funnier. I make a mental note. Later that day, I meet with Heather in a word study center. She can use the sound board to replace the onset and create different words. However, without the visual and tactile movement of letters, Heather's confidence wanes.

Although many students come to school with strong phonemic awareness, I see Heather could use additional support. Many times, we may see that certain class members could benefit from additional phonemic awareness and/or phonics instruction. Conferring and small-group lessons are ideal structures to support these students.

Students use their bodies (human "counters" on a rug made of sound boxes) and music to help hear, count, and identify sounds.

BACKED BY THE EXPERTS

Even 11 to 15 hours of phonemic awareness training in an appropriate time frame will yield meaningful results (Honig, 1995).

Phonemic awareness develops alongside students' understanding of how the spelling system works. Phonemic awareness, word recognition, decoding, and spelling improve together and will continue to support one another (McKenna & Stahl, 2015).

Sample Lesson to Develop Phonemic Awareness: Jumping Beans

WHO?

Use this with any student or group, especially:

- Students continuing to build up their phonemic awareness

- Those who are developing confidence with recognizing, comparing, and contrasting sounds in words

- Students continuing to develop a home language while also learning English

HOW?

1. Gather a group of students ready to bolster their phonemic awareness skills and have them sit on the perimeter of a meeting area.

2. Show students a "life-sized" sound board. This is easily made with taped-out boxes, carpet squares, stepping stones, balance cushions, or flat rubber shape mats. In this routine, *people* act as the manipulative that goes inside the sound boxes created.

3. Model choosing a word (from a word card) representing a sound/pattern being studied. Say the word out loud, segment the sounds in the word, and count how many different sounds you hear with your fingers. Say the word again. As you say the first sound, step on the first dot/inside the first box. As you say the second sound, step or hop to the second box, and so on.

4. Invite a few student volunteers to try using other words currently being studied.

5. Model turn taking, careful stepping/hopping, and appropriate actions. Discuss some actions that need to be avoided (for safety reasons).

6. Invite students to try this routine when it is their turn for a phonemic awareness center.

WHY?

- Research reminds us of what we know: Students need to move their bodies. Free play is an important part of each day, but we can also find ways to build playful movement into classroom learning.

- Auditory and kinesthetic learners will particularly enjoy this routine.

TIPS

- Be available and close by the first few times students visit this center.

- Have students generate a list of safety guidelines and post a reminder sign in this center.

- Make it musical: As a twist on this routine, substitute gross body movement for music! Students can also practice segmenting sounds in a word using musical instruments (including their voice). Students can hit a drum, xylophone, or shake a maraca (homemade works) each time they hear/say a different sound in a word.

PHONICS

One morning, I was leading the class in a shared reading. We were using a rhyming poem (proudly written by last year's class). The day's focus for shared reading was word study, and following a short model, the students turned and talked with their partner, trying to identify the rhyming words in the poem. I listened in and noticed that in order to find the rhyming words, Sam was repeating the poem to himself, listening to the way the words sounded. He did not look up at the letters on the chart and did not appear to be using "how-the-word-looks" clues. Later, in our writing workshop, I noticed Sam pull out his alphabet chart right away. He consulted the chart each time he tried to spell a word. Sam is an example of a motivated and hard-working student who can hear, stretch, and separate sounds but is not yet secure in his understanding of which letters make which sounds.

BACKED BY THE EXPERTS

"Explicit phonics instruction, when done effectively (i.e., not rote, but active and thought-provoking instruction), is a transitory phase of learning to read and never keeps kids from reading and engaging with high-quality trade books."

—Wiley Blevins (2016, p. xvi)

Shared reading and partner reading of short texts such as poems and songs are playful, supportive, and authentic ways to incorporate phonics.

Sample Lesson to Support Phonics: Singing Sounds

WHO?

Use this with any student or group, especially:

- Students who are continuing to build up their phonemic awareness while also focusing on developing confidence with letter–sound matching

- Those who are continuing to develop a home language while also learning English

HOW?

1. Gather a group of students who you feel are ready to solidify their understanding of letter–sound relationships. Explain that today you are going to use the rhythm of a song to help focus on the sounds some letters make.

2. Share a *familiar* song, chant, or rhythmic rhyme with the students. Sing it aloud.

3. Discuss a targeted letter (or letters) highlighted in the text. Together, identify each time you see this letter. Talk about both the sound and look of this/these targeted letter/letters.

4. Sing the song again, emphasizing the sound of this letter.

5. Sing the text multiple times with students, each time doing something different with your voice when you get to the targeted letter (whisper voice, loud voice, deep DJ voice, celebration voice, etc.).

6. Have a short discussion about the experience, the students' knowledge of the letter, and "where else" they hear and see this letter.

7. Repeat as needed with different songs and letters.

WHY?

- Singing and playing with words is interactive, engaging, and fun.

- Songs and poetry use rhythm, rhyme, and repetition, thereby naturally encouraging development of phonological awareness.

- Songs and poetry are filled with rhyme and alliteration. Rhyming builds auditory discrimination and is a component of phonemic awareness and phonics.

TIPS

- You may decide to use a song, rhyme, or chant you have studied or are currently using for shared reading. This will allow students to bring some background knowledge and confidence to this small-group experience. Consider this an "added" small-group shared reading session, focusing on what these students most need.

- This same routine can be done as a phonemic awareness routine, focusing on listening for, identifying, and singing a particular *sound* in the song.

- This routine can also be done as a spelling routine, focusing on a particular *pattern or word feature* repeated in the song.

SPELLING

When I taught sixth grade, Brianna was one of the students who was always soaking in new information. She read in her free moments and was quick to impart some new (random) information on a wide range of topics. I was not sure how her brain held onto so many different words and facts, but I appreciated her passion! Brianna had a vocabulary that was both extensive and impressive, but she struggled with spelling. During spelling-based sorting activities, Brianna's ideas were not consistent. Although Brianna added new words to her speaking, listening, and reading vocabulary, there

was little evidence of transfer of *spelling* learning in her writing. Sometimes, this common scenario can be a sign warranting further investigation. Other times, all a student like Brianna needs is some additional targeted instruction and well-rounded spelling practice.

Partners lend support by asking each other the Three Key Questions.

BACKED BY THE EXPERTS

"Spelling is critical for literacy, and it makes writing much easier—allowing the writer to focus on the ideas to be conveyed, not the letters needed to put those ideas on paper. . . . Linguistically explicit spelling instruction improves spelling of studied words and novel words . . . explicit instruction gave students the knowledge of spelling patterns that they needed to more accurately spell novel words."

—Malatesha Joshi, Rebecca Treiman, Suzanne Carreker, and Louisa C. Moats (2008–2009, p. 6).

Photo by Linda Day

When meeting with a small group, we can ask ourselves the Three Key Questions to help us transfer word study learning to our writing.

Sample Lesson to Upgrade Student Spelling: Three Key Questions

WHO?

Use with any student or group, especially:

- Students with a strong "meaning" foundation but who are ready for additional practice with spelling new words

- Those who consistently spell correctly in spelling and look for strategies to transfer knowledge of spelling to their writing

HOW?

1. Gather chosen students during either their word study or writing instruction time. Share and celebrate what is going well (getting ideas onto paper and doing some exciting risk-taking with their inclusion of interesting words). Explain that since this is already in place, you feel students are ready for taking the next step—using what they already know about words to make their work conventionally correct and easily readable.

2. Ask students to share some of the patterns, ideas, and habits they have developed in word study. Explain that we want to show off our word knowledge not only in word study, but all the time—and that our writing provides the perfect opportunity to transfer all we know.

3. Model rereading some of your own (quickly prepared) work and noticing any words you are not confident are spelled correctly. Use think-about to model the four steps (and three key questions) we ask when we encounter this situation:

    1) NOTICE IT: Does that look right?

    2) SAY IT ALOUD: Does that sound right?

    3) THINK: What do I already know that can help me be sure?

    4) USE IT: Apply previous word learning.

Continue to model using a known word, word part, or pattern to troubleshoot and attempt to "fix" an error.

4. Ask students to jump in and help you in one or two other "tricky" spots of your writing. Support students in taking the time to think through the three key questions.

5. Invite students to reread a recent entry in their writing notebook and highlight any word they think may not be correct and try out the new strategy.

WHY?

- By having students role-play the steps, they become part of their repertoire. First, students may imitate your actions, but then they will internalize the *what*, *why*, and *how* of this process and use it to improve their writing across all content areas.

- Time spent working and playing in word study is important, but students also need time to use these strategies in context.

- It is important for students to be able to write (and read) words with ease and fluency, as this frees up their brain to take on the rigorous thinking involved in composing text.

TIPS

- No time to compose your own text? Use student work (names removed) from a previous year.

- Hand out a student-sized checklist as a "takeaway tool." Or better yet, provide a few minutes for students to create their own visual reminder of the strategy, using the words and icons that will best help them to remember the *what*, *when*, and *why* of the strategy presented.

- Lead a similar strategy lesson that focuses on decoding words while reading.

MEANING-BASED VOCABULARY BUILDING

Speaking and listening are two critical components of literacy but are a part of every subject
and everyday life. I recently worked with a group
of teachers interested in studying classroom talk.
Together, we explored and tried out a variety of
speaking and listening structures in all subject
areas. One teacher was interested in trying out
the Conversation Stations I mentioned previously
in an anecdote about teaching a kindergarten
enrichment class. We decided to try content area
Conversation Stations where students visited a
center, read a passage, looked at a map or image,
or watched a video and then talked about their
ideas and learning. Students were asked to try to
naturally use the language of an expert in that subject area, using Tier II and III words as they shared
ideas with peers. We also added word study words
to their conversation "word bank." Something
interesting happened.

Photo by Linda Day

Photo by Linda Day

After helping this triad choose a few words for
their conversation, one student tallied how
many times the other group members used
identified words and other pattern words in their
conversation.

BACKED BY THE EXPERTS

*"A man with a scant vocabulary
will almost certainly be a weak
thinker. The richer and more
copious one's vocabulary and the
greater one's awareness of fine
distinctions and subtle nuances
of meaning, the more fertile
and precise is likely to be one's
thinking. Knowledge of things
and knowledge of the words for
them grow together. If you do not
know the words, you can hardly
know the thing."*

—Henry Hazlitt (Sennholz, 1916/1993, p. 51)

Students could use social studies words in social
studies, math words in math, and science words
in science. However, as we coded the conversations, we noticed there was little use of the
word study words. The students could spell these
words and read these words, but they were not
using these words. In our later reflective conversations, several students shared that although

Two fifth-grade students practice using studied pattern words in a FaceTime conversation using available classroom devices.

they "kinda knew" what the words meant and had "heard them before," it was challenging to use the word study words appropriately. The students' understanding of the words was vague and surface. They did not "own" the words. My follow-up conversations and sessions with this teacher started to also focus on a greater emphasis on meaning-based practices in word study in the hope that students would not only recognize or "sorta know" words, but instead, add words that were studied to speaking, listening, reading, and writing vocabularies. The lesson that follows will jump-start this important transfer for your students.

Sample Lesson to Augment Vocabulary: Talkin' the Talk

WHO?

Use this with any student or group, especially:

- Students who are working on transferring their word learning to their speaking and listening vocabulary

- Those ready to explore the meaning of words being studied and the contexts in which using these words would be appropriate

HOW?

1. Start the group by repeating your first-day *word introduction* routine (*Yep! Maybe . . . Huh?* or *None to Some*). Review any words that students are not completely comfortable defining and using. Share not only student-friendly definitions, but also supplement them with student-friendly contexts for when this word might be used.

2. Choose five words students know very well. Lay out those word cards. Start a conversation with group participants. Conversationalists will attempt to authentically and appropriately use these five words in the conversation. Tally the number of times the words are used. Change the topic of conversation. Try a new conversation (on the completely new, unrelated topic) with the same five words.

3. Choose a new set of five words, this time combining some high-comfort words and some lower-comfort words. Repeat the activity in Step 2.

4. Reflect on what was fun, easy, and challenging about this experience.

5. Encourage students to add this routine to their "meaning day" choices.

WHY?

- Recognizing, decoding, and spelling a word correctly isn't enough. To truly own a word, students need to be able to access its meaning. Only then will students add this word to their vocabulary, using it conversationally, fully understanding it while reading, and incorporating it into their writing.

- In order to add a word to our vocabularies, we need repeated exposure to the word, understanding of where and when to use it, and opportunities to insert the word—especially orally.

TIPS

- For added tech fun: Have students record their conversation, then listen back and tally how many times each participant used a pattern word or how many times they collectively used a pattern word. Alternatively, students might sit on separate sides of the room and FaceTime each other or participate in a Google Hangout with a person, partnership, or group in another class!

- For groups of three: Take turns either participating in the conversation or being a "word recorder." Partners will talk for an allotted amount of time while the third person records the pattern words used.

- For investigative fun: An observer can try to "guess the pattern" the partners were practicing in their conversation.

- Visit student partnerships/groups as they begin to try this out with greater independence. Observe and provide feedback afterward, coaching only when needed.

Building a Culture and Curriculum of Talk

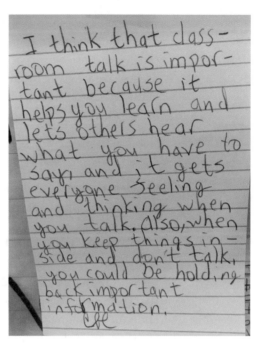

Sheila #8
I think that classroom talk is important b/c when others talk it can inspire other ideas for you and when you talk about your idea it inspires more people ect. Classroom talk is also helpful b/c if someone is confused you can use classroom talk to help them out.

I think that classroom talk is important because it helps you learn and lets others hear what you have to say, and it gets everyone feeling and thinking when you talk. Also, when you keep things inside and don't talk, you could be holding back important information.

Russian teacher and psychologist Lev Vygotsky believed that language is essential in furthering thinking, developing reasoning, and supporting reading and writing. Moreover, he believed that through conversation, students establish frameworks for thinking on their own (1962, 1978). When students engage in meaningful talk, their thinking becomes more rich, coherent, and grounded. When we prioritize time to talk in our classrooms, we prioritize the human need to connect with others *and* help the learners in our room build strong, trusting, positive relationships. Although time to be social and share casually is an important component of any classroom culture, here I am talking about purposeful classroom talk. This type of classroom talk needs to be not only valued but also explicitly taught. Doing so is not necessarily quick and easy, but it is *always* amazing.

We can explicitly teach what purposeful talk looks like, sounds like, how it works, and why it is valuable. Peter Johnston reminds us, "The language that teachers (and their students) use in the classroom is a big deal" (2004, p. 10). Once proficient in this type of talk, students become present conversationalists, capable of truly listening to classmates. They respond to others' ideas and further develop these thoughts to deepen understanding. They respectfully push back on theories and thinking that differs from their own perspective. Classmates expect and value other opinions and see them as an opportunity to grow. Students with this skill set not only talk together, they think together. After learning, practicing, and engaging in such purposeful talk, it becomes second nature. No one says it better than William Isaacs: "By changing the way we talk, we change the way we think, not just as individuals, but all together" (1999, p. 210).

This type of talk mirrors what Allington and Johnston (2002) saw in exceptional classrooms. Moreover, once this type of talk is in place, students naturally become each other's teachers, coaches, and cheerleaders. Our physical presence is not as needed! We are given the gift of time, freed up to hold the small groups and engage in the one-on-one conferring conversations that we know are the hallmark of quality, personalized instruction. When our students know how to talk together, we can spend our time supporting learners in our classroom with greater intention and equity.

Writer, consultant, and change leader Margaret Wheatley once wrote, "Conversation creates the condition for us to rediscover the joy of thinking together" (2009, p. 38). I could not agree more. So much of this book is centered around bringing joy to the study of words. In the launch to word study, initial lessons were provided to start up talk in the classroom. However, "one and done" will not create the community of talk needed to sustain strong and lasting collaborative learning. I regularly hold whole-class minilessons and small-group sessions on continuing to build up purposeful talk. I prioritize coaching partnership and small-group conversations not only at the start of the year, but also throughout the course of the year. Once talk has gotten going, I also force myself (so hard sometimes!) to step back and give students the time and space to get themselves "unstuck" from conversational lulls and challenges. Most importantly, I consistently model the type of talk I hope my students will try out and use. A curriculum of talk permeates every part of the day—in each subject area and in every moment in between. Regular modeling, teaching, coaching, and vast opportunities to talk saturate each day of the school year. The chart on pp. 158–160 shows some If/Then scenarios for coaching conversation partnerships.

Building this culture of talk will lift the level of everything you do in your classroom. It will also lift the level of all you imagine possible in your pursuit of having students learn about words (becoming more proficient in reading, writing, and using words) and understanding the power words provide. I love the line in Markus Zusak's novel *The Book Thief*: "The best word shakers were the ones who understood the true power of words. They were the ones who could climb the highest" (2007, p. 442). This heightens the importance of the time and effort we are putting toward lifting the level of word study in our classrooms and buildings. Furthermore, conversation also provides the conditions that support students the most in *using* their word learning! *When students engage in talk, they are using words*—and in word study, this talk is largely centered around the patterns, learning, and actual words they are studying and have studied. The impact of talk in word study is synergistic!

TEACHER TIP

Keep reading for additional ways to support partnerships and small groups in their continued efforts in lifting the level of talk!

I think that talking is important because you can learn about other peoples prospectives and mybe you never thought about it or it changed your thinking about the person.
NR

Classroom talk is important for 3rd graders, you can share your ideas on stuff and Group work needs talk or else you couldn't PLAN, CREATE your presentation. Or learn to be SOICAL which is a life skill and is good manners. Classroom talk is in partner-ships, triads (3 people group) And Groups (4 or more people)

I would suggust that students should talk one another. This is because, I don think anbody wants t sit in a quiet classr all day. It is fun t have a nice conversa in a classrom.

I think talking is good because it helps us bound togther. It also becomes a habit so its part of our life.

Thoughts from nine-year-olds about talk in the classroom.

Inviting Inquiry

In *What Do I Teach Readers Tomorrow? Nonfiction* (2017), Goldberg and Houser recommend that when talk is new, it can be useful to lead a class inquiry in conversations. Teachers can kick-start this inquiry by observing class conversations, sharing observations, and encouraging thoughtful class discussion. By personalizing the "initial data," student interest will likely be piqued. This will spark meaningful discovery into how and why we might prioritize learning to become engaged conversationalists. Goldberg and Houser also include lesson ideas (such as "Partner Ponder" on p. 137) to build talk.

COACHING PARTNERSHIPS AND SMALL GROUPS: IF/THEN CHART

IF I see this happening . . .	THEN It might be . . . and we can say . . .
Students sit with books closed, resources put away, and not studying words together, feeling that they are "done" for the day.	*It might be:* These students are not confident in knowing how to make the most of their time or how to become more persistent in committing to and continuing a conversation. *We might say:* "I have also been there. When I am not sure how to keep going, I . . ." "Something I have tried when I am not sure what to say next (or don't feel like continuing) is . . ." "Would it help to watch another partnership work and talk together? Perhaps you can ask them about what they do to keep talk going." "What do you think is making the conversation get stuck?" "Is there something around the room that you can use to help get yourselves unstuck?"

IF I see this happening . . .	THEN It might be . . . and we can say . . .
Students use "parallel play" talk structures: I say something, you nod or shake your head. You say something, I nod or shake my head. There is little in-depth exploration of ideas.	*It might be:* These students would like support in building trust, taking risks, or knowing how to build off someone's ideas. *We might say:* "What's the first thing that popped into your head when your partner said ___?" "What do you think might happen if you disagreed with or had a thought different from your partner?" "Can you each share one thing that you appreciate and admire about your partner?" "What might we say here that seems a little risky?" "Let's set a goal together on how we can say more during partner time. I would be happy to help you with it!" "I'd love to help you understand the power of one simple phrase: *What else?* Can we work on this together?"
One student takes the lead and the other student passively follows directions.	*It might be:* One partner is uncomfortable with silence and talks to fill up that quiet space, one partner could use support in learning to take the lead, *or* both students might appreciate knowing how to ask questions to nudge their partner to say and do more. *We might say:* "How does it feel when your partner ___?" "Do you have any ideas for how we can balance out the talk and work in this partnership?" "You work so hard at thinking through your ideas. Let's work together on how you can become more confident in sharing your thoughts." "If you envision an equal-parts partnership, what do you see? How can we work together to make this a reality?" "Let's create some commitments to each other to make this partnership grow."
Both students try to "outdo" each other with silliness.	*It might be:* These students are feeling frustrated by the word work and are avoiding feeling unsuccessful, are bored with their current routines, or don't "feel" the value of word study. *We might say:* "Here's what I am seeing: ___. This makes me wonder if ___. I'd like to work on this together." "Do you mind if I sit in and observe you work for a bit? I'm interested in your thinking and how things are going for you."

IF I see this happening . . .	THEN It might be . . . and we can say . . .
	"I'm wondering if you aren't feeling engaged or excited about word study. Do you remember a time when it was something you enjoyed or felt was valuable? Let's talk through this." "I want to make sure everyone in the room has the space to do their best work. Let's set a goal to help make sure you are remembering and respecting everyone around you."
Students actively work together, but ideas are nontraditional, and in some cases, may not seem "correct."	**It might be:** These students could use more support with the content—or maybe we teachers need to get more comfortable with seeing things more than one way. ***We might say:*** "Can you say more about this part here? I am not sure I understand." "What made you think that?" "Interesting. I never even considered that. Can you tell me about how you came up with this?" "I have to be honest. I never thought of it that way before. Can you explain it more so I can expand my own thinking?" "What made you think to try it this way?" "Have you considered ___?" "What would happen if you ___ or started with ___?"

WORKAROUNDS

CHALLENGE I: I have a large class. I am not sure how I will manage meeting with all students each week.

POSSIBLE WORKAROUNDS

This is a common concern we have all felt at one time or another. Having a plan in place can be helpful.

☐ Consult Appendix E. Use the provided schedules as a mentor text for how you might organize your time. Make needed tweaks, give it a shot, and continue to revise until you find what works for you.

☐ Transfer what's in place to word study. How do you meet with students at other times of the day? Look at what works for you in math, science, social studies, reading, and/or writing. Use this to help you plan your time during word study.

☐ Create a plan, but be flexible and adjust in the moment. If you plan to meet with a small group on a Wednesday, but when it comes someone is absent, two kids are at the nurse getting lice checks, and someone is at speech, scrap it and reschedule for Thursday!

CHALLENGE 2: I get nervous about conferring with students. I am not sure what to say or how to help. I prefer more planned instruction.

POSSIBLE WORKAROUNDS

☐ Read a professional text on conferring or sign up for some professional learning. Knowledge is power and will provide confidence. My two favorite go-to conferring resources are Carl Anderson's *How's It Going?* (2000) and Gravity Goldberg's *Mindset and Moves* (2016). There are a *ton* of other worthwhile sources and plenty of shorter articles and blogs on providing effective, meaningful feedback.

☐ Keep it focused on the student. Try to insert more "you" and take the "I" out of the conversation. Help students see what they are already doing and the impact of their actions. By sharing what's in place, why it is beneficial, and why students should continue to do this, we help create conscious competence.

☐ Relax and breathe. If this is new for you, start by simply walking around and checking in with students. Really, conferring is a conversation—it's person to person. You talk with your students all day long. This is no different. In the words of Glinda the Good Witch in *The Wizard of Oz*, "You've always had the power, my dear. You just had to learn it for yourself" (Fleming et al., 1939).

PRACTICAL PRIORITIZING

☐ Review results of the most recent spelling inventory, preassessment, and/or student work. Look for what is already in place and prioritize next steps for the class, small groups, and individual students.

☐ Read through additional suggested routines. Decide which routines best fit current class and/or specific groups of classroom learners.

☐ Create a few different "meet-with-students" schedules. Plan when you will introduce new routines to students.

☐ Start meeting with students, trying on the different schedules you created. See what works and make needed adjustments. Keep going.

☐ Celebrate all along the way. *Way to go!*

CHAPTER EIGHT

Releasing Responsibility

Goal Setting, Reflection, and Celebration

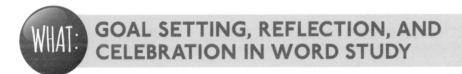

It is important to set goals because if you don't you really don't know what you're doing the subject for. It's also kind of fun because it's like you hitting a checkpoint in a video game when you complete a goal.

—Ty, age 9

Now that students have a repertoire of meaningful word study routines to practice and we are working hard to notice and nurture next steps, it's time to check in and see how things are going. Or more importantly, it's time to step back in our role as "checkers" and have our students take on more of the work in creating goals, checking on progress, and celebrating the hard work and growth happening. In this chapter, I provide a blueprint for building in time for these independence-nudging practices.

WHAT: GOAL SETTING, REFLECTION, AND CELEBRATION IN WORD STUDY

The goal setting–reflection–celebration cycle is part of classroom learning and *always* in play. As is true in our personal lives, goals give us vision for what can be attained through consistent, focused effort. We build purposeful goals by looking at what is already in place and using those strengths as our starting point. We prioritize and decide upon which "next steps" make the most sense for the here and now.

163

In school, when we set goals we develop what I call a First–Next–Then Staircase of Learning. It's a stepped plan to help students meet that goal. This process takes time. For example, if we notice a group of kindergarteners have strong phonemic awareness, are able to separate sounds in a word, and are revved up about writing, we might set a long-term goal of helping them label their sketches in writing. We would first work toward solidifying letter–sound relationships. Next, we would regularly explore, sort, and play with actual words to build greater understanding, fluency, and automaticity. Then, we might teach how to use a tool (e.g., an alphabet chart) to help students recognize and jot learned sounds and letters as they write. Imagine this **first, next,** and **then** as steps leading upward—this is the image I have in my mind as I continually roll out and revise responsive instruction: a staircase—ah, or maybe an escalator.

Let's look at another "staircase." If we notice a group of sixth graders has a strong understanding of using word parts to figure out meaning (-*ed* and -*ing* often signals that this word is a verb; -*able*, -*al*, and -*ful* often signal that this word is an adjective; -*ly* often signals that this word is an adverb; -*sion*, -*tion*, and -*ness* often signal that this word is a noun) we might **first** set a goal around learning about additional affixes**.** We could introduce a few words with a particular affix and foster curiosity by asking students to try to figure out the meaning of the word part. We might follow up by providing a few more words so students can test their theory. **Next,** we would explicitly teach the meaning of the affix, beginning to create connections and contexts for using these words. We might repeat this process, adding a second and third affix. We might provide support while students embark on a more in-depth exploration of the way these chosen beginnings and endings work within actual words. **Then,** when students can read, spell, and use words with these affixes during word study, we would then encourage them to take the crucial next step of using this expertise to help them apply this knowledge to reading, thereby decoding and clarifying meanings with greater confidence.

In a third scenario, if students at any age recognized that they could choose and work on a selected routine with stamina and independence but had a hard time staying organized as they worked, we might **first** work toward teaching the student how to find a work space appropriate for a chosen task. Once this was internalized, we could **next** share how to physically set up and use needed materials, remaining aware of our neighbors working nearby. **Then,** we would teach strategies for cleaning up and putting away word study materials.

When I share this first–next–then concept with teachers, they sometimes will ask, Is it always just three steps? And the answer is . . . no, not really. Sometimes there are ministeps and side steps as students strive to work on growth, but, first–next–then has helped me and students with goal setting.

If we set goals and never look back, the learning may not happen. Reflection, when done all along the way, helps us figure out how things are going and what might need to be adjusted. Many of us do this naturally. For example, when we provide directions to a class and notice a sea of confused faces staring back, we backtrack and try it a new way. Let's teach this important life skill to students. We can easily build in ways to quickly reflect: *What went well for you today? What felt tricky for you?* We might share how to make changes before challenges get too big: *What went so well today that you will you do it again tomorrow? What will you do to make the part that didn't go so well a little easier tomorrow?* We might also provide a tool (such as those provided in this chapter) to help make this process more concrete for students. A minute here and a minute there help build a reflection habit!

Goals are met as students work, reflect, and celebrate. The importance of celebration can never be forgotten. If we wait until "the end" to celebrate, the motivation to work toward loftier long-term goals will be lost. Regular reflection helps us celebrate what's going well: *What went well today? Think about HOW that happened. Share with a neighbor what you are proud of.* Two-minute reflection and celebration practices also help honor the small steps toward a larger goal: *Was there a time you felt frustrated today? What did you do? How did that help you? Let's name that as a celebration. It might sound something like, "Today, I was feeling frustrated when ___ but then I ___, and I want to celebrate that!"*

When teachers and students work as a team to create, work toward, reflect on, and celebrate goals, every positive outcome is heightened! Look ahead for lessons and ideas to help incorporate this cycle into your classroom.

WHY: GOAL SETTING HELPS US PRIORITIZE INSTRUCTION

As teachers, we can plan backwards using student goals as our end vision/success criterion. In this way, we are using a thoughtful and intentional "backwards design" approach to student learning (Wiggins & McTighe, 1998). There is nothing like the joy of watching a student feel accomplished. I once worked with an incredibly thoughtful, inquisitive, off-the-charts hard worker named Erika who also happened to be eligible for a wide range of interventions. She had a goal: to acquire enough word-solving strategies to read *Ruby's Sleepover* by Kathryn White (2012) on her own, and enjoy the process of doing so. Together, we doubled-down on our efforts in both word study and reading. And, of course, that book was in my Amazon shopping cart the moment Erika mentioned it. It was pretty great seeing the wide, bright eyes when I showed Erika the new classroom book. But, it in no way compared to the goose bumps and elation I felt watching Erika excitedly share her book recommendation for *Ruby's Sleepover* with the rest of the class. Every pattern introduction, every small group, every conferring conversation, without a doubt, was well worth it!

The Harvard Initiative of Learning and Teaching supports this process; their report shares that goal setting increases motivation and achievement. They conclude that goal setting most certainly increases and enhances learning. Dewett's findings (2007) also support these methods, sharing that when students are invested in goal setting, they also demonstrate greater creativity, persistence, and risk taking. Consequently, these students are more likely to reach their goals. Not only is there an increase in positive learning attributes, but in 1990, Schunk found that setting specific and clear goals makes students less likely to experience the effects of anxiety, frustration, and disappointment. This study also reports that challenging, high-quality goals also increase students' sense of self-efficacy. What makes a high-quality goal? Building off strengths! In this way, planned "next steps" are in a student's zone of proximal development (Vygotsky, 1978). To sum up, using student strengths (as observed in inventories, assessments, student work, casual conversation, or good old kid-watching) and creating goals based on what's going well helps all classroom members, teachers included.

Best-practice research is great, but a student's thoughts on *why* we set goals (here, referred to as *learning risks*) can mean just as much!

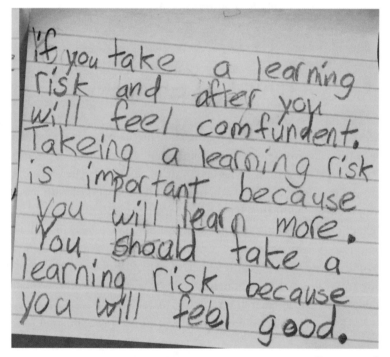

If you take a learning risk and after you will feel comfundent. Takeing a learning risk is important because you will learn more. You should take a learning risk because you will feel good.

—Sunny, age 8

WHEN: INCORPORATING GOAL SETTING, REFLECTION, AND CELEBRATION INTO OUR REGULAR ROUTINES

The goal setting–reflection–celebration cycle is always in motion. Goals are often set at the start of each unit of study. If you do not work in word study units, I suggest setting goals about once every two months. Once goals are set, they are visited at least once a week. Reflection and celebration recognize the progress being made. It is essential not to wait until the end to reflect and celebrate. Both reflection and celebration are critical in keeping motivation, engagement, and a willingness to persevere intact. Confucius shared wise ideas that still stand true today. He believed learning without taking the time for reflection was meaningless—and reflection without putting in the necessary effort for learning was dangerous. John Dewey later added his support to this sentiment: "We do not learn from experience, we learn from reflecting on experience" (1933, p. 78). The goal setting–reflection–celebration cycle is *always* in play.

SAMPLE LESSONS FOR GOAL SETTING, REFLECTION, AND ACCOUNTABILITY

In the following pages, you'll find some ideas that you could choose to do whole class, small group, and/or as a conferring conversation.

Goal-Setting Lesson: Ready-Set-Goal!

WHAT?

In this lesson, the class prioritizes two goals and creates a brief action plan to meet these goals.

HOW?

1. Ask students to join you in the meeting area. Play a short, engaging video clip to inspire students and kick off a conversation about a learner's mindset and how to set and work toward goals. One video I love and recommend is Gatorade's 2017 "The Secret to Victory" commercial.

2. Review previous conversations, read-alouds, and/or personal anecdotes exemplifying a growth mindset.

3. Share a sample word study checklist (these address work habits and word study concepts; see Appendix F for sample checklists). Ask students for suggestions on how they would like to modify the checklist to make it feel "just right."

4. Discuss what students feel is already a strength in place. Model looking at and using recent work as "proof." Working from this strength, together choose one *habit goal* and one *word-competency goal* to work toward as a class.

5. Create a simple "action plan" to meet these goals. Add in "checkpoints" for when and how students will reflect on progress toward these goals. Post these goals and plans for all to see.

6. Soon afterward, have students glue the modified version of the checklist into the goal section of their word study notebooks. Depending on the age of students, they can either glue or copy the class goal and action plan into the goal section.

WHY?

- It's a best practice! In 2001, Klauser found that people who write down their goals and share them with others are 33 percent more successful in accomplishing these goals.

- Goals need an action plan; without an action plan, goals are likely to be forgotten or abandoned.

- Goal setting is not an inherent skill; students need to be taught how to create meaningful and attainable goals.

TIPS

- For the first unit, month, or trimester, model goal setting as a class. When students are ready, begin removing scaffolds to empower students to create more specific and personalized goals. Later, word study groups and/or partners can create goals. Eventually, students will feel confident creating their own individualized goals.

- I recommend sitting with small groups, partners, and individuals to have a "goal-setting conference" each time goals are set. These meetings are often brief, but the conversation helps students to understand the importance of and process to creating important yet reachable goals.

A student works in the goal section of her word study notebook.

Reflection Lesson: How *You* Doin'?

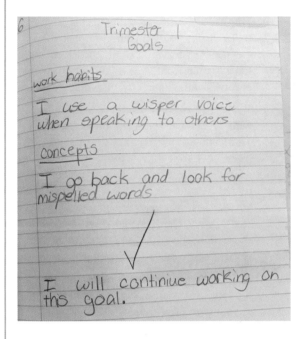

WHAT?

In this lesson, we support a habit of reflection by modeling how to reflect on progress toward a goal.

HOW?

1. Call students together: Start with a quick hook activity (see "Tips" for a few options) to get students thinking about reflection.

2. Review the two class goals (see *Ready–Set–Goal!*). Talk about what actions have been taken. Model finding, showing, and talking about "evidence" for progress toward goal. For example, if it is a material management goal, look through class word study materials and check out the organization, or if it was a spelling goal, have students look through their notebook to see how many times they spelled a selected word (or two) correctly.

3. Participate in a reflection conversation together and emphasize the importance of honesty.

4. Look back at the word study checklist. Together, decide whether the class is ready to move forward. *I think we did meet this goal because ___. I think we didn't meet this goal because ___.*

5. For students in kindergarten through second grade, do a bit of interactive writing to craft a short reflective piece. For Grades 3 and up, after the conversation have students go back to their own notebooks and write for a few minutes with reflections about their own work toward the class goal.

6. Set aside time regularly (at least once a week) for reflection.

WHY?

- It's a best practice! In 2014, Di Stefano, Gino, Pisano, and Staats reported that learning from direct experience is more effective when partnered with reflection, that reflecting on learning makes experiences more productive, and that reflection builds confidence in reaching goals, which also translates to higher rates of learning.

- Thinking about our process and progress helps us move forward.

- It is important to build in snippets of reflection and celebration throughout the process. Reflection that happens *only* at the end (of a cycle or unit) will not yield the same level of fruitful results.

(Continued)

(Continued)

TIPS

- *Primary reflection hooks*: Create cards of silly tasks for you to do in front of the class (e.g., hop on one foot for 30 seconds while also clapping your hands together above your head). Afterward, let the kids reflect and give you feedback on what you did well—and not so well.

- *Elementary reflection hooks*: Put up a piece of student work (from a previous year with names removed or something you created "as a student"). Ask students to point out what was done well—and not so well—using respectful language.

- *Upper-elementary and middle-grade reflection hooks*: Pose several debatable scenarios. Have students decide if they think they would learn more by doing it or thinking about what happened. Discuss each scenario and provide time for people with different viewpoints to share their opinions. Some examples could be playing the football game (playing an instrument in the concert, participating in a partnership fishbowl conversation, etc.) or watching back the tapes of the football game and talking about what happened.

- *Quick daily reflection:* End word study with a reflective share—choose an identified goal. Think about how you did with that goal today. Assess yourself (thumbs-up/side/down,1–5 scale, emoji chart, etc.). Turn and tell a partner what you will do tomorrow to become even stronger in this work.

- *End-of-the-week reflection:* End word study with a reflective share—choose one goal. Think about how you did with that goal this week. Look for evidence of work toward that goal in your notebook. Highlight, star, or underline evidence of your work toward your goal. Talk to your partner about what you see, how you think you are doing, and what you will do the same and differently next week.

- *End-of-unit/month/trimester reflection:* Prepare for your next goal-setting conference. Look at your current goal. Look through your notebook for evidence of work toward this goal. Talk to your partner/group and get their perspective. Write a short narrative paragraph about what went well and what didn't. Bring the reflective piece and "evidence" to the upcoming goal-setting conference.

My goal was . . .
So far I think . . .
I would still like to . . .
Could you help me with . . .?
OR
My goal was . . .
I have done well with . . .
So now, my new goal is . . .
So far I have . . .
Could you help me . . .?

Take a moment to reflect, celebrate, and refocus.
How did you do with your goal today?
Did anything else come up that you are proud of yourself for?
What is your goal for tomorrow?

Here are some prompts to help students to talk with their partner/group about their work toward a goal.

Accountability Lesson: I'm My Own Boss

Photo by Linda Day

A first-grade student holds herself accountable by using the word wall—not a teacher—to check her spelling.

WHAT?

In this lesson, we support students to become accountable for their actions and goal achievement.

HOW?

1. Gather students. Share a short anecdote that seems appropriate. Perhaps it is of your three-year-old son reminding you, "You're not the boss of me!" as he refuses to eat broccoli or your teenage daughter exclaiming almost the same thing when you suggest an outfit for a family gathering. Discuss frustrations felt when someone tries to tell you what to do and/or when you work hard to overcome obstacles and meet goals.

2. Share that as much as teachers, classmates, and partners are there to lend support, results ultimately come down to what we are willing to put in to accomplish our goals. After first taking the risk yourself, ask those who are comfortable to share times they let themselves down and what they could have done differently.

3. Invite students to empower themselves and be brave enough to hold themselves accountable. Ask students to review their goals and recent reflections and then honestly answer these questions: How are they doing? What did they do to cause these results? What can they do to continue or change these results?

WHY?

-   It's a best practice! Daniel Pink (2010) reminds us that the three factors leading to both personal and performance satisfaction are autonomy, mastery, and purpose. We want to empower students to create this for themselves; goal setting, reflection, and self-accountability will help students feel this satisfaction.

-   Teachers, classmates, and partners are wonderful supports. However, we want to bolster students' intrinsic motivation whenever and wherever we can.

TIPS

-   Introduce and revisit self-reflection, assessment, and accountability often but carefully remove heavy scaffolds of regular teacher and partner support in this work. Teacher and partner work will not be extinguished, but we do want students to begin to do this work for themselves.

-   Consider working as a class to set a goal not related to academics and monitor progress toward this goal (through reflection and self-assessment) to model the role of accountability in success.

-   See Appendix F for examples of student checklists.

Photo by Linda Day

Use class work (shared writing done together) to model the process of checking our own work and reflecting on "how we are doing." Fifth graders benefit from this work, too!

Ideas for Reflection and Celebration

Little to No Prep/Time	Medium Prep/Time	A Good Deal of Prep/Time
Post-it Progress Note: Look through your notebook. Put a Post-it on a page that shows progress toward a goal. Share with a neighbor or partner.	*Classroom Display:* Boast about progress. Each student creates his or her own part of a classroom display by completing these sentence starters: *I used to ___.* *But now I ___.*	*Word Parade:* Have students look back at recent patterns studied and pick a word that follows that pattern. Students come to school dressed up like that word and participate in a parade around the school.
Give One, Get One: Students meet with word study group members, sharing gratitude with each peer. Students thank one another for the different ways they helped make word study more meaningful, interesting, fun, and so on. Each student receives as many snippets of gratitude as they give.	*Card Creating:* Invite each student to make a card for a word study partner or group member. Share gratitude and a compliment.	*Student-Run Ed Camp:* Groups of two or three plan and facilitate different "Ed Camp" sessions to share their expertise with others and build upon this expertise with others' insights. Students collaborate to plan sessions around material management, goal setting and reflection, specific routines, targeted patterns, and the like. Sessions take place over two days; each student has one day to facilitate a session and one day to take part in someone else's session.
Buddy Day: Invite another class into the room for a word study session. Each student "buddies up" with a member of the second class and teaches this buddy all about the word study routine they are doing that day. Buddies complete the routine together.	*iMovie Trailer:* Work together as a class to create an iMovie Trailer—spread the word about the joy and learning of this stepped-up approach to word study! Share in a school assembly, at a faculty meeting, or with caregivers and families.	*Student-Created Digital Resources:* Students use technology to create a digital version of the printed minicharts for each routine (Show Me and Screencastify are elementary friendly; Flip Grid is often used in the middle grades). Students tell about and show the process of a learned routine. Video clips can be uploaded and added to the classroom website, Google Classroom, or any other appropriate platform. Student videos become resources for other students to refer to and use.

I think celebrating is an important part of learning because it gets people motivated & excited to work harder. I think we celebrate our work for two reasons: 1. to make people feel good about their hard work.

2. to motivate others to try even harder. Celebrations help to motivate me because when others appreciate my work, I try to do my best work, & try again, & again.

We should celebrate our learning because it is great to learn something new. The more things you learn the better. If we didn't celebrate our learning we might not want to learn more because we won't be encouraging ourselves to learn more.

—Simon, age 9

STARTING UP

Although I loved all of the recommended celebration ideas, this year I tried out the celebration ideas that required little or no prep time. Students enjoyed them. We did these celebrations about once every two months, so I repeated each suggestion twice.

—Sonja, Middle School Teacher of Special Education

STEPPING UP

We used a variety of these suggested routines. In my classroom, we did a little-or-no-prep routine about once every two weeks. I made a list of the medium- and high-prep ideas and had the students choose a "big" celebration three times across the school year: one in the late fall, one in the winter, and one at the end of the year.

—Sawyer, Grade 5 Teacher

WORKAROUNDS

CHALLENGE: *My students chose a class goal that I don't really feel is most important.*

POSSIBLE WORKAROUND

☐ Go with their goal! The actual first goal isn't too important. Instead, emphasize modeling the process of goal setting, creating an action plan, working toward a goal, and regularly reflecting on that goal. Your instruction will highlight what you know students most need, but recognizing and acknowledging student input are extremely important.

CHALLENGE: *I don't have a lot of time. Can't I just use the word study checklists provided?*

POSSIBLE WORKAROUND

☐ You could use the provided checklists. However, you could also co-create a class version using the provided checklists as a "mentor text." Together, decide which parts everyone likes, agrees to, and wants to keep. Tweak and switch out other parts to personalize the checklist for your current group of learners. Ideally, each new group of learners will create a personal version of this tool.

PRACTICAL PRIORITIZING

☐ Reread the suggested routines in this chapter. Consider which routines you will teach to keep engagement high and nurture and nudge classwide word learning.

☐ Create a mentor goal, action plan, and reflection/self-assessment tool.

☐ Think of ways to celebrate that seem developmentally appropriate, accessible, and exciting. Share a few options with students to gauge their interest and gather additional ideas.

☐ Remember: This is the *fun* part! Keep this work lighthearted and bask in the successes sprouting up all around you every day!

A TOUR OF WORD STUDY IN ACTION

20 Minutes of Focused Fun and Teaching Language

On these two pages, I try to capture the spirit and the swift steps of what you say and do—and what your students do—on a typical day of word study. Teachers often ask me, what do you say? How long do you check in with an independent small group? When do you find time to meet with a student who needs support? Use these anecdotes to envision your own plate-spinning word study sessions! If you keep these basic moves in mind, and move through these routines knowing they are cyclical, and flexible, you can import virtually all the lessons and practices in this book into these 20-minute powerhouses of word learning.

THE FIRST 3 MINUTES

"Okay . . . Today, the red group is working on a meaning routine. The blue group is meeting with me on the rug—you don't need to bring anything. Green group, today you can play a quick word game or build words using any material you like. Make sure you are careful setting up and putting away materials. Thumbs up if you know what you are doing today. . . . Word collectors, before we get started on word study today, take a moment to reread your goal. Think about what you will do today to work toward this goal. Before you move or get any supplies, quickly share your plan for the day with a friend. Then, let's get to it."

THE NEXT 8 MINUTES

"Blue group, please sit down and make a rainbow facing me so you can easily see and hear me. Today I will be introducing a new group of words. Please watch me and listen. You know how this goes . . . Put up I to 5 fingers as I share each word. I will review any words for which we want a clearer picture or understanding. Here's the first word . . . Now that we have reviewed all our new words, it is time to go off and work on preparing your word cards. Please remember to use your chosen color and throw out your scraps."

5 MINUTES MORE

"Green group, you are looking good. Keep it up. Red group, I'm coming over to see how it is going with your meaning routine today . . . Harmony, may I interrupt your work for a minute so we can chat about how things are going?"

3 MINUTES OF WRAP UP

"Word explorers, there were a few things I noticed about word study today. First, the green group worked independently. If there were any issues, I didn't even know. I appreciate you being solution seekers because this allowed me to meet with the blue group and a couple of people from the red group. Thank you! Harmony, you discovered something kind of cool while working on your "I might be . . ." routine. Could you share what you discovered? I think it would be a great tip for everyone."

Instructional Routine	What It Is	Purpose	When It Happens	Notes
Short Whole-Class Instruction (aka minilesson)	Brief (5-15 minutes) whole-class instruction to explicitly show students one strategy or routine and have learners give it a first try.	We use minilessons to introduce a new routine or address a whole-class need or next step.	Regularly during the launch, occasionally during the rest of the year.	Much of this book includes examples of whole-class lessons. Therefore, one was not included in the scenarios shown here.
Small Group	The teacher meets with a few students to work on a specific strategy, routine, or work habit.	We use small groups to efficiently nurture the next steps and practices used by a portion of the class.	Small group instruction happens while the rest of the class is working on their own word study routines.	Small group lessons typically last 5–10 minutes.
Conferring Conversation	The teacher meets 1:1 with a student to provide explicit strength-based feedback.	When we share with students what they are doing well, they tend to keep doing it. We help students grow by explicitly sharing next steps based off of these strengths.	Conferring conversations happen while the rest of the class is working on their own word study routines.	Conferring conversations are casual AND short and sweet. They typically take anywhere from 1–5 minutes each.
Goal Setting and Reflection "Check-In"	These check-ins are quick, frequent reminders of chosen goals, and reflection to see the progress made.	Setting, reflecting on, and sharing work toward goals builds motivation and ownership.	Checking in on goals can happen anytime and anyplace. When there is no whole-class lesson, goal check-ins may start or end a word study session.	Checking in on goals could take as little as 30 seconds! It is so easy to sneak this practice into whatever time is available.

PART III

Teaching for Transfer

In this class we make decisions. Mrs. K once told us her job is to teach us how to learn. Then we can learn anything! We make a goal, take risks, + think A LOT! This works in every subject. I'm really good at this now. Our whole class is. This is my favorite part because I feel like I'm in charge!

—Peter, age 9

The Wind by James Steph...

The wind <u>stood</u> up an...
He <u>whistled</u> on his
<u>Kicked</u> the whi...
and <u>thumped</u> the
And <u>said</u> that he
And so he will and

Photo by Linda Day

Conversation

Photo by Katie McGrath

Connecting the Dots
Word Study in Reading and Writing

> We do this word study routine called
> use it or lose it. It's kind of the
>
> same thing → using what we know
> about words all the time. If we don't
> use what we have learned, it might
> just poof! Dissapear from our
> brains!

—Dajirah, age 8

When I say to teachers, with my trademark chipper, glass-half-full mindset, *"Go for word study all day!"* they give me this knowing smile, as if to say, there Pam goes again. Once I really put them over the edge by proving my point by reading aloud Tony Fucile's picture book *Let's Do Nothing!* The two main characters, Frankie and Sal, challenge each other to do nothing. After a few humorous attempts, the boys have a moment of reality when they realize it's impossible to do nothing and that they are always doing *something*. It is easy to draw a parallel to word study. Go ahead—take a few moments and try to think of something we do that does not involve words in *any* way. Now, challenge yourself further to think of something we do in school that does not involve reading, writing, speaking, or listening. Can you recall anything that does not require us to make meaning from or use words in any way? Given the importance of words, it is shocking that so little of our time is dedicated to the pursuit of studying words!

As twenty-first century educators, we try to help students not only accumulate strategies and knowledge but also know how and when to apply and use these strategies. The great Russian writer Anton Chekhov once shared an idea about knowledge being of no real value unless it is put into practice. In Part III, we will explore ways to authentically embed word study into all facets of the day. In this chapter, we start with embedding word study into the instruction of reading and writing.

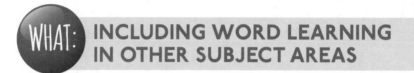

WHAT: INCLUDING WORD LEARNING IN OTHER SUBJECT AREAS

There are two main ways to advance word study in the content areas:

1. We teach students to remember and apply the actual letter, sound, and word knowledge practiced in word study.

2. We teach them how to study the lingo of any specific content area.

WHAT DOES IT MEAN TO APPLY WORD KNOWLEDGE?

One of the greatest challenges teachers face when it comes to word study is transfer. If past experiences tell us word knowledge hasn't "stuck," then we can (and will) find ways to consistently prioritize words across the day. We need to model and teach students *how* to use their gained expertise not only in the few minutes we spend exclusively on studying and exploring words—but in all parts of our day. There's no real magic to making word study stick; but it's magical when intentional and focused learning opportunities make this actually happen. In this chapter and Chapter 10, I outline simple, efficient ways to do just this!

WHAT EXACTLY IS CONTENT AREA LINGO?

In their tiered model of vocabulary development, the oh-so-brilliant Beck, McKeown, and Kucan (2013) classify words into three groups:

1. Tier I: These are common, everyday words (*boy*, *girl*, *table*, *floor*, *pencil*, etc.). Most students come into school knowing these words, and we often do not need to prioritize teaching time to address these words.

2. Tier II: These are important words that appear across content areas and subjects (*analyze*, *facilitate*, *persevere*, etc.). This academic vocabulary is what some students have referred to as "smart-sounding words." This tier of words is worth our teaching time! Most research shares that this is the most important class of words to not only teach, but to *teach well*. We want these words to become part of a student's vocabulary.

3. Tier III: These are our content-specific vocabulary words (*photosynthesis*, *cotangent*, *isotope*, *velocity*, *quotient*, etc.). Tier III words are often bolded in informational texts and are regularly found in glossaries. They reflect the lingo of a unit of study and may not be commonly used outside of that setting. We often teach these words during our content area work with students.

WHAT CAN I DO TO TEACH CONTENT LINGO SIMPLY AND EFFICIENTLY?

Beck, McKeown, and Kucan (2013) have research-backed, practice-shifting suggestions on how to choose, teach, and practice vocabulary. I highly recommend reading their work. Until then (and even after), know that the routines shared in previous chapters for studying words in word study can also be used to study and learn Tier III words in the content areas. That is, by using the same routines I shared in earlier chapters in your content area teaching, you free up time to focus on the content. We do not need to teach an entirely new way to study words; we can simply transfer (with no or minimal tweaks) word study routines for use in the content areas. Examples of these exciting practices are included in both this chapter and the next.

WHY: IT'S TIME TO CHANGE UP CURRENT PRACTICES THAT AREN'T STICKING

Why? Because we have all seen and/or experienced this before:

- Incorrect spelling of simple, straightforward words after patterns have been explicitly taught

- Students coming to us waaayyy too often to ask, "How do you spell ___?" or ignoring red, squiggly lines under their words when typing

- Students turning away from reading because the decoding becomes frustrating

- Students shying away from writing because their knowledge of spelling is not yet conventional, or students choosing "easier" (and bland, less precise) words when writing because they are unsure how to spell a more interesting word

- Students disengaging from all types of learning and social experiences because of their confidence and competence in making sense of and/or using words in some way

Why? Because research is telling us this:

- According to Rasinski (2017), 31 percent of fourth graders, 24 percent of eighth graders, and 27 percent of twelfth graders scored below the "basic" level in reading.

- The Survey of Adult Skills by the Organization for Economic Cooperation and Development (OECD) found that even though adults in the United States have higher-than-average levels of educational attainment, we have below-average basic literacy and numeracy skills. According to the 2013 OECD survey, the United States ranked 16th out of 23 countries in literacy proficiency, 21st in numeracy proficiency, and 14th in problem solving in technology-rich environments (Rogers, 2013).

- Data shows that almost two-thirds of today's high school students may be struggling readers (Lexia Learning, 2017).

- Students who don't have sufficient literacy skills as fourth graders are four times more likely to drop out of high school (Dell'Antonia, 2012).

- In 2014, the Annie E. Casey Foundation reported that only one-fifth of fourth graders from low-income households are "reading at a proficient level, compared to more than half of high-income children" (Potts, 2014). This is particularly upsetting because as educators we know that school becomes even more text dependent and demanding as students move into middle and high school.

- Some studies have reported that 85 percent of all juveniles who have contact with the juvenile justice system are "functionally illiterate" (Rosario, 2015).

WHEN: EMBEDDING WORD LEARNING IS *OUR* "NEXT STEP" GOAL

Throughout this book, I have suggested an intentional, one-step-at-a-time rollout of word study. Once word study is up and running in the classroom (i.e., you feel *fairly* secure and *reasonably* confident in using the practices recommended in Part I and

Part II of this book), it is time to take on these *next-level necessities*. We are ready to work to instill transfer and greater independence in practice across the day. There is no need to rush to this point, but there is also no reason to hold back once you feel the class is ready! As many of my mentors have said, "Don't let perfect get in the way of good." If we reflect on how things went as we started up or stepped up our approach to word study, we may recall the initial ebb and flow. Things in a classroom never go exactly as expected! However, we tried, we tweaked, we lived, and we learned. The same will happen as we start infusing word study throughout the day. There may be some bumps and missteps, but it is all worth it—because by intentionally promoting and teaching into transfer, we are providing experiences to truly make word study stick!

Infusing Word Study Into Reading

As readers, we need to recognize words and word parts. We need to decode with fluency, competency, and relative ease. We want to appreciate the beauty of words, the impact of words, and the meaning of words in the texts we encounter and choose to read. We also strive to understand the words and what it is these words are coming together to say. Moreover, we hope to be moved by words and feel and/or do something because of words.

Whether we are reading text, writing about something we read, or engaging in discussion about something read, we need to apply our word knowledge! As people become curious about words, engage in studying words, and begin to accumulate words, their competency and love of reading soars. There are infinite worthwhile practices to help support transfer of word knowledge in reading. Here are a few of my most efficient and high-impact favorites!

SHARED READING: PROVIDING VISION FOR WHAT TRANSFER LOOKS AND SOUNDS LIKE

Shared reading is an instructional practice in which we provide vision and support for students. Teachers do most of the work, and students watch. After seeing us in action, students are invited to, right then and there, try out whatever we have modeled. More specifically, shared reading is a structure in which we show or project an enlarged (short) text so the whole class can see the words. We read the text aloud, and students follow along with their eyes. Sometimes students are invited to read parts of the text along with us. Shared reading happens in cycles. Typically, these cycles are composed of a few "short and sweet" sessions. In each session, the class revisits the same short, enlarged text. Each session/day has a different focus (literal comprehension, word work, fluency, and inferential thinking are common focus areas), and each session lasts 5 to 15 minutes. Shared reading is often used when content or a process is new and students would benefit from *seeing* what it looks like when a competent reader (us) does the work. We might also plan and implement a cycle of shared reading when we notice students are having difficulty—or really, any time we want to build classroom community and support learning!

How might I organize a cycle of shared reading?

Each session in the cycle has a different focus. Typically, a cycle starts with some sort of literal comprehension work on Day 1 or Session 1. In the middle of the cycle, the teacher will have a different intention each day. Common areas of focus include concepts of print, phonemic awareness or phonics work, word solving (decoding), word solving (vocabulary), word noticing (pattern/spelling work), grammar/language work, and fluency. Often, the last session focuses on extension work (talk, deeper inferential thinking, or response writing). During shared-reading lessons, the teacher reads the text and shows the students how they do the work, using extremely explicit modeling and plenty of think-aloud. Each day, the students are invited to "dip in" and try a bit of the work, often through turning and talking with a partner.

What kind of text might be used?

This is not the time to read a whole book. If we want to read, show, and perhaps have students try—in 5 to 15 minutes—the text needs to be short. Often, the chosen text is just a notch or two above what is most comfortable for students to read independently. When shared reading is done during our *reading* block, we might read and repeatedly revisit the following:

- Nursery rhymes
- Poems
- Songs/song lyrics
- Articles or short pieces of texts
- One or two pages from a longer text

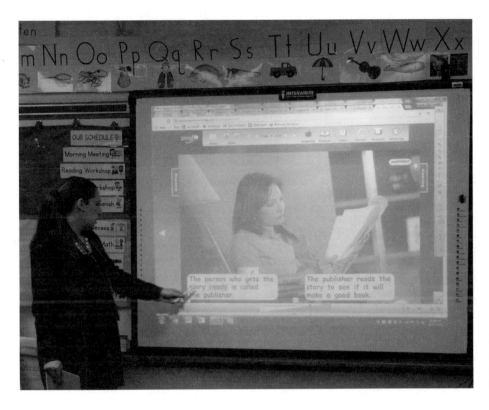

Heather leads a "word work" focused shared-reading session with her first-grade class.

SAMPLE CYCLES OF SHARED READING

Title and Author of Text: Unit of Study:		
Day/Session I	Comprehension	EX: Preview text and get mind ready to read.
Day/Session 2	Concepts of Print	EX: Notice spaces between words, read one word for each word written, and return sweep.
Day/Session 3	Spelling Pattern Word Work	EX: Notice a word part studied in word study, find all words with this pattern, and generate a list of other words associated with the pattern.
Day/Session 4	Fluency	EX: Use echo reading followed by choral reading.
Day/Session 5	Extension	EX: Infer how a character is feeling, share what in the text helped reader to figure that out, and make a connection to own experiences.

Title and Author of Text: Unit of Study:		
Day/Session 1	Comprehension	EX: Retell or summarize text orally.
Day/Session 2	Vocabulary	EX: Notice a studied word, talk about meaning, and think about synonyms or antonyms.
Day/Session 3	Spelling Pattern Word Work	EX: Notice a tricky word that is related to a pattern studied, use the self-monitoring cycle.
Day/Session 4	Fluency	EX: Repeat choral reading, and read pattern words in different "silly" voices.
Day/Session 5	Extension	EX: Use key words from the text to help write a synthesized summary and/or response.

Title and Author of Text: Unit of Study:		
Day/Session 1	Comprehension	EX: Identify text structure and use it to help share most important parts of text.
Day/Session 2	Vocabulary	EX: Use word parts (prefix, suffix, root) to help solve the words, understand connotation of the words, and share different contexts where this word would (and wouldn't) be used.
Day/Session 3	Spelling Pattern Word Work	EX: Use word parts (prefix, suffix, root) to help solve other words.
Day/Session 4	Grammar/Language	EX: Sort sentences (simple, compound, and complex) and notice use of conjunctions.
Day/Session 5	Extension	EX: Debate reaction to text—reader's perspective vs. author's perspective or one reader's perspective vs. another reader's perspective.

TEACHER TIP

The sample shared-reading cycles can be used with almost any poem, short text, article, and the like. There is no "magic" text any teacher needs to use for a cycle of shared reading. Choose texts you know, love, and have. Keep your eye out for engaging texts that students will enjoy revisiting again and again each day across a cycle!

WHOLE-CLASS INSTRUCTION: TEACHING HOW TO TRANSFER WORD KNOWLEDGE

In shared reading, we show students what it looks like for a competent reader (us) to use a strategy. In a "how-to" lesson, often called a minilesson, we explicitly teach students the procedural knowledge for using a specific strategy. During this time, we often show authentic, in-context use of the strategy (what it looks like when we are reading!). We show students the steps of the strategy, we coach students as they try out the process of the strategy, and we end by reminding students when and why they would use this strategy. We also invite and encourage students to regularly practice using this strategy in their own reading, knowing this work can happen with virtually any book! Here are a few of the endless strategies we might teach, paired with one example of procedural knowledge that would help students try out this strategy while reading:

Readers solve and read tricky words by looking for a part they know:

1. Notice the tricky word in the text.

2. Look inside—find a *part* you know.

3. Go back and try the whole word.

Readers solve and read tricky words by trying the vowel sound two ways:

1. Notice a HUH word.

2. Try the vowel sound two ways (short and long).

3. Think: Which sounds right and makes the most sense?

4. **KEEP READING!**

Readers solve and read tricky words by using clues to help:

1. Notice and stop at the tricky word.

2. Look at the first letter(s) and say the sound of that letter/those letters.

3. Look at the picture—find the parts of the picture that start with that letter.

4. Try that word in the sentence.

5. **KEEP READING!**

Readers solve tricky words by using all they know and learned:

1. *Notice it:* Stop at the tricky word.

2. *Think about it:* Does that word have a letter or part that I learned about in word study? How is this word like other words I already know?

3. *Use it:* Use your word study learning and prior word collecting to solve the word and move on.

4. **KEEP READING!**

Readers use three important questions to make sure they are reading the words just as the author wrote them:

1. Notice the tricky word. Stop and use a strategy (or strategies) to solve it

2. Ask yourself, *Does that make sense? Does it look right? Does it sound right?*

3. Yes to all three? KEEP READING! No to any of them? Try again!

Readers take the time to go back and check to make sure a word makes sense:

1. Notice a tricky word: *Huh?*

2. Try a strategy: *What do I know? What can I do here?*

3. Go back and s-l-o-w c-h-e-c-k: *Let me reread and make sure this looks right, sounds right, and makes sense.*

4. If OK, *then* move on and KEEP READING! (If not, go through the whole cycle again!)

SMALL-GROUP WORK AND/OR CONFERRING: SUPPORTING STUDENTS AS THEY GIVE THIS A GO

Only in books and on TV are there classes full of kids all ready for the same strategy and learning at the exact same time! In real life, we know this is rarely, if ever, true. As educators, we often support and extend learning for individuals through small-group work and one-on-one conferring conversations. In reading, this small-group work and conferring often resembles these commonly used structures:

1. **Guided Reading:** This is small group instruction in which a teacher supports students while reading an instructional-level text. Teachers provide guidance as students learn and apply new reading strategies. Most typically, the teacher chooses the text, and all the students in the group are reading the same text. Often, teachers use the *Fountas & Pinnell Continuum of Literacy Learning* (2016) to make strategic choices about how best to support different groups of learners during guided reading.

2. **Strategy Group:** This is small-group instruction in which a teacher can support students' work on a specific strategy they are ready for. The teacher forms this short-term, flexible group because the chosen students have a similar strength in place and a common readiness for a next step. The teacher models a "step-up" strategy and then coaches students as they try it out in their own reading. The students are often reading different texts during a strategy lesson.

3. **Small-Group Shared Reading:** This is small-group instruction that mirrors the whole-class structure of shared reading noted earlier in the chapter. A teacher may choose to use small-group shared reading to provide additional support to a group of learners so that they are more confident in trying new or challenging work with greater independence.

4. **Conferring Conversations:** This is one-on-one talk time between a teacher and a student. During this time, a teacher shares something the student is already doing well. The teacher then, as in a strategy group, models a "step-up" strategy the student is ready for and coaches the student through the first try of that strategy. Before leaving, the teacher may provide an oral or visual reminder of the strategy practiced and/or review once again when, why, and how to continue to try using that strategy.

Photo by Julie McAuley

Supporting word
learning during a
guided-reading lesson.

Photo by Julie McAuley

Leading a small group
on using learned word
parts to help decode
tricky words in an
informational text.

In any and all of the aforementioned differentiated supports, teachers can highlight and infuse new word learning and transfer of word learning. For example, in guided reading, teachers may teach into a new "type of word" that often appears in these new, cool books students are beginning to read. In a strategy group, small-group shared reading, and conferring conversation, teachers can support and extend students' knowledge of in-context word solving, self-monitoring, vocabulary development, and fluent reading of words. In *all* the previous structures, teachers can also intentionally speak using pattern words studied in word study. Teachers can ask students to thoughtfully and appropriately use these types of words when talking about texts. Students might also be supported in transferring word learning while jotting or writing about the books they are reading.

Word Study in Writing

As writers, we need to know about words and word parts so we can communicate our ideas to an audience. We also hope to encode with fluency, competency, and relative ease so we can focus on our ideas. We want to use precise, meaningful, "just-right" words to spark different feelings and reactions in our readers. We hope that an audience will be moved by words to feel and do something because of our writing.

Many teachers feel students are not consistently applying all they know about words while writing. Well, where there's a noticing, there's a way to address it with our instruction! There are countless high-impact practices to help support transfer of word knowledge to writing. Here are a few of my favorites!

SHARED WRITING: PROVIDING VISION FOR WHAT TRANSFER LOOKS AND SOUNDS LIKE

Shared writing is an instructional practice that provides both vision and support for students. Using the gradual release model of I Go–We Go–You Go, it falls in the "we go" range, but it is very close to the "I go" side because the teacher does the majority of the "heavy lifting" work. This is a structure where a class plans out and composes a text together, bit by bit over several sessions. In each session, the teacher models a different part of the process by using think-aloud and doing all the writing/composing of the text. Students contribute by sharing ideas at specifically chosen points in each session with a partner. Just as in shared reading, each session in a cycle is about 5 to 15 minutes, and a cycle frequently is composed of three to seven sessions, with about five sessions being most typical. Because this is such a high support and scaffolded instructional practice, it is often used when either the genre, the content, or a process are new and/or tricky for students.

How might I organize a cycle of shared writing?

It helps to think of shared writing as the "mirror" of shared reading. Just as in shared reading, each session has a different focus. Very often, a cycle starts with *generating ideas* on Day 1 or in Session 1. In the middle of the cycle, the teacher will have a different intention each day. Common areas of focus include planning a piece of writing, quickly drafting a piece of writing, elaborating on ideas, and enhancing writing. Frequently, the last session focuses on polishing the piece to make it clear and understandable for the reader. Each day, the teacher uses think-aloud as he or she rehearses to write and actually writes. The teacher shows the students how to do the work, using extremely explicit modeling. Students are invited to "dip in" and try a bit of the work *aloud*, often through turning and talking with a partner.

SAMPLE CYCLES OF SHARED WRITING

Genre/Text Type: Unit of Study:		
Day/Session 1	Generate Ideas	EX: Share and list possible topics for procedural "how-to" writing using shared expertise (washing hands, unpacking backpack, lining up for lunch, saying the Pledge of Allegiance).
Day/Session 2	Plan	EX: List steps in order across fingers. Touch pages of booklet saying the same steps in the same order. Use "order words" as saying steps aloud.
Day/Session 3	Rehearse	EX: Quickly sketch across pages, using sketches to show the most important part of each step.
Day/Session 4	Enhance	EX: Add details to turn sketches into teaching pictures.
Day/Session 5	Polish	EX: Add labels to parts of the sketch. Stretch words, use taught strategies, and record as many sounds as possible for each word so writing is understandable for others.

Genre/Text Type: Unit of Study:		
Day/Session 1	Generate Ideas	EX: Share and list possible topics for procedural "all-about" writing using shared expertise (town live in, school attending, specials at school, etc.). Vote on one topic to write about together.
Day/Session 2	Plan	EX: List "parts of" the topic across fingers. Touch pages of booklet, saying the same parts (subtopics) in the same order.

Genre/Text Type: Unit of Study:		
Day/Session 3	Draft	EX: Quickly sketch across pages. Go back and add details and labels to sketches. While labeling, stretch words, model remembering, and use taught strategies and patterns.
Day/Session 4	Elaborate	EX: Use labels in sketch as a word bank. Together, compose sentences on each page to teach the reader about the topic. While writing, model remembering and using taught strategies to spell words conventionally.
Day/Session 5	Enhance and Polish	EX: Go back and model process of noticing and checking spelling of specific (pattern?) words on each page. While revising content and editing, model using taught patterns and strategies while writing.

Genre/Text Type: Unit of Study:		
Day/Session I	Generate Ideas	EX: Share and list possible topics for "shared-experience" personal narrative. Choose one to write about together.
Day/Session 2	Plan	EX: Use a timeline, story mountain, or other planning structure to plan out how the story will go.
Day/Session 3	Draft	EX: Use plan to quickly draft. While drafting, model remembering and using taught strategies and patterns "in the moment."
Day/Session 4	Enhance	EX: Revisit draft, finding drab words and parts. Replace with more precise, interesting, and descriptive words. Model taking word risks and infusing all that has been taught and practiced to write creatively, conventionally, and correctly.
Day/Session 5	Polish	EX: Model process of reading work and checking spelling of specific (pattern?) words. While revising content and editing mechanics, model using tools to support conventional and correct use of taught patterns.

INTERACTIVE WRITING: STUDENTS DIP IN AND TRY . . . JUST A LITTLE BIT

Interactive writing is a structure in which a class plans and works to create a text together, typically in one setting/session. The teacher shows the thinking behind the writing happening and does *most* of the writing/composing of the text. In this instructional practice, students take on a bit more of the work. For example, students contribute by sharing ideas with a partner, but they *also* participate by dipping in and doing some of the writing at specifically selected points. These points intend to have students practice using conventional spelling and grammar. Just as in shared reading and shared writing, when using the gradual release model of I Go–We Go–You Go, it falls in the "we go" range. However, interactive writing is truly "we go" since students are not only contributing ideas but also doing some of the writing! I love this instructional practice for so many reasons, but it is particularly awesome for fostering the application of word and grammar learning while writing.

To give you greater vision of this one-and-done (often 10–20 minutes) practice, here's a sneak peek of how the session would look: The teacher or class decides on a topic to write about. Together, the teacher and students compose a short piece of writing. Every so often, the teacher pauses, asks students to recall prior learning and try to apply that learning to the writing at hand. Common stopping points include these:

- Spelling of high-frequency words

- Spelling of any words containing a studied pattern or word part

- Spelling of learned words

- Applying and using conventional capitalization, punctuation, or other taught grammar skills

Students are involved and easily engaged throughout the process.

WHOLE-CLASS INSTRUCTION: TEACHING HOW TO TRANSFER WORD KNOWLEDGE

If we do not take the time to teach students how to apply their word learning, it likely won't happen. Whole-class lessons are a wonderful opportunity to explicitly teach students the procedural knowledge for using a specific strategy. This is an ideal time to remind students of prior word learning and how to apply it while writing. During this direct instruction, teachers show the students the steps of the strategy, coach students as they try out the process of a strategy, and end by reminding students when and why they would use this strategy. Teachers encourage students to practice using their word learning in their own writing and then hold them accountable for doing so. The following are a few of the strategies we might teach, paired with one example of procedural knowledge that would help student in trying out this strategy while writing:

Writers work toward their word study goals by also trying out this work while writing at other points in the day.

1. Think, remember, and say a word study goal.

2. Tell yourself, *Do this while writing today!*

3. Do it!

4. At the end, look back and check for it. Celebrate!

Writers make sure their work is understandable by using word learning to help them spell correctly while writing.

1. Write, write, write!

2. Notice when you get to a pattern word or learned word.

3. Ask yourself, *What do I know that can help me here?*

4. Use your prior learning.

5. Continue to write, write, write!

Writers make sure their work is understandable by using word learning to help them make sure they spelled words correctly.

1. Write, remembering to use all you know.

2. Look back. Find all the words you wrote that have a word part you have studied.

3. Ask yourself, *Did I use what I know? Does it look right? Does it make sense here?*

4. YES? Celebrate! NO? Fix it up and then celebrate!

Writers make sure their work is understandable by using a tool to help them make sure they spelled words correctly.

1. Write, write, write!

2. Look back. Highlight, circle, or underline any word you are unsure of.

3. Use something to check the spelling/word usage of each identified word: a partner, a chart, a word wall, a hard-copy or online dictionary or thesaurus.

4. Celebrate your hard work and commitment!

SMALL-GROUP WORK AND/OR CONFERRING: SUPPORTING STUDENTS AS THEY GIVE THIS A GO

Our classes are comprised of incredibly unique and special learners with varied strengths and areas of readiness. As educators, we can support and nurture the "just-right" next steps of classroom members through small-group work and one-on-one conferring conversations. In writing, this small-group work and conferring often resembles these commonly used structures:

1. **Strategy Group:** This is small-group instruction in which a teacher can support students' work on a specific strategy they are ready to try in writing. The teacher forms this short-term, flexible group because the chosen students

have a similar strength in place and a common readiness for a next step. The teacher models a "step-up" strategy and then coaches students as they try it out in their own writing. The students are all working on writing their own pieces during a strategy lesson.

2. **Small-Group Shared/Interactive Writing:** This is small-group instruction that may mirror the whole-class structure of shared writing described earlier. However, sometimes a teacher does a hybrid version of shared and interactive writing in a small-group setting. A teacher may choose to use this hybrid small-group practice to provide additional support while also releasing some scaffolds so that students more slowly take on more and more of this work. Over a few short-and-sweet sessions, the group works to generate ideas, plan, compose, and enhance a piece of writing. However, the teacher asks the students to do more and more of the work (including some of the actual writing) in each session.

3. **Conferring Conversations:** In writing, teachers often check in with individual students during the time the class is independently writing. The teacher talks with the students and/or looks at their recent writing. The teacher then names something they are already doing well. The teacher then models a "step-up" strategy and coaches while they try that strategy. Before leaving, the teacher may provide an oral or visual reminder of the strategy practiced and/or a review once again of when, why, and how to continue to try using that strategy.

Check out a few examples of teachers, students, and partners working to apply their word learning during writing time:

Photo by Julie McAuley

In this conferring conversation with a fourth-grader, Karen models a strategy for applying word learning while writing.

Here, I am conferring with a sixth-grade student who is ready to work on stepping up word choice in her opinion writing.

Photo by Linda Day

Student partnerships work together to increase accountability. They are checking to make sure they have applied their word learning to their writing.

WORKAROUNDS

CHALLENGE: *I am not sure where I can find texts with pattern words for shared reading.*

POSSIBLE WORKAROUNDS

☐ It is so much easier than you think! If you are in the elementary grades, pretty much every text will have multiple examples of whatever pattern you want to highlight: starting and ending sounds, vowel sounds, *r*-controlled vowels, *-s, -es, -ing, -ed, -tion, -le*, open and closed syllables, compound words, contractions, and so on—you *will* find these types of patterns in texts more easily than you ever imagined.

☐ Thankfully, stages of spelling development are loosely aligned to reading levels. Therefore, it is quite common for the patterns students are studying in word study to be in "typical" texts read at that grade level.

☐ Grab a text you already have handy and accessible and then look for examples of spelling patterns in that text. No "decodable texts" necessary! Use authentic texts you know, have, love, and think the students will enjoy.

CHALLENGE: *I am used to correcting student writing and then having them recopy. Can't I keep doing that?*

POSSIBLE WORKAROUNDS

☐ Let's be honest: When we correct student work, who is doing the work? (*Hint:* It is not the student!) The person doing the correcting (not simply copying) has the brain doing the learning.

☐ When we correct student work, we are telling students, "I know better" and that their voices and efforts don't matter: The editing process becomes dreaded, powerless, and pointless. People often do not feel positive about themselves or writing in general after getting a page back that is filled with corrections (in *any* color, not only the stereotypical red pen).

☐ Feedback helps students not only learn but take ownership of their process. Model strategies (like those recommended in this chapter) for transferring word learning to writing and mentor students so that they become more and more proficient with this process. This helps students not only spell *this* word correctly on *this* page of *this* piece, but *more* words correctly on *more* pages and across *more* pieces.

☐ Make it a "Win! Win! Situation": Provide in-person feedback and support at school—and enjoy your time with friends and family at home (because you are *not* sitting on your couch correcting student work)!

PRACTICAL PRIORITIZING

- ☐ Look closely at upcoming reading and writing units. List out the "lingo" of each unit—especially the Tier II and III vocabulary words related to the topic being studied. Plan to try out one word-study routine in the content areas, using content area lingo.

- ☐ Create or rework plans for *one* cycle of shared reading or writing, this time incorporating word work more prominently in the cycle.

- ☐ Try *one* whole-class or small-group lesson on using word study knowledge while reading and/or word knowledge while writing. Use the anchor charts provided in this chapter for guidance.

- ☐ If you use the framework of reading or writing workshop in your school, think about how you could incorporate more word work into your conferring conversations. Hint: Some teachers like choosing *one* day of the week (e.g., Tuesday) and having all conferring conversations that one day be about next-step word work.

- ☐ Remember—a little goes a long way. Take baby steps and add in more and more word work as you feel comfortable and ready!

CHAPTER TEN

Sealing the Deal With Word Learning in the Content Areas

I was researching for our group inquiry project and I realized — the new vocab I came across was almost exactly the same as the words other people in my group also found. All of a sudden — we got it! If we were going to be learning, writing, talking, or teaching about this topic — THESE were the words we would use. We discovered the EXPERT words. HUGE lightbulb moment!

— Devon, 6th grade

—Devon, age 11

Words surround us. We are literally immersed in a world of words. Words extend beyond our literacy blocks. Content area lingo is "real world" and relevant. For example, in math, words such as *dimension*, *volume*, and *vector* slide naturally off an architect's tongue as they create and share blueprints for skyscrapers and more modest and functional homes. And for those of us who don't design jaw-dropping buildings . . . we use words such as *interest*, *deductions*, and *depreciation* in our everyday lives. Astronomers look at the night sky and speculate, using terms such as *celestial coordinates*, *transparency*, and *ephemerides* as they describe their noticings. As novices, we marvel as we look through a telescope and chat about a *blue moon*, *asteroid*, or *lunar eclipse*. An archaeologist digging in ancient ruins might record ideas related to the *stratigraphy* or *assemblage*. As lay people, we may have a once-in-a-lifetime opportunity to shine a flashlight on a cave wall in Dordogne (or perhaps more likely,

201

take a virtual field trip to this part of France) to check out art from the Ice Age, seeing and discussing the mammoth images created an unimaginably long time ago. The power lingo and language provide across disciplines (and beyond school walls) is both inspiring and exciting. *This* is what we strive to have students see and celebrate. They will only be able to do this, though, if we take the time to prioritize it. In this chapter, I propose ways for students to study, use, and apply their knowledge of words—and the way words work—in all subject areas.

Word Study in Math

As a child, I felt lost in math. My head would spin as I tried to replicate the processes the teacher modeled on the blackboard. Forget bullies, frenemies, or mindless homework: *word problems* were my greatest nemesis. I remember sitting at my second-grade desk (first row, second seat from the right), completely frozen in fear as we were asked to solve that week's four word problems. I ended up literally making myself sick to get out of doing word problems the next two weeks. Things didn't get any easier for the rest of elementary school. I was in eighth grade when a dedicated and engaging teacher cracked my math code and the lightbulb finally turned on. (Thank you, Mr. Zweig!) He not only brought a little playfulness to math, but he also increased my confidence. Mr. Zweig introduced me to the language of math. Ahhh . . . math as a language—filled with plot lines, characters, problems, solutions, and all sorts of decodable vocabulary. I was hooked.

For some students, though, what made everything suddenly clear to me is what makes math so tricky for them! Those who "see" numbers and compute naturally may feel intimidated by language. It is likely that many of us have students like these, students like me, and students everywhere in between in our math classes. I imagine we all have practices in place to nurture and nudge each of these types of mathematicians. Here are a few additional practices I have used with great success.

SHARED READING OF WORD PROBLEMS

In the past, I presented students with word problems and manipulatives and hoped they would figure out what to do. I anticipated the students would all use the math tools to help them visualize, make sense of the problem, and discover the learning themselves. A few students "got" it and not only got going, but stayed going. But others stalled out, and some even avoided starting, unsure of where to begin. I began to think about these noticings and more recently shifted my thinking. Because of this reflection, I now feel better prepared to anticipate the differentiated guidance students might need. I understand the need to be flexible in how and when I scaffold. There are times I know a discovery-based approach is more natural and needed. There are other times when I prioritize more explicit instruction in how to make sense of word problems.

I found using a modified version of shared reading helped my students understand the language of word problems and how to apply their literacy learning in math. This practice supported greater confidence. Students displayed increased readiness to tackle and discover what we came to call "partner perseverance problems."

We would read the same word problem (our "text") multiple times, each time with a different focus. It was different from traditional shared reading because it *often* took place in one 5- to 15-minute session.

- First, students and I might focus on a literal understanding of the scenario posed in the word problem.

But in subsequent reads, we might work on the following:

- Making sense of content-specific vocabulary

- Synthesizing the information in a provided chart/model/infographic

- Sorting needed and extraneous information

- Identifying the question asked (and any hidden questions we need to first answer), visualizing the problem and creating a model to "show" the situation, or even planning the steps we would take to solve the problem

Here are a few examples:

Sawyer was sending invitations for her birthday party. She planned to invite four friends from school and five friends from her soccer team. How many friends altogether was Sawyer inviting to her party?	Read 1: *Math & Literal Comprehension* Read and identify the people, situation, and problem.
	Read 2: *Math & Word Work* Read. Together, locate the high-frequency words. Highlight. Then, model rereading the problem fluently, reading the high-frequency words in a snap.
	Read 3: *Math & Word Work* Read and hunt for the number words in the problem. Make a picture/model to show each number. Read and find other "math" words (*altogether*) and decide on an operation.
	Read 4: *Math & Grammar & Fluency* Reread and search for the question mark. Chorally read the problem in a voice that reflects the punctuation. Discuss: *What is this question asking?* Have partnerships discuss and share different ways to solve this problem.
	Solve the problem. Together, list the steps used across fingers and share "how you know for sure."

Devon wanted and just got a puppy! He went to the pet store and purchased several items.

Refer to the chart to find the total number of items Devon purchased for his new dog.

Item	Number Purchased
Leash	One
Collar	One
Bowls	Two
Bags of food	One
Toys	Three
Bones	Six

Read I: *Math & Literal Comprehension*

Read and visualize the important information provided in the problem.

Read 2: *Math & Word Work*

Reread the problem. Find all past tense verbs. Sort words (add –*ed*, add –*d*, irregular/word is changed).

Find and discuss number and math clue words in the problem. Use word knowledge to explicitly state what the problem is asking.

Read 3: *Math & Reading a Text Feature*

Look at the chart and use think-aloud to model making sense of information included.

Read 4: *Math & Jotting Thinking*

Use think-aloud to model making a visual model to show the problem, write a number sentence, and share the steps used in solving the problem.

Invite partnerships to use their whiteboards to replicate your process OR think about and create their own model and number sentence to solve the problem. Select a few partnerships to share their work.

You are finally getting an allowance! You put $15 into your bank account in January, $30 into your bank account in February, and $60 into your bank account in March. If this pattern continues, how much money will you have saved by the end of the year?

Read I: *Math & Literal Comprehension & Fluency*

Read the problem fluently, paying attention to punctuation used throughout. Identify the key information/facts included in the problem.

Read 2: *Math & Word Work*

Reread and notice **ou** and **ow** words (pattern recently studied by one of the word study groups).

Reread and pull out number words and math clue words. Discuss number forms.

Read 3: *Math & Inferring*

Model thinking to figure out/infer hidden questions that need to be found and answered before answering the question *actually* asked in the problem. Make a plan for answering any hidden questions *plus* the question actually asked.

Read 4: *Math & Jotting Thinking*

Work in partnerships to create a visual model and number sentence to show and solve the given scenario.

Read 5: *Math & Sharing Thinking*

Take turns using number talks to share processes used to solve and check the problem. In number talk, use both math and word study words (i.e., **ou** and **ow** words, *pattern, total, sum, double*, etc.).

INTERACTIVE WRITING OF A MATH EXPLANATION

Today in math, it is not enough to compute. We also want students to then explain their strategies, thinking, process, connections, and learning. Interactive writing helps us scaffold this process for students. As previously mentioned, during an interactive writing session students dip in and help the teacher compose parts of a text. Here in math, the topic of the text being composed would be either our math thinking or processes. Because math writing is such a rich and comprehensive skill, I recommend first starting with less intimidating "oral" explanations of math thinking—which come in the form of number talks. Number talks, a thoughtful practice taught by Jo Boaler (2016) and others, offer great rehearsal for writing. Number talks provide a regular (weekly, if not daily) opportunity for students to share the different ways they solved a problem, often naturally infusing rich math vocabulary. They are a strong stand-alone practice but also offer an opportunity to seamlessly shift into writing about math.

When using interactive writing in math, I often start with a few number talks to hear the strategies employed by different classroom mathematicians. This provides the content of our reflective math writing. When we begin writing this content, I ask students to share the first step. I jot their ideas and ask them to "dip in" and share in the writing at specific and intentional moments. These moments may be to write "math words," aka Tier III content-specific vocabulary. I also ask them to jump in whenever we get to a word that provides an opportunity to apply and transfer our more general word study learning. By doing so, transfer is modeled, highlighted, emphasized, and practiced!

Stefanie's class prepares for interactive writing in math by showing the different strategies they used to solve a tricky problem. One of these methods will be explained in the piece composed together by the class.

Here, a third grader participates in the interactive writing of a math response. Not only is math vocabulary infused, but the students also work to include the patterns recently studied by some class members.

TEACHING AND PRACTICING CONTENT AREA VOCABULARY

Students need regular, playful, and low-stakes practice using content vocabulary. By providing these opportunities, content words make their way to long-term memory and become part of their larger vocabulary. Increased vocabulary has countless benefits for students. The practices used in word study naturally lend themselves to math! Here are a few of my favorite word study routines and how they can be used in math.

Routine	Used in Math By . . .	Looks Like . . .
Yep! Maybe . . . Huh?	A preassessment of content vocabulary for a new unit of study, topic, or chapter.	

Routine	Used in Math By . . .	Looks Like . . .
Backwards Scattergories	Students make connections between content-specific vocabulary words, based on meaning.	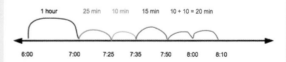
Word Hunts	Students hunt for content words and/or pattern words in their math reading (directions, word problems, etc.).	**WORD STUDY: Contractions** **MATH: Elapsed Time** **not is have will** **MODEL:** (FIRST- READ & HUNT) Pam should've been at Hamilton School at 8:00 AM. She woke up at 6:00 AM and exercised for one hour. Then, she took a shower and got dressed. This took 25 minutes. Pam then ate breakfast for 10 minutes and hung out with her kids for 15 minutes before leaving the house. It takes Pam 20 minutes to get to Hamilton School. Was she there on time? Explain how you know. 1 hour 25 min 10 min 15 min 10 + 10 = 20 min 6:00 7:00 7:25 7:35 7:50 8:00 8:10 THEN- WRITE & INCLUDE: No, Pam wasn't on time. She got to Hamilton School at 8:10 AM, which is 10 minutes late. She should've woken up 10 minutes earlier. I know this because I made an open number line and started at 6:00 AM. It took Pam one hour to exercise which brings her to 7:00 AM. Next, she took a shower and got dressed for 25 minutes, which brings the time to 7:25 AM. Pam finished eating 10 minutes later (7:35 AM) and then spent time with her kids for 15 minutes. This means she didn't leave her house until 7:50 AM. It takes 20 minutes to get to Hamilton school. Pam got to Hamilton School at 8:10, but she should've been there at 8:00 AM. There's the problem!

Routine	Used in Math By . . .	Looks Like . . .
Picture It	Students show their understanding of math vocabulary by visually representing words and their meanings.	
Word Webs and Riddles	Students use a combination of phonics, spelling, and meaning information to create webs or riddles about math words.	

Routine	Used in Math By . . .	Looks Like . . .
		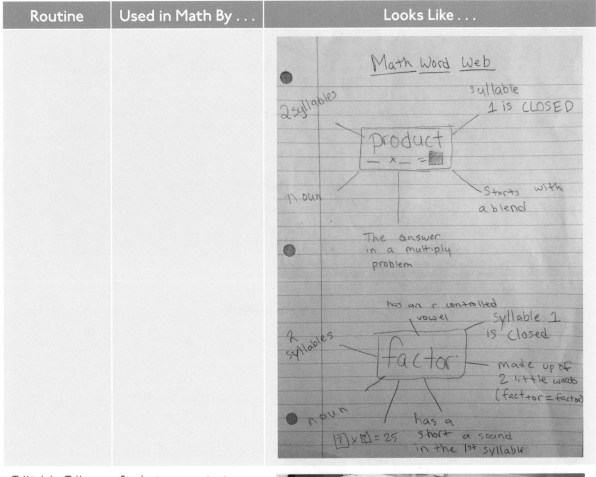
Talkin' the Talk	Students use content vocabulary when working with peers, when talking in math, and when writing in math.	

Word Study in Social Studies and Science

In most of our stem challenges, we build or construct something. I have learned the most important part of building something is usally the base it need to be strong and sturdy word study is like the base in a stem challenge. Being strong with words helps us construct our learning in all other areas.
—Zachary age 9

—Zachary, age 9

INTEGRATED SHARED READING

Teachers can twist and tweak the typical structure of shared reading described in this book by using a text tied to the topic being studied in the content areas. This text could be a page of an informational text, a webpage, a blog, an infographic, a primary document, a lab report, or anything else of the teacher's choosing. Here are some general guidelines:

Day 1	Focus: Comprehension of content included in the text
Day 2 and Day 3	Focus: Word work
	Focus of Day 2: Decode and talk about content area vocabulary
	Focus of Day 3: Notice, talk about, and extend thinking about pattern words found in the text
Day 4	Focus: Read the text (rich with content vocabulary and pattern words) fluently
Day 5	Focus: Extend and deepen thinking; talk or write using appropriate content vocabulary and pattern words

In this way, we are naturally integrating social studies or science with reading and word study. This helps us to use our instructional time with greater efficiency and helps foster thoughtful transfer of word learning.

INTEGRATED SHARED AND INTERACTIVE WRITING

Shared and interactive writing provide a wonderful opportunity to intentionally infuse writing and word study into the content areas. In shared writing, the class could work over a series of sessions to compose a piece of writing tied to content area learning. If the teacher is connecting informational writing and content area learning, the class might compose a piece of informational writing on a content area topic. If the teacher wants to connect opinion writing to content area learning, he or she may work to develop a theory and prove that using content-specific facts (and vocabulary). Perhaps the class can decide they have much in common with Lenape children and prove that using specific content area learning. They may also look at lab results and draw conclusions about if a substance was an acid or a base—and again, prove that theory using content learning. If the teacher is connecting the dots between narrative writing and the content areas, perhaps they may compose a historical fiction piece together or craft a "small-moment story" from the perspective of someone who witnessed something historically relevant. In interactive writing, the class could work to create a model lab report or work on paraphrasing and taking notes on information acquired while researching. The possibilities are endless! Again, in each of these experiences, teachers are using limited time and resources and maximizing their impact. Reading, writing, word study, and the content areas come together with such a specific purpose. Students learn how to carry over strategies learned in word study. Everyone is deepening and extending their knowledge of content vocabulary and studied patterns. It is an overall win for everyone!

A sixth grader combines word study patterns and science vocabulary as she works on an interactive writing piece with her classmates.

TEACHING AND PRACTICING CONTENT AREA VOCABULARY

Transferring routines typically used in word study for both social studies and science invite students to bring a similar level of curiosity, interest, and deep practice to studying words in the content areas. Inquiry-based practices are plentiful in the content areas—why not infuse the inquiry-based word learning practices previously mentioned in this book to complement the inquiry-based work happening in other parts of the day? Here are how a few favorite word study routines look in social studies (SS) and science.

Routine	Used in SS/Science By . . .	Looks Like . . .
Yep! Maybe . . . Huh?	Students share their schema, self-assessing their existing knowledge of content vocabulary for a new unit of study, topic, or chapter	 Photo by Linda Day
Talkin' the Talk	Students rotate to different stations to view short videos, examine photographs or primary documents, or read short poems, texts, or songs related to content area learning. They work to use content vocabulary and pattern words as they discuss their observations, wonders, thoughts, feelings, and reactions with classmates.	

Routine	Used in SS/Science By . . .	Looks Like . . .
Word Scavenger Hunts	Students hunt for content words and/or pattern words in their SS and science reading (directions, research, etc.).	
Picture It	Students show their understanding of content area vocabulary by visually representing words and their meanings.	

Routine	Used in SS/Science By . . .	Looks Like . . .
Word Webs and Riddles	Students use a combination of phonics, spelling, and meaning information to create webs or riddles about SS and science words.	

Science Word Webs (Lukas, 3-6)

I start with an ē sound.
I end with "Or"
I have 3 syllables.
I am a pretend line that circles Earth but you can see me on a globe.
I am imaginary.
— EQUATOR

Means ½ of the Earth.
3 syllables
Little words inside: He, is, Sphere, and Here.
It has 3 "e"s
In the middle, it has a PH that sounds like F.
— HEMISPHERE

Science Riddles

1. I have 5 syllables
2. I end with the /shen/ sound
3. I am the process of water turning into a gas. Who am I?
EVAPORATION!

1. I have 3 syllables
2. I have a first part that means "water"
3. My second part is a math 3-D figure with no edges or sides.
4. I mean all the water on, under, & above Earth. Who am I? Hydrosphere!
CAYLEIGH

Routine	Used in SS/Science By . . .	Looks Like . . .
Word Scavenger Hunts	Students hunt for both Tier III/content-specific words and patterns studied in word study in content area texts, thereby continuing to study and collect words in the content areas.	(handwritten chart)
Interactive Writing	The class writes about topics related to science and social studies learning, intentionally trying to appropriately include both content vocabulary and pattern words.	

More Options to Encourage Transfer of Word Learning

MATH

- In writing workshop, use class shared writing (with a math twist) to model the recursive writing process in an informational writing unit. As a class, plan, draft, enhance, and polish either "how-to" procedural writing or "all-about" informational writing about a math topic learned in class.

- Create more meaningful, "blurred content lines" assessments: One example of an integrated performance task is to ask students to create "how-to" procedural writing or "all-about" informational writing about a math topic learned in class. By doing so, this one piece would help us glean instructional information we could use in math, writing, and word study!

- Use an interactive bulletin board (on classroom walls or digitally): Students write math word problems for other classmates to solve. Word problems include correctly spelled and used word study pattern words and math content vocabulary.

SOCIAL STUDIES/SCIENCE

- In writing workshop, use class shared writing to model the recursive writing process in an informational writing unit. As a class, plan, draft, enhance, and polish "all-about" informational writing about a topic learned in SS or science.

- In writing workshop, engage in content area research writing. This can be done independently, in partnerships, or with small groups.

- Go on content and pattern word "hunts" in informational texts. Double challenge: Are any content words also pattern words? How many words can the class collect?

- Have students identify, discuss, compare, and contrast the Tier II and Tier III words they find while reading and researching in the content areas.

- Display content words and recently studied word study patterns prominently. Encourage students to regularly use these words in their content area discussions and writing: classwork, lab reports, research, "going public" shares from inquiry research, and so on.

What else might you add to this list?

Photo by Linda Day

WORKAROUNDS

CHALLENGE: *I don't teach math, social studies, or science. We are departmentalized, and I only teach literacy.*

POSSIBLE WORKAROUNDS

☐ Option I: You can integrate reading, writing, word study, and language/grammar as frequently as possible using the techniques suggested in Chapter 9.

☐ Option 2: Support your colleagues! Talk to the content area teachers on your team. Chances are, they are also scrambling, trying to make the most of each minute. Is there a way you could support one another? Could you "flip flop," integrating each other's subject learning into your own content learning? It may be even more important to forge this connection for students if the teachers and classrooms are different. We can work together to make transfer happen!

CHALLENGE: *The students in my room study different patterns with their word study groups. We don't have a "common pattern" that the whole class is studying. How do I decide which group's pattern words to highlight in the content areas?*

POSSIBLE WORKAROUNDS

☐ Option I: Highlight any pattern any student has studied, even if it is not shared by the whole class. This increases the exposure *all* students have with different patterns and words!

☐ Option 2: Rotate which group's patterns you will highlight while doing content area work. This way everyone gets some reinforcement of word learning—and as already mentioned, others will get exposure to additional words and patterns.

☐ Option 3: Choose patterns that you have noticed the class needs support with, even if no one has studied these patterns with you. This is a great place to introduce tricky words students are likely to encounter and to reinforce learning from previous years that may not yet be cemented in students' minds!

☐ Option 4: Do what's easiest and what seems most natural. Look at a text you already plan on using for math, social studies, or science and identify/teach whatever pattern you see is there and waiting to be studied—maybe it is one group's pattern, maybe it is an "easy" pattern students don't yet own, maybe it is something you feel is worthwhile to introduce, or maybe it is something else. All word learning is valuable word learning . . . and the transfer of word study techniques and word collecting strategies is always worthy of our time and effort!

PRACTICAL PRIORITIZING

☐ Create a list of the lingo (content area vocabulary) of upcoming units: math, social studies, science, and so on.

☐ Look through subject area materials for examples of letters, sounds, patterns, and parts studied in word study.

☐ Make a list of pattern words that connect with current content area topics. Keep this list handy and practice using these words as you talk and write across the day.

☐ Start considering ways to connect and integrate subject areas. Consider and list how you already study content area vocabulary. Ponder which of the suggested methods you will add to enrich content area word study.

A TOUR OF WORD STUDY IN ACTION

A Sneak Peek of Content Area Word Learning

On these two pages, catch the buzz and breeziness of word learning all day long! Here, you will get the opportunity to listen in and hear how skillful yet simple word exploring might go. As you wander around these pages, I encourage you to make connections between these sound bites and the lessons and ideas shared in the previous chapters.

INTERACTIVE WRITING IN MATH

"I enjoyed hearing about the different ways you all solved this perseverance problem today! I appreciate that you made an extra effort to use not only math words but also some of the pattern words we have been exploring in word study. Now we are going to choose one method and write down our math thinking. I am going to need your help. You will come up with the ideas. I will take responsibility for writing your thoughts on this chart. Here's the fun part: When we get to either a math word or a pattern word, I am going to have you all write that word on your slates. We will then take turns having some classroom mathematicians come up and write those special math and pattern words. So that we don't forget this is about math, writing, *and* word study, I put our math words in this pocket chart, and I also put in a large card to remind you of the patterns different groups are currently studying in word study. Let's get started! Our first job is to choose one person's number talk to write up."

SHARED READING IN READING

"Today, we are going to look back at the same two pages of our new favorite book. I am going to have you go on a hunt for a special word that is one of our recent pattern words. It starts with the same sound as *rrrrowdy*. It has a doubled consonant before adding the *-ing*. A word with a similar meaning is *jogging*. Can you find it? Whisper it to your partner. . . . Now, shout it out! Let's play around with this word. First, when might we run? Hmmm, it might be a time we needed to get somewhere fast. Or maybe while we were playing a specific sport? Hmmm . . . When might I run? Turn and talk. List different times you might be running. . . . I heard ___. Now, let's think of lots of words that, like *jogging*, have a similar meaning to *running*. Then, we will order them and see how many words we can include in our shades of meaning. I will start and you can all jump in and help in a moment."

A WORD INTRODUCTION IN SOCIAL STUDIES

"My, my, my social scientists! You already discovered that our new unit is all about geography and how where people live impacts their lives. We will be doing a lot of researching and discovering in this unit. There is a lot of lingo—or words that have to do with geography—that we will be learning about and using. In order to figure out how some of this word teaching and learning might go, I am going to introduce these words to you now—just like I introduce new words in word study. When I hold up the word, I want you to share one of our signals that tell how comfortable you are with this word. The first word is *equator*."

SHARED WRITING IN SCIENCE

"We watched some really interesting things happen with our magnets! We talked with our partners about what we observed, what we thought, and what we wondered. I feel excited and ready to do some jotting and thinking. Let's take a moment to really remember what we observed. Replay it in your minds. Pay attention to all the details you are seeing—they are what we will need to include in our sketch. Let me start. OK, I remember. I am seeing ___. Now, you try. Turn and talk with your partner. Give as many details as you can because this will help us plan out what we want to include in our sketch. I heard you say ___, so let me start sketching those parts. Now, we need to add some labels to this sketch. Let's think about our science words. Let's also think about words we could use to describe what we saw—because scientists work to be very precise when they jot. What parts of the sketch might we label, and what words would we use? . . . Scientists—we observed, remembered, sketched, and labeled. Tomorrow, we will be ready to use our sketch and labels to help us begin to write."

Instructional Routine	What It Is	Purpose	When It Happens	How We Incorporate Words
Shared Reading	Brief (5–15 minutes) series of lessons that takes place over 3–5 days. The short selected text is enlarged so all students can see and follow along as the teacher reads the text. Each session in the cycle has a different focus, and the teacher models before the students dip in and try.	We use shared reading to provide vision and support. Although shared reading can always be used, it is most frequently used when content is new or tricky. The teacher does most of the work; students are invited to take an in-the-moment, "low stakes" try with a partner.	Shared reading can happen in any part of the day! Often, it occurs at the end of a reading block, but it can happen in any subject, at the start of the day, or at the end of the day.	One or two of the sessions can be focused on studying, thinking about, or extending knowledge of letters, sounds, word parts, or whole words in the passage. Teachers might model these actions: • Decoding a word • Thinking about the meaning or connotation of a word • Finding and talking about a studied letter, sound, pattern, affix, or root, along with synonyms, antonyms, or "relatives" of a word • Connecting a word to different contexts • And much more!
Shared Writing	Brief (5–15 minutes) series of lessons that takes place over 3–5 days. Over the course of the cycle, the class helps the teacher compose a piece of writing. Each session in the cycle has a different focus and the teacher models before the students dip in and try.	We use shared writing to provide vision and support. Although shared writing can always be used, it is most frequently used when a genre of writing is new. While the teacher does most of the work, students are invited to contribute ideas so there is shared ownership of the composed piece.	Shared writing can happen in any part of the day! Often, it occurs during immersion (the start of a new unit) or at the end of a writing block, but it can happen in any subject, at the start of the day, or at the end of the day.	One or two of the sessions can be focused on remembering, thinking about, or applying knowledge of letters, sounds, word parts, or whole words while writing. Teachers might model these actions: • Encoding a word • Thinking about the most precise word that could be used • Talking about a studied letter, sound, pattern, affix, or root and intentionally finding a place to transfer this learning • Considering word choice to sound like an expert, create a mood, or paint a picture • And much more!

Instructional Routine	What It Is	Purpose	When It Happens	How We Incorporate Words
Interactive Writing	Brief (10–20 minutes) one-and-done lesson in which the teacher and students compose a piece of writing together, but students take a bit of a more active role than in shared writing. Here, the class helps the teacher compose the piece of writing by taking over some of the actual writing.	We use interactive writing to provide vision and support, as well as encourage students to use what they know about the language standards as they write. The teacher does most of the writing; students are invited to write certain letters, words, or conventions as the piece is being composed.	Interactive writing can happen in any part of the day! Often, it occurs during immersion (the start of a new unit) or at the end of a writing period, but it can happen in any subject, at the start of the day, or at the end of the day.	During the session, students are encouraged to generate and share ideas. They help with writing words that include sounds, letters, and word parts they have been exploring. For example, students could come up and write the following: • Words with the /sh/ sound • Any "long *a*" words • Any words in past tense • Any words with an open first syllable • Any Tier III content area vocabulary word
A Word Study Routine in the Content Areas	Use an already-learned word study routine in other subject areas to explore, talk about, and learn content area vocabulary.	Word study routines are already known, understood, and practiced, so students can transfer this expertise with minimal teaching and direction. This supports efficient use of instructional time, student ownership, and increased vocabulary competency.	Word study routines support the infusion of best practice instruction in all subject areas!	Often, teachers choose to use meaning routines (e.g., I Might Be . . . , Backward Scattergories, etc.), but any word study routine can be transferred to any subject area.

Conclusion: Word Power!

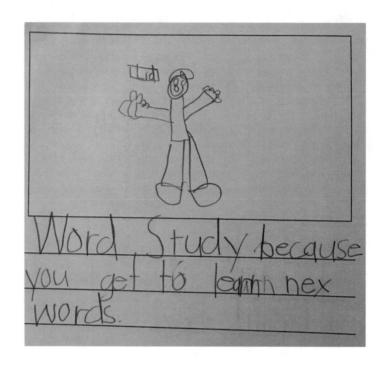

There's something quite ironic about my writing a book on word study. I often reverse the order of letters, position of letters, and at times, letters seem to jump around my page. As a child, I remember the time I spent rereading texts several times, recording and listening to myself reading, and then writing the words down as I listened to my recordings. I remember feeling disheartened looking at returned Scantrons and being able to clearly see the reading comprehension questions marked by a series of red underscores down the right side of the sheet. Much to my dismay, my study time far superseded that of my classmates and exponentially increased throughout my years of school. I think back to my childhood and wonder how no one noticed. But then, I remember that "back then" spelling was all about short-term memorization. We didn't do too much writing, and I had developed so many of my own compensating strategies that by the time I handed in final copies, my spelling did not appear problematic. There were fewer opportunities for teachers to notice these types of struggles, and there was not a great emphasis placed on addressing individual student needs.

I sincerely believe my own personal challenges and experience of one-size-fits-all, bland spelling instruction is what drove my interest in word study once I became a classroom teacher. I emulated my mentors, playing the parts of scientist and artist as I created multifaceted instructional plans that fit each student. I thought through instructional decisions and considered implications for different types of learners. I noticed when students soared and felt frustrated and tried my best to respond accordingly. I do not feel I was unique in any of these endeavors; however, I do feel that my own difficulties gave me greater insight into the processes students *were* using and *could be* using as they studied and learned words. My friend Patty McGee says that our struggles are our greatest gifts to our teaching. If this is true, and I would love to think it is, then my struggles were (and are) precious, as they have made me ready to better support each student I have the privilege to get to know!

Brené Brown writes that we need to be willing to give ourselves a break and "appreciate the beauty of our cracks or imperfections" (2016, p. 224). I am still often frustrated by the too-many red squiggles on my screen or when my written words don't immediately reflect those in my brain and heart. However, I would like to think my cracks and imperfections bring their own gift. They are reflected in the spirit, voice, and practices shared throughout this book. If a bit of this excitement about and interest in words could begin to ripple outward and reach hard-working, creative, and innovative educators near and far, I know together, we can make a difference in not only understanding specific words and patterns but also in better understanding each other. Together, we can push past mandates and move toward genuine curiosity and passion about the power and impact of words. We don't need to go it alone. As educators, our learning community transcends the walls of any building. Let's start collaborating and **start up** and **step up** "best practice" word study in *all* our classrooms, schools, and districts.

STAYING THE COURSE IS WORTH IT

Word collecting has never
been more meaningful or engaging!

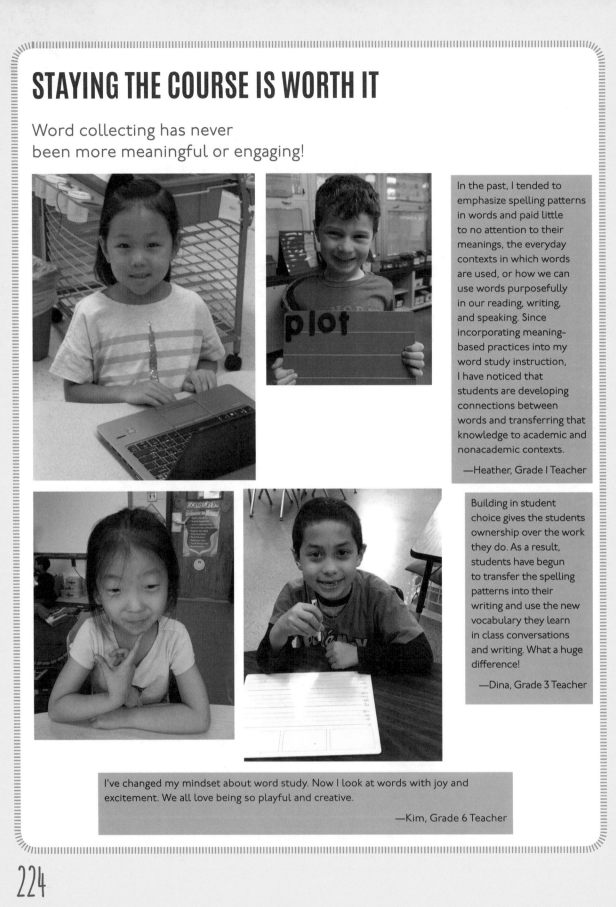

In the past, I tended to emphasize spelling patterns in words and paid little to no attention to their meanings, the everyday contexts in which words are used, or how we can use words purposefully in our reading, writing, and speaking. Since incorporating meaning-based practices into my word study instruction, I have noticed that students are developing connections between words and transferring that knowledge to academic and nonacademic contexts.

—Heather, Grade 1 Teacher

Building in student choice gives the students ownership over the work they do. As a result, students have begun to transfer the spelling patterns into their writing and use the new vocabulary they learn in class conversations and writing. What a huge difference!

—Dina, Grade 3 Teacher

I've changed my mindset about word study. Now I look at words with joy and excitement. We all love being so playful and creative.

—Kim, Grade 6 Teacher

I have noticed how excited students are when we do word study. It's fun to watch the engagement! I personally enjoy this approach, and after seeing the difference in motivation and learning, there is *no way* I would go back to my old ways.

—Sam, ENL Teacher

When my children are reading at home, they get excited and call out any pattern words, prefixes, or suffixes they find in their reading. This *never* happened before.

—Danielle, Caregiver

225

Appendix A

Go-To Resources

This book stands on the shoulders of the greats that have researched, synthesized, experimented, and shared for years! The following list includes the work of a few of the most knowledgeable and accomplished educators I rely on to learn about words. Their expertise, work, ideas, and writing have shaped my approach to word study.

Favorite Professional Texts*

- *Words Their Way: Word Study for Phonics, Vocabulary, and Spelling Instruction* (6th ed.) by Donald R. Bear, Marcia Invernizzi, Shane Templeton, and Francine Johnston

- *The Fountas & Pinnell Comprehensive Phonics, Spelling, and Word Study Guide* by Irene Fountas and Gay Su Pinnell

- *Word Matters* by Irene Fountas and Gay Su Pinnell

- *The Fountas & Pinnell Literacy Continuum, Expanded Edition: A Tool for Assessment, Planning, and Teaching PreK–8* by Irene Fountas and Gay Su Pinnel

- *You Kan Red This! Spelling and Punctuation for the Whole Language Classroom* by Sandra Wilde

- *Essential Strategies for Word Study* by Timothy Rasinski

- *Teaching Phonics & Word Study* by Wiley Blevins

- *A Fresh Look at Phonics* by Wiley Blevins

*Full citations can be found in the Reference section.

Spelling Programs This Book Augments

Word Study That Sticks can be used in conjunction with many of the phonics, spelling, and vocabulary resources already used in schools. If your school or district currently uses any of the following programs—or any others (whether homegrown or from an educational publisher)—I encourage you to spend some time with colleagues putting these chapters side by side with whatever program you are using to explore ways to use the routines in this book to deepen and extend student learning.

- *Words Their Way* (Pearson)

- *Fountas & Pinnell Phonics Lessons* (Heinemann)

- *Fundations* (Wilson Language Training)

- *Zaner-Bloser Spelling Connections* by Dr. Richard Gentry (Zaner-Bloser)

- *Everyday Spelling* (Pearson)

- *Houghton Mifflin Spelling and Vocabulary* (Houghton Mifflin Harcourt)

- *Scholastic Spelling* (Scholastic)

- *Sitton Spelling* (Egger)

- *Treasures Series Spelling* (Houghton Mifflin Harcourt)

- *Upcoming: TCRWP Phonics* (Heinemann)

Where to Find Words

If you find yourself wondering, searching, or asking, "What words will I use?" fret no more! Finding words is easy—there are endless options. It is the mindset we bring to studying words in general and what we *do* with the words we study that are the secrets to starting up or stepping up classroom word study.

- All of the previously listed programs offer word lists that can be purchased.

- There are *infinite* online resources! Type "spelling lists" into a Google Search and be amazed with the number of results.

- For *more* online resources, search "short-*a* CVC words," "words with *r*-controlled vowels," "words containing the prefix *re-*," and so on to compile your own customized lists for the students you are currently supporting.

- Use your head! Talk with colleagues, decide on instructional priorities, and brainstorm words together. Fill in as needed with any of the provided resources.

Here are some sample "scope and sequence" maps from the early grades through middle grades to give an idea of the kinds of patterns that might be studied. These maps were created based on knowledge of the developmental stages of spelling *and* displayed student readiness. Remember: classroom learning plans and priorities are created using a combination of formal and informal assessments. As such, yearly trajectories for word learning often differ classroom to classroom, year to year.

	Unit 1	Unit 2	Unit 3	Unit 4	Unit 5
Group A	Whole-class study (extended unit, 8–12 weeks)	Whole-class study:	CVC word families with /i/ and /o/	CVC word families with /e/ and /u/	Mixed short-vowel word families
Group B	High emphasis on phonemic awareness	Continued high emphasis on phonemic awareness and CVC (consonant-vowel-consonant) word families with /a/	Word families with /i/ and /o/	Word families with /e/ and /u/	Beginning and ending blends
Group C	Letter recognition		Word families with /i/ and /o/	Word families with /e/ and /u/	Exploration of simple short and long vowel sounds
	Letter–sound correspondence				

	Unit 1	Unit 2	Unit 3	Unit 4	Unit 5	Unit 6
Group A	Short-vowel CVC review (whole class)	Beginning and ending blends	Beginning and ending digraphs	Basic mixed short- and long-vowel sounds	Long-vowel patterns for *A*	Long-vowel patterns for *I* and *E*
Group B		Mixed digraphs and blends (Part 1)	Mixed digraphs and blends (Part 2)	Study of simple short and long vowel sounds and long-vowel patterns for *A*	Long-vowel patterns for *I* and *E*	Long-vowel patterns for *O* and *U*
Group C		Digraphs and blends (Part 2)	Study of simple short and long vowel sounds	Long-vowel patterns for *A* and *I*	Long-vowel patterns for *E, O,* and *U*	*R*-influenced vowel patterns

	Unit 1	Unit 2	Unit 3	Unit 4	Unit 5
Whole Class (New Routine Intro)	Whole-class patterns for launch:	Contractions	Compound words	Homophones	Homographs
Group A	Digraph and blend review	Long vowel patterns for *O* and *U*	Mixed long- and short-long-vowel patterns	*R*-controlled vowels	Diphthongs and other unusual vowel sounds
Group B	Basic long- and short-vowel review	Mixed long- and short-long-vowel patterns	*R*-controlled vowels	Diphthongs and other unusual vowel sounds	Inflectional endings for plural and past tense
Group C		Beginning and ending complex consonants and consonant clusters	Diphthongs and other unusual vowel sounds	Inflectional endings for plural and past tense	Open and closed syllables, basic juncture

	Unit 1	Unit 2	Unit 3	Unit 4	Unit 5
Group A	Options for whole-class patterns for launch unit:	Diphthongs and other unusual vowel sounds	Beginning and ending complex consonants and consonant clusters	Inflectional endings for plural and past tense	Open and closed syllables, basic juncture
Group B	Hard and soft *C* and *G* Homophones and homographs	Review of inflectional endings for plural and past tense	Vowel patterns in accented syllables	Vowel patterns in unaccented syllables	Prefixes
Group C	Words with silent consonants Unusual past-tense words	Review vowel patterns in accented and unaccented syllables	Prefixes	Suffixes	Roots

	Unit 1	Unit 2	Unit 3	Unit 4	Unit 5
Group A	Options for whole-class patterns for launch unit:	Vowel patterns in accented syllables	Vowel patterns in unaccented syllables	Prefixes	Suffixes
Group B	Review of words with silent consonants	Prefixes	Suffixes	Roots	Roots
Group C	Review of inflected endings for plural and past tense words Review of -le, -el, and -al Review of /shen/ sound patterns	Roots	Roots	Roots	Roots

Appendix B

Spelling Inventories

All teaching (in every subject area) comes down to three simple questions:

- What's in place?
- What's next?
- How can I help?

As educators, we look to the students in the classroom for direction in where to start and where to go. When it comes to determining children's word knowledge, we do a lot of it "informally" each day and across all subjects. We watch students, talk to students, and study student work. I cannot overemphasize the value of these daily observations in discovering what a learner has in place; it's this intel that you combine with formal assessments to make decisions. In word study, spelling inventories are one example of a more formal tool you can use to see what students already know and understand about the way words work. Taken together, *all* this data prepares us to provide responsive instruction.

Many teachers with whom I've worked say to me, "But isn't it the formal results that matter most?" A resounding *no*! We can only feel confident in our decisions and intentional about next steps in instruction when we are drawing from a deeper well of our day-to-day wisdom, too. It feels oh-so-good to know what we provide to students is based on what we see, know, and understand—not on what others who have never met our students or stepped foot in our classrooms feel *all* students at any one grade level should be ready for.

What follows is a list of some of the most commonly used spelling inventories using real words (not nonsense words). No matter what tool you decide to use, remember that results are a "snapshot" and part of an album of information we gather to fully understand all that our students know and are ready to learn.

Most Recommended Spelling Inventories

Pearson's *Words Their Way: Word Study for Phonics, Vocabulary, and Spelling* has three different inventories available—primary, elementary, and upper level.

Sylvia Greene's *Informal Word Analysis Inventory*

Richard Gentry's *Monster Test*

The Padlet resource *Phonics, PA, or Spelling Inventory Assessment Review*, created by mstruck01, lists some pluses and downsides of several different inventories.

References

Bear, D. R., Invernizzi, M. R., Templeton, S. R., & Johnston, F. (2012). *Words their way: Word study for phonics, vocabulary, and spelling instruction* (5th ed.). Boston, MA: Pearson.

Gentry, R. (2007). *Assessing early literacy with Richard Gentry: Five phases, one simple test.* Portsmouth, NH: Heinemann.

Greene, S. (2016). *Sylvia Greene's informal word analysis.* Retrieved from http://lincs.ed.gov/readingprofiles/MC_Word_Analysis.htm.

mstruck01. (2017). *Phonics, PA, or spelling inventory assessment review* [Padlet]. Retrieved from https://padlet.com/mstruck01/dqh3aacsn6my

Appendix C

Word-Rich Books Across the Grades

There are so many incredible books that help us all appreciate the beauty, power, and joy of words! We can always notice, pause, and discuss the words in a book. We may ponder the feelings and impact of the words the author has chosen to include. It is crucial to share texts across all subject areas, including word study.

- *WORDLESS BOOKS:* I love using wordless books across all grades. These accessible texts help students infer the words and create their own stories.

- *SILLY BOOKS*: Seek out some just-for-fun-books that are playful with the words they use and/or the "look" and format of the words on the page. Noticing, talking about, and discussing words are all meant to be fun! Laugh out loud together.

- *BEAUTIFUL BOOKS:* There are books we read that make us wonder how any person could possess such an incredible gift! These books beg us to stop and notice how words are strung together and crafted to elicit such impactful images and feelings.

- *POWERFUL BOOKS:* I am eternally grateful for the books that make us feel inspired and want to act! The words in these books have *power* over us—they help us to feel something . . . say something . . . do something. They remind us of the power we possess by spending time growing our word knowledge and sharing our thoughts and intentions with the world.

- *POEMS*: Any poem . . . every poem. I would take great pleasure in building an entire word study curriculum around poetry. It is so very possible! But until then, regularly sharing and enjoying poetry together will lift the level of all we do in word study each day.

To kick off text-rich word study and inspire you to collect more word-themed titles, here are some favorite books that teachers (including me) have woven into their word study block:

ALPHABET BOOKS

- *Carmine: A Little More Red* by Melissa Sweet
- *ABC NYC* by Joanne Dugan
- *A Is for Africa* by Ifeoma Onyefulu

- *Hip-Hop Alphabet* by Howie Abrams

- *Ah-Ha to Zig-Zag: 31 Objects From Cooper Hewitt, Smithsonian Design Museum* by Maira Kalman

- *Z Is for Moose* by Kelly Bingham

- *An Artist's Alphabet* by Norman Messenger

- *Rad American Women A–Z: Rebels, Trailblazers, and Visionaries Who Shaped Our History . . . and Our Future* by Kate Schatz (for older audiences)

WORDLESS

- *The Red Book* by Barbara Lehman

- *Lion and the Mouse* by Jerry Pinkney

- *Zoom* by Istvan Banyai

- *Unspoken: A Story From the Underground Railroad* by Henry Cole

- *Anno's Journey* by Mitsumasa Anno

- *Journey Trilogy* by Aaron Becker

- *The Arrival* by Shaun Tan

- *Wave* by Suzy Lee

SILLY AND PLAYFUL WORD BOOKS

- *The Book With No Pictures* by B. J. Novak

- *The Pencil* by Allan Ahlberg

- *Previously* by Allan Ahlberg

- *Guess Again* by Mac Barnett

- *Rhyming Dust Bunnies* and *Here Comes the Big, Mean Dust Bunny* by Jan Thomas

WORD-FOCUSED PICTURE BOOKS

- *Word Collector* by Peter Reynolds

- *The Word Collector* by Sonja Wimmer

- *13 Words* by Lemony Snicket

- *Thesaurus Rex* by Laya Steinberg

- *Little Red Writing* by Joan Holub

- *A Squiggly Story* by Andrew Larsen

- *The Alphabet Tree* by Leo Lionni

- *Fancy Nancy* by Jane O'Connor

- *Max's Words* by Kate Banks

- *The Boy Who Loved Words* by Roni Schotter

- *Thank You, Mr. Falker* by Patricia Polacco

- *Big Words for Little People* by Jamie Lee Curtis

- *One Word From Sophia* by Jim Averbeck

BOOKS WITH A "LANGUAGE" THEME

- *If I Were a Prefix* by Marcie Aboff

- *Eats, Shoots & Leaves: The Zero Tolerance Approach to Punctuation* by Lynne Truss

- *Exclamation Mark* by Amy Krouse Rosenthal and Tom Lichtenheld

- *Yo! Yes?* by Chris Raschka

CHAPTER BOOKS WITH A WORD FOCUS

- *Frindle* by Andrew Clements

- *Donovan's Word Jar* by Monalisa DeGross

- *Charlotte's Web* by E. B. White

- *The Stories Julian Tells* by Ann Cameron

- *Wishtree* by Katherine Applegate

- *Brown Girl Dreaming* by Jacqueline Woodson

- *Words of Stone* by Kevin Henkes

BIOGRAPHIES OF "WORD PEOPLE"

- *Noah Webster and His Words* by Jeri Ferris
- *The Right Word: Roget and His Thesaurus* by Jennifer Bryant
- *Some Writer! The Story of E. B. White* by Melissa Sweet
- *Martin & Mahalia: His Words, Her Song* by Andrea Davis Pinkney
- *A River of Words: The Story of William Carlos Williams* by Jen Bryant

POETRY

- *Out of Wonder: Poems Celebrating Poets* by Kwame Alexander and Chris Colerley
- *Read! Read! Read!* by Amy Ludwig Vanderwater
- *This Is Just to Say: Poems of Apology and Forgiveness* by Joyce Sidman
- *One Last Word: Wisdom From the Harlem Renaissance* by Nikki Grimes
- *The Land of Words: New and Selected Poems* by Eloise Greenfield
- *Old Elm Speaks: Tree Poems* by Kristine O'Connell George
- *Hip-Hop Speaks to Children: A Celebration of Poetry With a Beat* by Nikki Giovanni
- *Runny Babbit* by Shel Silverstein

WORDS HELP US ACT!

- *Cloudette* by Tom Lichtenheld
- *Come With Me* by Holly M. McGhee
- *Pass It On* by Sophy Henn
- *Be Kind* by Pat Zietlow Miller
- *Shaking Things Up: 14 Young Women Who Changed the World* by Susan Hood
- *Free as a Bird* by Lina Maslo
- *Malala's Magic Pencil* by Malala Yousafzai

Appendix D

Quotes About Words

In Chapter 3, I shared a lesson and recommended using thought-provoking quotes about words to kick off word study. However, sharing, discussing, and debating quotes about words can be done at any point in the year. This is a wonderful way to infuse an extra spark of excitement into word exploring.

- "Raise your words, not your voice. It is rain that grows flowers, not thunder." —Rumi
- "One kind word can change someone's entire day." —Unknown
- "Handle them carefully, for words have more power than atom bombs." —Pearl Strachan Hurd
- "Words have energy and power with the ability to help, to heal, to hinder, to hurt, to harm, to humiliate, and to humble." —Yehuda Berg
- "All I need is a sheet of paper and something to write with, and then I can turn the world upside down." —Friedrich Nietzsche
- "Don't ever diminish the power of words. Words move hearts and hearts move limbs." —Hamza Yusuf
- "Good words are worth much and cost little." —George Herbert
- "Your words have power. Speak words that are kind, loving, positive, uplifting, encouraging, and life-giving." —Unknown
- "No matter what anybody tells you, words and ideas can change the world." —John Keating
- "The best word shakers were the ones who understood the true power of words. They were the ones who could climb the highest." —Markus Zusak
- "Words have the power to both destroy and heal. When words are both true and kind, they can change our world." —Buddha
- "I know nothing in the world that has as much power as a word. Sometimes I write one, and I look at it, until it begins to shine." —Emily Dickinson

Quotes About Words
From Children and Adolescent Books

- "What's good is that there are many ways to get a point across, which I guess is why language is important. Maybe it's why language was even invented." —*Short* by Holly Goldberg Sloan, p. 134

- "So many things have gone out of date. But after all these years, words are still important. Words are still needed by everyone. Words are used to think with, to write with, to dream with, to hope and pray with." —*Frindle* by Andrew Clements, p. 100

- "Selig loved everything about words—the sound of them in his ears (tintinnabulating!), the taste of them on his tongue (tantalizing!), the thought of them when they percolated in his brain (stirring!), and, most especially, the feel of them when they moved his heart (Mama!)." —*The Boy Who Loved Words* by Roni Schotter

- "Different languages, different food, different customs. That's our neighborhood: wild and tangled and colorful. Like the best kind of garden." —*Wishtree* by Katherine Applegate, p. 54

- "Don't gobblefunk around with words." —*The BFG* by Roald Dahl, p. 28

- "So Matilda's strong young mind continued to grow, nurtured by the voices of all those authors who had sent their books out into the world like ships on the sea. These books gave Matilda a hopeful and comforting message: You are not alone." —*Matilda* by Roald Dahl/screenplay produced and directed by Danny DeVito

I feel like Jacqueline Woodson's *Brown Girl Dreaming* (2016) is, among other things, a love letter to words. A few of my favorite chapters are

- composition notebook
- on paper
- gifted
- writing # 1
- late autumn
- writing # 2
- reading
- the selfish giant
- too good
- how to listen # 10
- a writer

References

Applegate, K. (2017). *Wishtree*. New York, NY: Feiwel & Friends.

Clements, A. (1988). *Frindle*. New York, NY: Aladdin Paperbacks.

Dahl, R. (1988). *Matilda*. New York, NY: Viking Kestrel.

Dahl, R. (2007). *The BFG*. New York, NY: Puffin Books.

DeVito, D. (Producer/Director). (1996). *Matilda* [Motion picture]. USA: Sony Pictures.

Schotter, R. (2006). *The boy who loved words*. New York, NY: Schwartz & Wade.

Sloan, H. G. (2018). *Short*. New York, NY: Puffin Books.

Woodson, J. (2016). *Brown Girl Dreaming*. New York, NY: Puffin Books.

Appendix E

Expanded Sample Word Study Schedules

Sample Five-Day Cycles

PRIMARY

	Day 1	Day 2	Day 3	Day 4	Day 5
Routine	Meaning intro Color, cut	Meaning practice center	Pattern intro Pattern practice	Pattern practice: Fluency center	Phonemic awareness and phonics center

Consider different options for your word study cycle. Here, notice . . .

- High-frequency work is done at a separate time of the day.

- For your centers, create the most meaningful, playful, and developmentally appropriate options. Try to avoid busy work and assignments. No product or proof necessary. Center routines encourage deep thinking and transfer whenever possible.

- This model uses informal assessment—observation checklists and records.

ELEMENTARY

	Day 1	Day 2	Day 3	Day 4	Day 5
Routine	Meaning intro Color, cut	Meaning practice	Pattern intro Pattern practice	Pattern practice with emphasis on fluency	Extra phonemic awareness and phonics routine

Consider different options for your word study cycle. Here, notice . . .

- High-frequency work is done at a separate time of the day.

- For practice, do the routines most meaningful, playful, and developmentally appropriate for your grade level.

- This model uses unit assessments, not cycle assessments.

UPPER ELEMENTARY AND MIDDLE GRADES

	Day 1	Day 2	Day 3	Day 4	Day 5
Routine	Meaning intro Color, cut	Meaning practice	Pattern intro Pattern practice	Pattern practice with emphasis on fluency	Transfer routine

Consider different options for your word study cycle. Here, notice . . .

- For practice, use the routines most meaningful, playful, and developmentally appropriate for your grade level.

- A transfer routine is embedded practice in reading, writing, math, social studies, or science to encourage transfer of word learning to other subject areas.

- This model uses unit assessments, not cycle assessments.

Sample Six-Day Cycles

PRIMARY

	Day 1	Day 2	Day 3	Day 4	Day 5	Day 6
Routine	Meaning intro Color, cut	Meaning practice center	Pattern intro Pattern practice	Pattern practice center	Pattern practice: Fluency center	Phonemic awareness and phonics center

Consider different options for your word study cycle. Here, notice . . .

- High-frequency work is done at a separate time of the day.
- For centers, create the most meaningful, playful, and developmentally appropriate center options. Try to avoid busy work and assignments. No product or proof is necessary. Center routines encourage deep thinking and transfer whenever possible.
- This model uses informal assessment and observation checklists and records.

ELEMENTARY

	Day 1	Day 2	Day 3	Day 4	Day 5	Day 6
Routine	Meaning intro Color, cut	Meaning practice	Pattern intro Pattern practice	Pattern practice	Pattern practice with emphasis on fluency	Extra phonemic awareness and phonics routine

Consider different options for your word study cycle. Here, notice . . .

- High-frequency work is done at a separate time of the day.

- For practice, do the routines most meaningful, playful, and developmentally appropriate for your grade level.

- This model uses unit assessments, not cycle assessments.

UPPER ELEMENTARY AND MIDDLE GRADES

	Day 1	Day 2	Day 3	Day 4	Day 5	Day 6
Routine	Meaning intro Color, cut	Meaning practice	Pattern intro Pattern practice	Pattern practice with emphasis on fluency	Transfer work	Assessment and/or reflection

Consider different options for your word study cycle. Here, notice . . .

- For practice, do the routines most meaningful, playful, and developmentally appropriate for your grade level.

- This model uses cycle-based assessment and check-in routines.

Sample Seven-Day Cycles

PRIMARY

	Day 1	Day 2	Day 3	Day 4	Day 5	Day 6	Day 7
Routine	High-frequency word work center	Meaning intro Color, cut	Meaning practice center	Pattern intro Pattern practice	Pattern practice center	Phonemic awareness and phonics center	Informal assessment and/or center reflection

Consider different options for your word study cycle. Here, notice . . .

- High-frequency work is done as part of the cycle.

- For centers, create the most meaningful, playful, and developmentally appropriate center options. Try to avoid busy work and assignments. No product or proof is necessary. Center routines encourage deep thinking and transfer whenever possible.

ELEMENTARY

	Day 1	Day 2	Day 3	Day 4	Day 5	Day 6	Day 7
Routine	Phonemic awareness and phonics routine	Meaning intro Color, cut	Meaning practice	Pattern intro Pattern practice	Pattern practice	Assess and/or reflect	Extra phonemic awareness and phonics routine

Consider different options for your word study cycle. Here, notice . . .

- High-frequency work is done at a separate time of the day.

- For practice, do the routines most meaningful, playful, and developmentally appropriate for your grade level.

- This model uses cycle assessments.

UPPER ELEMENTARY AND MIDDLE GRADES

	Day 1	Day 2	Day 3	Day 4	Day 5	Day 6	Day 7
Routine	Meaning intro Color, cut	Meaning practice	Pattern intro Pattern practice	Pattern practice with emphasis on fluency	Additional meaning, spelling, or hybrid practice	Transfer work	Assess and/or reflect

Consider different options for your word study cycle. Here, notice . . .

- For practice, do the routines most meaningful, playful, and developmentally appropriate for your grade level.

- This model uses cycle assessments.

Sample Cycles With Sample Routines for All Levels

	Day 1	Day 2	Day 3	Day 4	Day 5
Routine	Meaning intro Color, cut	Meaning practice	Pattern intro Pattern practice	Pattern practice with emphasis on fluency	Assessment and/or reflection
Suggested practice routine options/choices	Intro: Yep! Maybe . . . Huh? Intro: None to Some Extension: Begin Backwards Scattergories	Backwards Scattergories Shades of Meaning Synonym/Antonym Go Fish Word Trees Picture It	Guess the Pattern Nice to Meet You Word Scavenger Hunts Word Webs and Riddles	How Fast Can You Go? Look, Say, Cover, Write, Check Read It–Build It–Write it Multisensory Fun and Games	Next-Level Sorting Challenge Explanation of Learning: Show Off (Part I) Interactive Writing: Use It or Lose It Find & Fix Up

Managing the Groups

The following is a schedule of how three different groups of students spend their time in one particular cycle in an elementary classroom.

	Day 1	Day 2	Day 3	Day 4	Day 5
Red	Small-group meeting: Meaning intro	Independent meaning work	Small-group meeting: Pattern intro	Independent pattern work	Occasional small-group meeting: Assessment/reflection
Blue	Occasional small-group meeting: Assessment/reflection	Small-group meeting: Meaning intro	Independent meaning work	Small-group meeting: Pattern intro	Independent pattern work
Green	Independent pattern work	Occasional small-group meeting: Assessment/reflection	Small-group meeting: Meaning intro	Independent meaning work	Small-group meeting: Pattern intro

Now, here is a sample schedule of how the *teacher* spends his or her time in that same cycle.

	Day 1	Day 2	Day 3	Day 4	Day 5
Red	Small-group meeting: Meaning intro	1:1 or table conferring conversations	Small-group meeting: Pattern intro	Work on own, without teacher	Quick small-group meeting: Assessment/ reflection (occasional)
Blue	Quick small-group meeting: Assessment/ reflection (occasional)	Small-group meeting: Meaning intro	Work on own, without teacher	Small-group meeting: Pattern intro	1:1 or small-group conferring conversations
Green	Work on own, without teacher	Quick small-group meeting: Assessment/ reflection (occasional)	Small-group meeting: Meaning intro	1:1 or table conferring conversations	Small-group meeting: Pattern intro

Appendix F

Sample Checklists

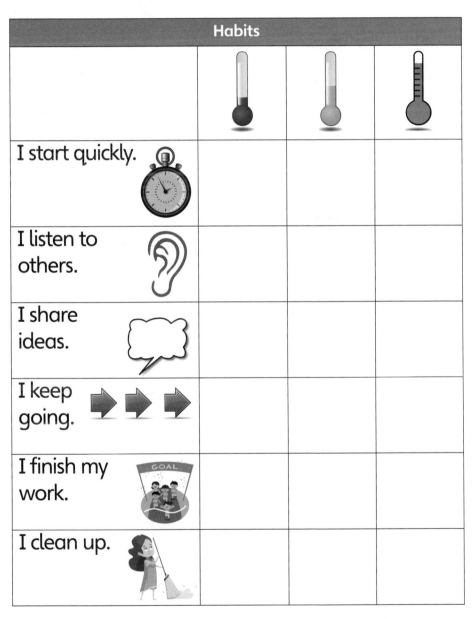

Habits			
I start quickly.			
I listen to others.			
I share ideas.			
I keep going.			
I finish my work.			
I clean up.			

Concepts			
I look at letters *and* listen for sounds.			
I use new words when I talk.			
I find and read new words.			
I use new words when I write.			
I reread, check, and fix up words.			
I use what I know all the time.			

Blue and orange thermometers: Art by gnokii; Red thermometer: Art by bartovan; Magnifying glass: Art by dacr; Boy and girl with speech bubbles: Art by GDJ; Boy with book: Art by oksmith; Student writing: Art by pietluk; Edit find replace: Art by warszawianka; Brain activity: Art by benoitpetit

Word Study Checklist: Primary

Habits			
	Sometimes	Usually	Consistently
I get materials quickly and quietly.			
I use a quiet voice.			
I listen to others.			
I share ideas.			
I keep going.			
I finish.			
I put away materials neatly.			

Concepts			
	Sometimes	Usually	Consistently
I use the word wall and other tools.			
I look at letters *and* listen for sounds.			
I practice talking with new words.			
I practice reading new words.			
I practice using new words when I write.			
I go back, look for, and fix up words.			
I use what I know all the time.			

Word Study Checklist: Upper Elementary

Work Habits			
	Sometimes	Usually	Consistently
I take out my materials and begin working quickly and quietly.			
I use an appropriate voice when speaking with others.			
I keep my notebook organized by dating each page, labeling the routine, writing neatly, and using pages in order.			
I work independently with focus and attention in order to complete chosen routines.			
I put away all personal and classroom materials neatly.			

Concepts			
	Sometimes	Usually	Consistently
When necessary, I use the word wall, my notebook, group members, and other resources to help me complete work.			
I use my knowledge of patterns and words in word study and outside of word study.			
I clearly explain my ideas to classmates.			
I go back, look for, and correct misspelled words.			
I review previously learned patterns to make sure I remember important learning.			

Word Study: Reflection and Self-Assessment Tool

Students use checklists to set goals and reflect on recent practice. The following reflection and self-assessment tool can be used in conjunction with checklists. This tool intends to invite students to take a greater role in their own assessment. On occasion, students can use the following *1–4* scale to evaluate their recent performance in each of the following areas:

- Work habits
- Correct spelling of words
- Correct use of words

After students use the *1–4* scale to quantify their reflections, they elaborate and explain these ratings using the provided prompts. The teacher then reviews these student thoughts before providing additional written feedback. Most ideally, the teacher then engages in a brief conversation with classroom learners to discuss the noted ratings and reflections.

Word Study That Sticks

1	2	3	4

• Developing
 	
• Starting
	• Getting there
	
	• Sometimes
		• Got it!
		
		• Doing it all
		  the time
			• Supporting
			  others, too
			
			• Consistently doing
			  more than asked

	Student	Teacher
Work habits		
Words spelled correctly		
Words used correctly		

I did really well with . . .

Today, I will spend a little time improving . . .

Teacher comments:

References

Achor, S. (2011). *The happiness advantage*. Cambridge, MA: Enterprise Media.

Allen, D. (2001). *Getting things done: The art of stress-free productivity*. New York, NY: Viking.

Allington, R. L., & Johnston, P. (2002). *Reading to learn: Lessons from exemplary 4th grade classrooms*. New York, NY: Guilford.

Anderson, C. (2000). *How's it going? A practical guide to conferring with student writers*. Portsmouth, NH: Heinemann.

Anderson, M. (2016). *Learning to choose, choosing to learn*. Alexandria, VA: ASCD. Retrieved from http://www.ascd.org/publications/books/116015/chapters/The-Key-Benefits-of-Choice.aspx

Annie. E. Casey Foundation. (2014). *Early reading proficiency in the United States*. Retrieved from http://www.aecf.org/resources/early-reading-proficiency-in-the-united-states/.

Applegate, K. (2017). *Wishtree*. New York, NY: Feiwel & Friends.

Baumann, J. K., & Kame'enui, E. J. (Eds.). (2004). *Vocabulary instruction: Research to practice*. New York, NY: The Guilford Press.

Bear, D. R., Invernizzi, M., Templeton, S., & Johnston, F. (2004). *Words their way: Word study for phonics, vocabulary, and spelling instruction*. Upper Saddle River, NJ: Pearson/Merrill/Prentice Hall.

Bear, D. R., Invernizzi, M. R., Templeton, S. R., & Johnston, F. (2012). *Words their way: Word study for phonics, vocabulary, and spelling instruction* (5th ed.). Boston, MA: Pearson.

Bear, D. R., Invernizzi, M., Templeton, S., & Johnston, F. (2016). *Words their way: Word study for phonics, vocabulary, and spelling instruction* (6th ed.). London, United Kingdom: Pearson.

Beaty, A. (2013). *Rosie Revere engineer*. New York, NY: Abrams Books.

Beck, I., McKeown, M. G., & Kucan, L. (2013). *Bringing words to life*. New York, NY: The Guilford Press.

Bell, B., & Cowie, B. (1999). A model of formative assessment in science education: Principles, policy, & practice. *Assessment in Education: Principles, Policy, & Practice, 6*(1), 101–116.

Blachowicz, C. L. Z., Fisher, P. J. L., Ogle, D., & Watts-Taffe, S. (2006). *Vocabulary: Questions from the classroom*. Newark, DE: International Reading Association.

Black, P., & Wiliam, D. (1998). Inside the black box: Raising standards through classroom assessment. *Phi Delta Kappan, 80*(2), 139–148.

Blevins, W. (2001). *Teaching phonics & word study*. New York, NY: Scholastic.

Blevins, W. (2016). *A fresh look at phonics: Common causes of failure and 7 ingredients for success*. Thousand Oaks, CA: Corwin.

Boaler, J. (2016). *Mathematical mindsets: Unleashing students' potential through creative math, inspiring messages, and innovative teaching*. San Francisco, CA: Jossey-Bass.

Bomer, K. (2010). *Hidden gems: Naming and teaching from the brilliance in every student's writing*. Portsmouth, NH: Heinemann.

Brown, B. (2016). *Daring greatly: How the courage to be vulnerable transforms the way we live, love, parent, and lead*. London, United Kingdom: Penguin Books Ltd.

Catlin, K., Lewan, G., & Perignon, B. (1999). *Increasing student engagement through goal-setting, cooperative learning and student choice*. (Doctoral dissertation). Retrieved from ERIC (ED433100).

Chall, J. S. (1983). *Stages of' reading development*. New York, NY: McGraw B. Hill.

Chomsky, C. (1971). Write first read later. *Childhood Education, 47*, 296–299.

Clements, A. (1988). *Frindle*. New York, NY: Aladdin Paperbacks.

Cornwall, G. (2017). *Jabari jumps*. Somerville, MA: Candlewick Press.

Cowie, B., & Bell, B. (1999). A model of formative assessment in science education. *Assessment in Education: Principles, Policy & Practice, 6*(1), 102–116.

Dahl, R. (1988). *Matilda*. New York, NY: Viking Kestrel.

Dahl, R. (2007). *The BFG*. New York, NY: Puffin Books.

Daniels, H. (2017). *The curious classroom: 10 structures for teaching with student-directed inquiry*. Portsmouth, NH: Heinemann.

Dell'Antonia, K. J. (2012, March 19). The link between reading level and dropout rates. [Blogpost]. Retrieved from https://parenting.blogs.nytimes.com/2012/03/19/the-link-between-reading-level-and-dropout-rates/?_r=0

DeVito, D. (Producer/Director). (1996). *Matilda* [Motion picture]. USA: Sony Pictures.

Dewett, T. (2007). Linking intrinsic motivation, risk taking, and employee creativity in an R & D environment. *R&D Management, 37*(1),197–2008.

Dewey, J. (1933). *How we think: A restatement of the relation of reflective thinking to the educative process*. Boston, MA: D.C. Heath & Co.

Dinnerstein, R. (2016). *Choice time: How to deepen learning through inquiry and play, preK–2*. Portsmouth, NH: Heinemann.

Di Stefano, G., Gino, F., & Staats, B. (2014, April 14). *Learning by thinking: How reflection improves performance*. Retrieved from https://hbswk.hbs.edu/item/learning-by-thinking-how-reflection-improves-performance

Duckworth, S. (2015, July 15). New #sketchnote: The iceberg illustration, inspired by Matthew. Retrieved November 4, 2017 from https://plus.google.com/SylviaDuckworth/posts/Vw5ZFs1Cb

Dweck, C. (2006). *Mindset: The new psychology of success*. New York, NY: Random House.

Dweck, C. S. (2012). *Mindset*. London, United Kingdom: Robinson.

Fisher, D., Frey, N., & Hattie, J. (2016). *Visible learning for literacy, grades K–12: Implementing the practices that work best to accelerate student learning*. Thousand Oaks, CA: Corwin.

Fleming, V., Langley, N., Ryerson, F., Woolf, E. A., Rosson, H., LeRoy, M., Garland, J., . . . Warner Bros. Family Entertainment. (1939). *The wizard of Oz* [Motion picture]. Place of publication not identified: Turner Entertainment.

Fletcher, R. (2017). *The writing teacher's companion: Embracing choice, voice, purpose and play*. New York, NY: Scholastic.

Fountas, I., & Pinnell, G. S. (2002). *Word matters: Teaching phonics and spelling in the reading writing classroom*. Portsmouth, NH: Heinemann.

Fountas, I., & Pinnell, G. S. (2016). *The Fountas & Pinnell literacy continuum, expanded edition*. Portsmouth, NH: Heinemann.

Fucile, T. (2009). *Let's do nothing!* Somerville, MA: Candlewick Press.

Fullan, M. (2001). *Leading in a culture of change*. San Francisco, CA: Jossey-Bass.

Funny Commercials. (2017, June 28). *Gatorade commercial 2017 the secret to victory*. Retrieved from https://www.youtube.com/watch?v=LgnB7NdBMDU

Gentry, J. R. (1982). An analysis of developmental spelling in GNYS AT WRK. *The Reading Teacher, 36*, 192–200.

Gentry, R. (2007). *Assessing early literacy with Richard Gentry: Five phases, one simple test*. Portsmouth, NH: Heinemann.

Gilbert, E. (2016). *Big magic: Creative living beyond fear*. New York, NY: Riverhead Books.

Gillet, J. W., & Kita, M. J. (1979). Words, kids, and categories. *The Reading Teacher, 32,* 538–542.

Goldberg, G. (2015, October 13). Taking on new teaching roles: The 4 *Ms* [Blog post]. Retrieved from http://corwin-connect.com/2015/10/taking-on-new-teacher-roles-the-4-ms/

Goldberg, G. (2016). *Mindsets & moves: Strategies that help readers take charge, grades 1–8.* Thousand Oaks, CA: Corwin.

Goldberg, G., & Houser, R. (2017). *What do I teach readers tomorrow? Nonfiction.* Thousand Oaks, CA: Corwin.

Graves, M. F. (2016). *The vocabulary book: Learning and instruction (language and literacy).* New York, NY: Teacher College Press.

Graves, M. F., Schneider, S., & Ringstaff, C. (2018). Empowering students with word-learning strategies: Teach a child to fish. *The Reading Teacher, 71*(5), 533–541.

Greene, S. (2016). *Sylvia Greene's informal word analysis.* Retrieved from http://lincs.ed.gov/readingprofiles/MC_Word_Analysis.htm.

Hirsh, L. (2013, January 31). Anne Burrell talks wedding plans and "chef wanted." Retrieved from http://www.etonline.com/news/129936_Anne_Burrell_Talks_Wedding_Plans_and_Chef_Wanted

Honig, B. (1996). *Teaching our children to read: The role of skills in a comprehensive reading program.* Thousand Oaks, CA: Corwin.

Isaacs, W. (1999). *Dialogue: The art of thinking together.* New York, NY: Doubleday.

James, W. (1958). *Talks to teachers on psychology and to students on some of life's ideals.* New York, NY: Norton.

Johnston, P. (2004). *Choice words: How our language affects children's learning.* Portland, ME: Stenhouse.

Joshi, R. M., Treiman, R., Carreker, S., & Moats, L. C. (2008–2009, Winter). How words cast their spell: spelling is an integral part of learning the language, not a matter of memorization. *American Educator, 32*(4), 6–16, 42–43.

Kame'enui, E. J., & Baumann, J. F. (2012). *Vocabulary instruction, second edition: Research to practice.* New York, NY: The Guilford Press.

Klauser, H. A. (2001). W*rite it down, make it happen: Knowing what you want and getting it.* New York, NY: Simon & Schuster.

Kohn, A. (2011). *Feel-bad education: and other contrarian essays on children and schooling.* Boston, MA: Beacon Press.

Kondō, M. (2015). *The life-changing magic of tidying up: The Japanese art of decluttering and organizing* (C. Hirano, Trans.). Waterville, ME: Thorndike Press.

Lexia Learning. (2017, October 30). What to do when adolescent literacy rates spell trouble [Blog post]. Retrieved from https://www.lexialearning.com/blog/what-do-when-adolescent-literacy-rates-spell-trouble

Lombardi, V. (2018). Famous quotes by Vince Lombardi. Retrieved from http://www.vincelombardi.com/

Looney, J. W. (2005), Formative assessment: Improving learning in secondary classrooms, *OECD Education Working Papers* (58), OECD. Retrieved from https://www.oecd.org/edu/ceri/35661078.pdf

Ludwig VanDerwater, A. (2016, July 26). *What is your signature dish?* Address presented at Paramus Summer Institute in East Brook High School, Paramus.

Malone, T., & Lepper, M. (1987). Making learning fun: A taxonomy of intrinsic motivations for learning. In R. Snow & M. J. Farr (Eds.), *Aptitude, learning, and instruction, vol. 3: Conative and affective process analyses.* Hillsdale, NJ: L. Erlbaum.

McGee, P. (2017). *Feedback that moves writers forward: How to escape correcting mode to transform student writing*. Thousand Oaks, CA: Corwin.

McKenna, M., & Dougherty Stahl, K. (2015). *Assessment for reading instruction* (3rd ed.). New York, NY: The Guilford Press.

Morris, D. (1982). "Word sort": A categorization strategy for improving word recognition ability. *Reading Psychology, 3*, 247–259.

mstruck01. (2017). *Phonics, PA, or spelling inventory assessment review* [Padlet]. Retrieved from https://padlet.com/mstruck01/dqh3aacsn6my

National Reading Panel. (2000). *Teaching children to read: An evidence-based assessment of the scientific research literature on reading and its implications for reading instruction—Report of the subgroups*. Washington, DC: U.S. Department of Health and Human Services.

Patall, E., Cooper, H., & Robinson, J. C. (2008). The effects of choice on intrinsic motivation and related outcomes: A meta-analysis of research findings. *Psychological Bulletin, 134*(2), 270–300.

Pink, D. H. (2010). *Drive the surprising truth about what motivates us*. Edinburgh, Scotland: Canongate.

Potts, M. (2014, February 12). Stress, poverty, and the childhood reading gap [Blog post]. Retrieved from http://prospect.org/article/stress-poverty-and-childhood-reading-gap

Quaglia Institute for Student Aspirations. (2014). *My voice: National student voice report (grades 6–12)*. Retrieved from http://www.qisa.org/dmsView/My_Voice_2013-2014_National_Report_8_25

Quaglia Institute for Student Aspirations and Teacher Voice and Aspirations International Center. (2015). *Teacher voice report, 2010–1014*. Thousand Oaks, CA: Corwin.

Rasinski, T. V. (2017). Readers who struggle: Why many struggle and a modest proposal for improving their reading. *The Reading Teacher, 70*(5), 519–524.

Rasinski, T. V., Padak, N., Newton, R. M., & Newton, E. (2008). *Greek and Latin roots: Key to building vocabulary*. Huntington Beach, CA: Shell Educational.

Rasinski, T. V., & Zutell, J. (2010). *Essential strategies for word study: Effective methods for improving decoding, spelling, and vocabulary*. New York, NY: Scholastic.

Robb, L. J. (2017). *Read, talk, write*. Thousand Oaks, CA: Corwin.

Roberts, K., & Roberts, M. B. (2016). *DIY literacy: Teaching tools for differentiation, rigor, and independence*. Portsmouth, NH: Heinemann.

Rogers, M. (2013, October 8). Troubling stats on adult literacy [Blog post]. Retrieved from https://www.insidehighered.com/news/2013/10/08/us-adults-rank-below-average-global-survey-basic-education-skills

Rosario, R. (2015, November 12). Troubled youths get a message of hope. Retrieved from https://www.twincities.com/2010/11/13/ruben-rosario-troubled-youths-get-a-message-of-hope/

Scheinerman, R. (2013, July 7). *What my beagle does when are not home: Beagle gets into hot oven* [Video file]. Retrieved from https://www.youtube.com/watch?v=_ym0rxisOpw&feature=youtu.be

Schotter, R. (2006). *The boy who loved words*. New York, NY: Schwartz & Wade.

Schunk, D. H. (1990). Goal setting and self-efficacy during self regulated learning. *Educational Psychologist, 25*, 71–86.

Scriven, M. (1967). The methodology of evaluation. In R. W. Tyler, R. M. Gagne, & M. Scriven (Eds.), *Perspectives of curriculum evaluation* (pp. 39–83). Chicago, IL: Rand McNally.

Sennholz, H. F. (1993). *The wisdom of Henry Hazlitt: A collection of essays by Henry Hazlitt.* Auburn, AL: The Foundation of Economic Learning.

Sinek, S. (2009, September). *Simon Sinek: How great leaders inspire action* [Video file]. Retrieved from https://www.ted.com/talks/simon_sinek_how_great_leaders_inspire_action

@simonsinek. (2010, July 6). Rule books tell people what to do. Frameworks guide people how to act. Rule books insist on discipline. Frameworks allow for creativity [Twitter moment]. Retrieved from https://twitter.com/simonsinek/status/17881092539

Sloan, H. G. (2018). *Short.* New York, NY: Puffin Books.

Spires, A. (2014). *The most magnificent thing.* New York, NY: Kids Can Press.

Stahl, S. A., & Nagy, W. E. (2006). *Teaching word meanings.* Mahwah, NJ: L. Erlbaum.

TMBbrand. (2011, March 13). *TMB Panyee FC short film.* Retrieved from https://www.youtube.com/watch?v=jU4oA3kkAWU

Turkay, S. (2014). *Setting goals: Who, why, how?* Manuscript. VPAL Research Team, Harvard University, Cambridge, MA.

Vygotsky, L. S. (1962). *Thought and language.* Cambridge, MA: MIT Press. (Original work published in 1934)

Vygotsky, L. S. (1978). *Mind and society: The development of higher psychological processes.* Cambridge, MA: Harvard University Press.

Waber, B. (2002). *Courage.* Boston, MA: Houghton Mifflin Harcourt.

Wheatley, M. J. (2009). *Turning to one another: Simple conversation to restore hope to the future.* San Francisco, CA: Berrett Koehler.

White, K. (2012). *Ruby's sleepover.* New Milford, NJ: Barefoot Books.

Wiggins, G., & McTighe, J. (1998). *Understanding by design.* Alexandria, VA: Association of Supervision and Curriculum Development.

Wilde, S. (1992). *You kan red this! Spelling and punctuation for the whole language classroom.* Portsmouth, NH: Heinemann.

Woodson, J. (2016). *Brown Girl Dreaming.* New York, NY: Puffin Books.

Yates, K. (2015). *Simple starts: Making the move to a reader-centered classroom.* Portsmouth, NH: Heinemann.

Zusak, M. (2007). *The book thief.* New York, NY: Random House.

Index

Because...
ALL TEACHERS ARE LEADERS

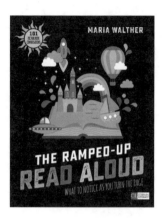

MARIA WALTHER

101 picture book experiences, a thousand ways to savor strategically. This is the book that shows how to use ANY book to teach readers and writers!

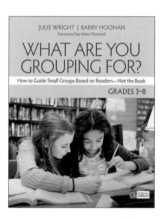

JULIE WRIGHT AND BARRY HOONAN

This book explains the five teacher moves that work together to support students' reading independence through small-group learning—kidwatching, pivoting, assessing, curating, and planning.

M. COLLEEN CRUZ

By flipping the traditional "reading first, writing second" sequence, these innovative books let you make the most of the writing-to-reading connection via 50 carefully matched lesson pairs in each book.

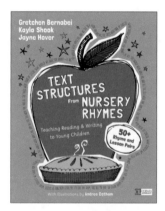

GRETCHEN BERNABEI, KAYLA SHOOK, AND JAYNE HOVER

In 53 lessons centered around classic nursery rhymes, this groundbreaking book offers a straightforward framework for guiding children to write in any style, from narrative to persuasive.

To order your copies, visit corwin.com/literacy

Do you have a minute? Of course not.

That's why at Corwin Literacy we have put together a collection of just-in-time, classroom-tested, practical resources from trusted experts that allow you to quickly find the information you need when you need it.

GRAVITY GOLDBERG AND RENEE HOUSER

With these books, discover how to move your readers forward with in-class, actionable formative assessment in just minutes a day with a proven four-step process and lots of next-step resources.

NANCY AKHAVAN

With 75 tasks on beautiful full-color pages, this book offers a literacy instruction plan that ensures students benefit from independent effort and engagement.

MOLLY NESS

Molly Ness's three-step planning process will help you create dynamic lessons that focus on the five most important think-aloud strategies.

PATTY McGEE

Patty McGee helps you transform student writers by showing you how to build tone, trust, motivation, and choice into your daily lessons, conferences, and revision suggestions.

A SAGE Publishing Company

Helping educators make the greatest impact

CORWIN HAS ONE MISSION: to enhance education through intentional professional learning.

We build long-term relationships with our authors, educators, clients, and associations who partner with us to develop and continuously improve the best evidence-based practices that establish and support lifelong learning.